Laylines
1980 – 1996

Laylines
1980 – 1996

Partial Views of
Church and Society

Seán Mac Réamoinn

DOMINICAN PUBLICATIONS

First published (1997) by
Dominican Publications
42 Parnell Square
Dublin 1

ISBN 1-871552-64-8

British Library Cataloguing in Publications Data.
A catalogue record for this book is available
from the British Library.

Cover design by Bill Bolger

Printed in Ireland by
ColourBooks Ltd

CONTENTS

PREFACE

'I'm thinking of suggesting to the Pope that the whole Church should be turned over to them for a couple of weeks.' The author of this unexpected encomium was an American journalist, Robert Hoyt, writing in 1968 in the weekly *National Catholic Reporter.*

It was to four Irish journalists, no less, that Hoyt was proposing to entrust the care of the Roman Catholic Church. They were Louis McRedmond (*The Irish Independent,* of which he was then editor), John Horgan (*The Irish Times*), Donal Musgrave (*The Irish Press*) – and Seán Mac Réamoinn, reporting for Irish T.V. and radio. Hoyt had met them when they and he were covering Vatican Council II and the 1967 Roman Synod of Bishops.

Hoyt went on to say of the four journalists: 'They might not be able to solve the crisis of faith or the crisis of authority, but they would at least postpone the crisis of boredom.'

He added, 'The man to put in charge of the whole operation would be one Seán Mac Réamoinn, who writes for Irish papers and talks for Irish television, and who is at once the most serious and the least stuffy of men. He has a round jolly face, a moustache as thick as is his brogue and a twinkle in his eye that should be patented and put on the market for the salvation of souls.'

We in Dominican Publications were delighted when Seán began brightening the pages of *Doctrine and Life* from February, 1980, with the first appearance of his Laylines column. In those days he had perforce to wear a literary disguise: he used the pen-name, Oisín. As the then editor explained, Seán was still a public servant at the time – he was on the staff of the national radio and television stations – and protocol dictated that he might not use his own name when writing about matters of national interest, which he would certainly want to do from time to time.

The editor went on to inform *Doctrine and Life* readers that 'Oisín' was 'a distinguished Irish layman who has much to offer in the way of insight, comment, gripe or suggestion.' More recently, when the same editor was presenting Seán for a special award from the Master of the Dominican Order, Fr Timothy Radcliffe, he said: 'Seán has managed to infuse into his writings that all too rare combination of seriousness and unstuffiness, that twinkle in the eye, coupled with a profound *sensus theologicus*, a sense of history, a love for the Church, for Ireland and things Irish, a courtesy and an elegance of expression.'

The Laylines column has proved to be so consistently thoughtful, so well-informed, so alert and so perceptive on a wide range of topics including theology, politics and the arts – and has always been so beautifully written – since it first appeared in February 1980 that it seemed to us it deserved a wider public. That's why, as part of the celebrations to mark the centenary of Dominican Publications (founded 1897), we bring out in book form a selection of pieces from the column.

What to include from the more than half a million words Seán has contributed over eighteen years provoked much heart-searching. If this book was not to be either clumsily unwieldy or impossibly expensive, more, far more, had to be excluded than could be included. The aim we set ourselves was to provide as representative a picture as we could of the range of themes and topics on which Seán has commented, and to give a flavour of how the column has related to the events of the day.

The work of selecting passages for inclusion and of preparing the selection for publication could not have been undertaken, nor would it have been brought to any kind of conclusion, without the expert help of Bernard Harris who also assisted in preparing the book for the press and compiled the index. We are deeply grateful for his contribution.

Though this book stops at the end of 1996, the Laylines column does not. During 1997 Seán has already commented on the Northern Ireland situation, on the Robinson presidency, and on the ministry of reading in Church. He has had a gripe about the use of the words 'racism' and 'racist' in regard to the treatment of Travellers and about the travails of using public transport. He has suggested the adoption of a basic income policy as a contribution to a progressive reduction of unemployment. In the September issue of *Doctrine and Life* his attention is on the value of the Seanad as a forum for having second thoughts, on probity in public life and on showing a welcome to strangers on our shores.

Laylines lives.

Austin Flannery, O.P.
Editor, *Doctrine and Life*, 1957–1988

Bernard Treacy, O.P.
Editor, *Doctrine and Life*, 1989 —   August 1997

1980

Hans Küng and the Vatican

When Hans Küng's *Infallible?* appeared in English in 1971, the reviewer in the London *Tablet* had this to say:

> What is requested from defenders of the traditional teaching is not a condemnation of the book but a refutation. If this can be provided, then a condemnation is unnecessary; if it cannot be provided, then a condemnation is unjustified.

That seems to me to put the case rather neatly. Granted that Küng is not the easiest in the world to dialogue with, and might well exhaust the patience of men even more saintly than the Congregation for the Doctrine of the Faith, still the more one thinks of the way they have handled the matter the more one is appalled at the sterile futility of the whole proceeding, as well as its very dubious propriety as far as justice 'being seen to be done' is concerned.

It seems to me that these are the real issues, and to feel and express concern about them need not imply agreeing with everything Küng has written. On the popular level I don't believe he has ever produced anything to match *The Council and Reunion*, which made him famous when it appeared in 1962. If labels are to be affixed I would think of him as 'liberal' rather than 'radical', and, indeed, as to the social implications of being a Christian, he is disappointingly conservative. But this is not the point: in fundamentals and accidentals alike, refutation rather than condemnation is (as the *Tablet* reviewer indicated) the only real answer to errors or ambiguities. And, even from a pastoral point of view, refutation must be something more, much more, than the criticisms embodied in the German bishops' defence of the Vatican ban.

However well-intentioned and humane in tone, it is hard to see the bishops' statement as going any real distance in allaying the well-grounded fears of concerned Christians (within and without the Roman obedience). For, while it shows an apparently genuine wish to avoid hasty action – in one way or another the affair has been dragging on since 1967 – what is missing is any recognition that the Vatican procedures are clearly at odds with ideas of justice and due process of law, now fairly universally accepted outside of totalitarian states. This is where the real scandal lies, and not to acknowledge it compounds it.

It is, I believe, important that interested persons and bodies should bombard Rome with protests and pleas for reform. This is all the more urgent because of the impending case of Professor Schillebeeckx.

By the way, the *Tablet* reviewer whom I quoted was one P.J. McGrath. He was then a professor at Maynooth.

(February 1980, vol. 30, no. 2, pp. 98-99)

The course of Irish ecumenism

A mild and cautious optimism about ecumenical prospects in Ireland has begun to replace the widespread depression of the past year or so. The election [on 25 February 1980] of Bishop John Armstrong as Church of Ireland Primate has been welcomed north and south: he returns to his native Ulster after a long ministry both in Dublin and in the pastoral archipelago of the South. He is widely liked and admired as an honest open Christian, and of proven commitment to unity.

The recent inter-church meeting at Ballymascanlon seems to have been an improvement on its predecessors. There appear to have been some real conversations, with the possibility of a follow-through in certain areas. Even a small advance along the road would raise the drooping spirit....

So Ballymascanlon 1980 deserves two cheers anyway. One of these must go to the decision to take a joint hard look at crime and punishment, with particular reference to the actual situation on both sides of the political border....

Surely it is high time for the Churches to confront society with one voice, if only to recall some of the clearer imperatives of that New Testament teaching which allegedly informs our social institutions. And it is also high time for us all to examine our own consciences in this matter....

I for one know that self-scrutiny (usually matutinal and inspired by hangover) reveals an appalling failure here. My record is abysmal on the personal level – I have never done anything for an individual prisoner – nor have I contributed anything to penal reform, a subject on which I have often talked at boring length. For instance: I happen to disagree with people who want political status for certain prisoners in the North, and have often proposed that the energies of those dedicated to this cause would be better redirected into seeking an improvement on the conditions of all prisoners. I can argue powerfully that special treatment for some is a blow against solidarity, and that the ritual humiliations of uniform and so on should be ended in all cases. But have I ever put my money (or time or whatever talent I have) where my mouth is? The answer is: no! And the fact that my fellow-citizens and coreligionists are for the most part as bad as I am is no help at all.

Not for the first time, one is led to that key passage in Matthew 25 which spells out what our final judgement will be. In whom does Jesus tell us he is to be found? The hungry, the homeless, the sick and handicapped – and prisoners. Here if anywhere is the cornerstone of our ethic, here we are told with great clarity how a Christian should behave, or rather how a real Christian is to be recognised.... Even 'official' Church preoccupations now include hunger and poverty, on the international as well as the immediate local level. But those in prison are rarely mentioned: it takes torture, or rumours thereof, or some other special kind of ill-treatment to earn the concern of those of us who have so far escaped social punishment for our crimes....

In the whole question of care of prisoners, as in so many other matters of Gospel precept our duty is twofold: personal and social. Each of us should find a way of doing some direct good to a brother or sister who is, or who has recently been, in prison. But we must do more.

Whether or not one holds (with the late Maurice Gorham) that a Christian must of necessity be a Socialist, one must surely recognize that some Christian objectives can only be achieved by political action. This need not and should not imply organizations and structures in competition with those of secular society; rather should Christians work in and through those secular structures. Individual prison-visiting, however desirable, cannot of itself bring about penal reform, any more than individual almsgiving will feed the hungry of the Third World. *Ecclesia 'semper reformanda'* applies to society as much as to the Church: structures need to be 'converted' as well as hearts.

(April 1980, vol. 30, no. 4, pp. 164-167)

Justice indivisible

Journeyings overseas led me to Tübingen and the hospitable apartment of Hans Küng. It was by coincidence the very day on which his letter outlining his present academic standing (the 'compromise' solution as it has been called) appeared in *The Irish Times*. None of us was then aware of this, and Küng gave me a copy for my own information but also for possible publication if the original had gone astray....

It might indeed be argued that if Küng is a victim of injustice, his situation is a comfortable and indeed an enviable one, compared to others whose witness, inside and outside the Church, has invited the displeasure of authority elsewhere. An ecumenical chair in a German university, it has been rather sourly pointed out, is preferable to a bed in a Soviet mental hospital, or a prison cell in Brazil (or Ireland) – not to speak of a martyr's grave in El Salvador.

This is true, but it's hardly the point. Justice like peace is indivisible, and while to deny it or skimp it may seem a small matter at times, especially in a larger context of oppression or social need, to do so always blots not just the page but the whole copy-book. And the Church is supposed to set headlines ...

(June-July 1980, vol. 30, no. 6, pp. 313-314)

Laicisation

'A kind of Limbo' was how Fr Brian D'Arcy, C.P., has described the situation of a number of Irish priests whose laicisation process has been held up in Rome. A less gentle man might have used a stronger name for it.

Fr D'Arcy was speaking at the annual meeting in Newry of the National Conference of Priests of Ireland, and his remarks were made in the context of an appeal to his fellow-priests on behalf of those who have already left the ministry. The size of the problem in Ireland is happily small, but it must be seen as a microcosm of a much wider one, whose urgency cannot be gainsaid.

In the long-term, of course, the question of laicisation could be seen as an irrelevance. Indeed the phrase 'reduction to the lay state' is not just insulting to those of us who are not in Holy Orders: it implies a deep confusion between ministry and 'clerisy'. The very ambiguity of the word 'clerical' in contemporary usage should put us on our guard, but in fact we seem to have accepted as God-given and for all time the existence of a clerical 'class' within the Church, and that all ministry, not to say priesthood, is contained within it. Indeed it's not so long since the Church itself was, at least in popular thinking and parlance regarded as co-terminous with the 'clergy'.

In trying further to reform our own thinking, and ultimately our practices and structures, we cannot ignore nearly two thousand years of history. The clerical Church of the West may have been all a great accident, but in the event it provided a framework, however imperfect, for the preaching of the gospel and the growth of the sacramental community.

However, *semper reformanda* is the watchword. I do believe that the declericalising of ministry is one of the most urgent tasks facing the Church today. Its achievement could create a new situation in which such apparently intractable problems as the ordination of women and married men would assume a new perspective. But this, however desirable, is not the main reason for attempting what must be, admittedly, an enormously difficult and complex reform. For what is really at stake is the realisation of that 'priestly community' (*Lumen Gentium*) which is the *Laos*, the People of God, and the ordering of ministry within it. We need to consider and make manifest not just the priesthood of the laity, but the lay-hood of the priest.

(June-July 1980, vol. 30, no. 6, pp. 314-315)

Challenge at Glenstal

Like most such events, this year's Ecumenical Meeting at Glenstal (the seventeenth) will have meant different things to different people. The subject was Authority – thorny to some, exasperating to others, a comfort to others still, and perhaps to a (lucky?) few a matter of no great weight. I found the main lectures too divergent in approach and 'level' to be of much help in trying to find a common ecumenical way forward: but, as usual, liturgy, hospitality and personal encounter made the journey worthwhile. I had almost come to settle for that much for this year when, on the final morning, mind as well as heart were raised by two splendid contributions. One of these was the remarkable summing-up, not to say synthesis, of the proceedings offered by Fr Gabriel Daly, O.S.A. – a challenge to the intellectual and moral sloth of our theologizings in the matter of unity.

This was matched by an even more radical challenge by the

homilist at Mass, Fr Raymond Kennedy, C.S.Sp., who called on the apostolic witness of the early Church to confront us with the fundamental importance of the principle enshrined in the often-quoted but rarely-practised triad about 'unity in essentials, freedom in what is doubtful, and charity in all things'. Where Fr Kennedy got under our skins was in forcing us to face up to the question of what is really and undeniably essential. And he managed to be both blunt and courteous on such notoriously delicate issues as intercommunion and the indissolubility of marriage, and to raise questions (in a homily!) on Catholic teaching and practice about both. It was the bravest and the most honest pulpit-talk I've heard for a very long time, and I have a feeling it will be remembered for an equally long time....

If dissensions are bad things, differences are not – but, again we confuse the two, like unity and uniformity. And I would go further and say that even the differences bred by dissension can be good in themselves: this is true in politics and culture, and perhaps especially in religion. Anyone who doesn't believe me should get hold of a copy of Michael Hurley's *Praying for Unity*, the pioneer publication of the Irish ecumenical movement, which rehearses some of the specific virtues of the divided Christian traditions. The insights and meditations and heroisms – yes, and the martyrdoms – that are the very fruits of the sin of disunity, wherever and whenever committed, can in God's good time turn the sin itself into a *felix culpa*.

All the Christian Churches have sins to confess and repent of and make amends for: but each of them has also gifts to offer to the community of tomorrow. And let us never forget that whatever the theological differences the main troubles almost certainly lie in non-theological areas....

At the very beginning of the Glenstal meeting Cardinal Tomás Ó Fiaich offered a challenge – to his fellow-Catholics. Encouraging all to a greater ecumenical effort he coined the singularly happy phrase: 'As the Roman Catholics are the largest community in numbers, so we should be the largest in generosity'.

This is heart-warming stuff, as was indeed the general burden of the Cardinal's opening address, although he spoke with sober realism of certain recent set-backs to unity among Irish Christians. He obviously looks forward in hope, and his cautious but positive references to certain new departures on the interchurch marriage front carried conviction. He spoke too with obvious affection of his now retired fellow-Primate, G.O. Simms and of Archbishop Simms's successor John Armstrong, a long-time pillar of the Glenstal conference.

Cardinal Ó Fiaich would not profess to be an ecumenical theologian. His own subject is Irish history which has its own lessons to teach, even in the theological areas, and he is also an authority on and enthusiast for the Gaelic literary tradition of his native Ulster. But this does not put him out of sympathy with Ulstermen who share neither his scholarship nor his *pietas*, as the scores of 'all sorts and conditions' who have experienced his hospitality in Armagh will attest. I do not know his ultimate view of unity, or whether it provides for pluralism, but I am quite certain that no Irish churchman is more genuinely devoted to breaking down those fears and suspicions and hatreds which still strangle us.

We heard the Cardinal speak again, with a rather different emphasis, but again with great warmth and enthusiasm, in the ruined chancel of Old Mellifont on the Sunday after St Benedict's Day. A new abbot for New Mellifont Abbey was being blessed within the historic wall of the medieval foundation, where our first Cistercians settled nearly 850 years ago. Cardinal Ó Fiaich's predecessor at the time, in the see of Armagh, was the great reformer Malachy, friend of Bernard of Clairvaux, and it was this friendship that brought those first monks to a part of Ireland dedicated to worship, pagan and Christian, since the Stone Age.

The Mass and abbatial blessing at Mellifont was one of the great events of the Benedictine Year, celebrated all over the world but especially in Europe, of which St Benedict is patron. Benedictine and Cistercian monks and nuns are all collaborating in the fifteenth centenary of their common founder – 'There's ecumenism for you!' remarked a Jesuit who shall be nameless.

(August-September 1980, vol. 30, no. 7, pp. 353-356)

The communication gap

'The Church has nothing to fear from the truth'. This was the excellent (if self-evident) proposition with which Bishop Agnellus Andrew appealed to the fathers of the present Synod of Bishops for a frank, non-whitewashing approach to the media, at the opening session – and let us say in parenthesis how pleased all his former colleagues are to see a real communicator in the Vatican at last. Honesty is of course the only policy, but it is alas! not enough. There is a great gulf of credibility and of intelligibility to be crossed not alone between the magisterium and a post-Christian world, but even between the most amiable of institutional voices and the faithful living in that world. To say that the problem is a cultural one helps to identify it but doesn't go very far in solving it.

It is nevertheless essential to grasp this point if we are to make any progress. For it's not just a matter of clarity of expression, of stripping away outworn rhetoric and fustian, of being 'up-to-date'. Language has been well compared with money in that as well as being a means of exchange it is also a store of value. This shows up most often perhaps in translating from one language to another without remembering that one is also translating from one culture to another....

It would be easy to exaggerate the extent of the communication gap, but it would be tragically stupid to pretend it doesn't exist. Whole areas of presupposition, of shared symbol, of familiar referral are being demolished and are being replaced, at times by shoddy prefabs constructed partly from the new sciences and pseudo-sciences, partly from the new hedonism: but there are other new constructs being built to last, especially in the southern half of the world. Whether the new successor cultures are shoddy or solid the Church must come to terms with them, and keep trying to find intelligible language in which to preach the gospel.

(November 1980, vol. 30, no. 9, pp. 508-509)

Synod on the Family

As to the Synod, it is understandable that its impact should differ widely in different parts of the world: the preoccupations of the Christian family in America, or even in Ireland, are not those of their counterparts in Brazil or Tanzania. But it would be too easy to accept such simple equations as are sometimes proposed, e.g. Third World objectives correspond to traditional Christian values (no contraception) – the selfish West means closing the doors to life. There remain such awkward 'exceptions' as the Indonesian Church which seems to accept 'artificial' techniques of family planning as a *sine qua non* of social sanity.

The one aspect of the Synod that I feel I must refer to is the distasteful, not to say scandalous, question raised by the blandness of its voice. Was it really so smooth?

I am personally sick to death of the cliché that the Church is not a democracy: maybe it isn't, but need it always seem to model its deliberations on those of a Stalinist Supreme Soviet? From the reports that issued out of what was allegedly a gathering representative of the local Churches, dealing with matters lying at the very heart of Christian living, one had an impression of the worst kind of 'managed' assembly. There were indeed some differences of emphasis, but a huge and smug unanimity of adherence to doubtful norms seemed to be the final outcome. One was reminded of the Duke of Wellington's remark about certain of his troops: 'I don't know whether they'll frighten the enemy, but, my God, they frighten me!' ... Saddest of all perhaps were those synodal fathers who were determined to speak the truth in love – like the Archbishops of Malines-Brussels and Westminster – for even they seemed to find it necessary to clothe their simple and honourable witness in language less than direct. The briefest and plainest speaker of all, the Archbishop of Durban, was apparently too plain to be included in the official report.

(December 1980, vol. 30, no. 10, pp. 564-565)

Cardinal Hume and the Hunger Strike

Cardinal Hume's interventions have been widely and justly praised. His more recent remarks on the H-block hunger strike have been greeted with less general enthusiasm, in Ireland at any rate. In this matter the difference of emphasis between him and Cardinal Ó Fiaich attests to the very real depth of moral feeling which divides Christians in these islands. Certainly it would be deplorable to say or do anything which would represent as an issue of Church politics ('Catholics split on H-block') something which is a challenge to Christian conscience.

It is for this very reason that while avoiding instant comment on each new stage in the deterioration of a tragic situation, we must, I believe, try to reach some position on which Christians can agree, whatever their political prejudices and predilections. And this can only be done if we look at the facts – historical, social, and psychological – and then reflect on these in the light of our gospel tradition. Thus it is essential for all of us to admit to ourselves as well as to others that murders (however euphemised) have been done; that some at least of the judicial processes have been of dubious validity; that ill-treatment to the point of torture (again however euphemised) has continued in the

cause of 'Beating the Terrorists'; that the 'Blanket' campaign
with its consequent hunger-strike action was equally freely chosen; that there is an urgent need for prison reform for all.

Which brings us to the heart of the matter. If reform can be
seen to be good and necessary can there be any moral justifica-
tion for postponing it, just because it may seem to be a concession
to murderers and other criminals? To argue that there can seems
to me to be a kind of end-justifies-the-means morality in reverse.
The imperatives implied in Matthew 25 are surely not to be
ignored for fear of being misunderstood.

(December 1980, vol. 30, no. 10, pp. 565-566)

The Liberator and the Legion

Daniel O'Connell was the first Irish layman to leave his mark, as
a layman, on the history of the universal Church. He had no
successor for a hundred years: the other seminal names of the
nineteenth century – Rice, McAuley, Aikenhead – chose to
'become religious'. An authentic lay voice came only with the
establishment of an Irish state, and indeed from within that
state's first bureaucracy.

Frank Duff was not the best known or best loved of Irishmen,
at home or abroad. To point to him as heir to the warm,
flamboyant, rhetorical and all too human O'Connell might seem
incongruous. Duff lacked all the more obvious qualities of
leadership. Yet a leader he was, a pioneer and a maker. What he
made may or may not live long after him, it is already changing
in many places, and will probably change more radically still; but
the witness and apostolate of the Legion of Mary is one of the
great facts of twentieth-century Christianity.

I write as an outsider, one who, while respecting the movement, has never found it attractive, spiritually or culturally. Even
at a time when quasi-military language was used more
uninhibitedly than today, I disliked the vocabulary of the Legion,
and, on quite a different level, I was always uneasy with what I
would regard as an over-emphasis on Marian devotion. We have
been told that the present Pope, when he received Frank Duff
before his ninetieth birthday, greeted him as a fellow disciple of
Grignion de Montfort. This can only be a stumbling-block to
those of us who regard Grignion de Montfort's writings as not
alone distasteful, but an apparent distortion of Gospel teaching.

But if there were distortions in Frank Duff's Christian charity and apostolic zeal they were hardly visible, the merest blurs on a great shining life, lived to the full for others. He was a man of his time as we all are, and his vision was not unlimited: but it was strong and clear, and where it led he followed without flinching. And where he led, there followed a vast *meitheal* of men and women who brought the Good News to many a dark corner at home, and abroad, to the very ends of the earth: without them the Church in our time would have known a poorer harvest. *Beannacht Dé le hanam an tsíoladóra.*

(December 1980, vol. 30, no. 10, p. 563)

1981

Lapsing and light from the East

Losing the faith, leaving the Church, not going to Mass, dropping out, lapsing, drifting away. Whatever we call it (and there are differences of degree and of kind implicit in the different phrases), or however we explain it, it's happening. Happening especially among the young. The statistics may be still quite reassuring, and the churches still look reassuringly full, but every concerned parent knows that it's widespread. It hasn't hit my house yet, it's next door and I can hardly hope for perpetual immunity....

I wonder to what extent difficulties and apparent failures in this regard in Ireland, just now, are related to the minor 'population-explosion' which we've been experiencing. I've been accused of attributing all our present problems to the fact that something like half our population is under twenty-five: I don't, but I do suggest it has crucial cultural implications. My thesis is that in times of rapid population growth, the normal rhythms of cultural transmission are seriously disturbed, so that the wisdom of the tribe may be partly lost or distorted. And I would guess that this is not just true of purely oral cultures....

The Gospel has always subsisted in human culture(s), and a Christianity that is not culturally conditioned is an impossibility: the Word that was made flesh, however transcendent, bears the mutations of the flesh. Perhaps all I'm saying is that we shouldn't be too worried by the breakdown which is not really of faith, but of one mode of transmission of that faith. This doesn't, of course, make the search for new modes less urgent....

What is puzzling to many of us is this: that while losing the faith may (most often?) mean losing all religious sense, and usually rules out formal religious practice, a significant minority turn to non-Christian cults, usually of eastern provenance. These range from authentic Buddhism in various forms, to more dubious teachings and teachers, some quite recently 'revealed'. These replacements for the religion of baptism, home and school often evoke only a passing enthusiasm, but sometimes they lead to a deep and lasting commitment....

The whole question of eastern non-Christian religions and cults, bound up as it is with mysticism (and mystification!), needs a much fuller and more urgent study than we have hitherto given it, as well as a mature and sensitive discernment of spirits. We are, I believe, becoming ever more aware of the fact that the great world religions have a place in God's plan, and that the uniqueness of Christ and his saving power should not lead us to undervalue the insights and values and charisms not alone of Judaism (to which we are linked by adoption) and Islam, but also of Hinduism, Zoroastrianism, and Buddhism.

A casual reading of a rather lightweight but sensitively written book on Thomas Merton which I came across recently has convinced me of how stupid I was to dismiss Merton many years ago on the strength (or weakness) of his early work *Elected Silence* (*Seven Storey Mountain*). It also made me aware, for the first time, of his remarkable spiritual pilgrimage in later life, lit by Zen Buddhist insights.

There is indeed a dizzy tightrope to be walked here, and many an unskilled enthusiast has toppled. More dangerous still are the 'simplicities' of some latter-day gurus whose appeal seems to me to correspond in a weird way – with, of course, enormous differences – to that of certain fundamentalist voices nearer home. And not all 'Christian' fundamentalists owe their ancestry to post-Reformation developments.

(January 1981, vol. 31, no. 1, pp. 43-47)

Politics for the Kingdom

There is a very real sense in which the Christian must try to be a reformer and a revolutionary at the same time. The Gospel is about revolution, and not only in our hearts. But on the road from Jerusalem to Jericho we cannot neglect the present victim for fear of postponing a future glory.

The disabled, the mentally handicapped, the depressed, all who are sick in mind and body, have a claim on us. As have the poor, the old, the lonely, the tortured, the persecuted, the dispossessed, the untouchables. The claim is Christ's claim, and it's never enough to answer 'Lord, Lord!' Nor is the penny on the plate enough: nor even the National Collection. If it means going into the political kitchen we mustn't mind the heat. Hell will be hotter. As indeed is the hell on earth which in many parts of the globe has come about through political inactivity.

This inactivity, the social laziness of men and women whose private lives are decent and benevolent, is objectively one of the grave sins of our time. Subjectively, of course, it is possible to excuse it on many counts: disillusion with previous failures, disgust with the machinery and methods of politicians in many countries, innocent unawareness of injustices or of creeping tyranny. But the bleak state of international affairs in this mild Spring of 1981 might cause us to suggest that Poland is not the only country where organised popular protest and actions are needed to bring down corrupt structures and corrupt men. The belligerent bawlings coming from Washington since the new Administration [of President Ronald Reagan] took over may be so much swashbuckling, but even the more 'moderate' voices of the new Conservatism in the U.S.A. (as in the U.K.) must cast a chill.

That the greatest free nation in the world should busy itself with the support of tyranny and torture, from El Salvador to South Korea, is something to which we have become long accustomed: it didn't start with Reagan, nor even Nixon. But that a high officer of state should, in so many words, decry the importance of human rights is quite literally shocking – far more so than the windy hypocrisies of the Soviets in justifying their own aggressions.

(March 1981, vol. 31, no. 3, p. 175)

Back to school

Open-minded observers outside Ireland, as they try to make sense of the unhappy situation in the North, find it hard to understand the Catholic insistence on denominational schooling. They are especially baffled when this insistence is expressed not just by the clergy and devout laity, but by individuals whose personal religious commitment may be slight, and admittedly so. What they fail to grasp is that even 'Catholic agnostics' fear the proselytising influence of the 'nondenominational' school: but what they fear is a loss or weakening of culture, not of religious faith. This is what gives such general popular support to the negative attitude of the Catholic Church leadership to integration: religious and cultural concerns share a common position and while some radical Catholics strike out bravely against the stream, their attitude is regarded as eccentric and even dangerous by most of even their nominal coreligionists.

Before dismissing the majority line as hopelessly obscurantist and reactionary, there are two unpalatable truths which have to be faced. The first has to do with the nature of 'national' culture in the north. Some of its constituent elements, from food to folk music, belong also to the colonist culture. Others, relating to work as well as to leisure, in both town and country, are seen as characteristic of 'us', not of 'them'. But the distinctive and binding factor is religion.

Once it might have been the Irish (Gaelic) language, although it was never exclusively confined to the native population and the Gaelic of many of the Scottish planters was close enough for mutual intelligibility. But English has been the vernacular of both communities for at least a hundred years (with a few 'islands' of Gaelic survival here and there).

The point is worth noting because, in fact, the seventeenth century planters were the first wave of 'invaders' not to have become culturally assimilated – Vikings, Norman French, pre-Reformation English, all became 'More Irish than the Irish themselves: *Hibernicis ipsis Hiberniores*'....

Inevitably then, in the cultural vacuum of post-Famine Ireland (and in many places even earlier), the Roman Catholic Church was the one 'native' institution of power and prestige and its influence was enhanced by the popular religious cultures which helped to mould the lives, and lifestyles, of its adherents. I use the plural 'cultures' because there were (and still are) two at least: the traditional Irish, rooted in the remote past, a remarkable fusion of the austere and the fanciful, of penance and poetry – often of great beauty – and the new devotionalism, imported from Italy and France, usually via Britain. And unfortunately it was this latter article that was 'sold' by the majority of the more zealous preachers and teachers of the time. It has influenced the non-religious elements of 'native' culture in the North far more than is commonly realised.

There is however a tougher strain in that culture, the heritage of deprivation, injustice and contempt which the Ulster Catholic carries in his heart and his memory. Which brings me to the second unpalatable truth about possible educational integration: as long as 'the others' are on top, there is little doubt but that 'nondenominational' schooling would mean, in the main, schooling on British rather than on Irish concepts, traditions, beliefs and that the teaching of history, literature, perhaps even geography would present British perspectives, British prejudices, British values. There would be very few exceptions for a very long time.

...

Having said all that, I will now declare myself for integration. For, in spite of all the dangers and difficulties with which the prospect bristles, I believe it to be a *sine qua non* of any real advance to building one human community in Northern Ireland. In the Republic I regard it as desirable, but outside of Dublin and one or two other places, it is hardly a burning issue.

But let me add at once that religious or confessional integration isn't worth a damn without social integration as well. And that's as true in the south as in the north. Education based on class-structures is a sickness we need to get rid of, and, where class differences and confessional differences are used (or allowed) to maintain and perpetuate each other, what we have is a cancer. The housing ghettoes of Derry and Belfast, for instance, are particularly foul and noxious examples.

Catholic Church leaders are perfectly right when they point out that separate schools are not the only structures of apartheid in the North. But it is disingenuous to point to the schools as one element in a ghetto imposed from without, while at the same time refusing to countenance integration for reasons of religious principle. In any event the arguments for a 'full Catholic formation' ring rather hollow when put in counterpoint to the savageries done by young men, very young men, the products of this formation.

The time has long come for us all to take a long hard look at the whole educational situation, and see what we mean or should mean by 'formation'. And we must begin to take seriously what we so often pretend to believe, that the educational process cannot be confined to the school, that it must also involve the home, the Church, and all those agencies of community which touch young people's lives. It is vital to establish a harmony between all of these.

Even in times and places where there is no apparent crisis or conflict, this harmony is often less than complete: too often there are grave discrepancies in the values and standards to which the young are exposed, deliberately or accidentally in the various areas of their 'formation'. I do not, of course, suggest that education should be totalitarian and that 'outside influences' should be kept at bay: that parents and priests and teachers and social workers should speak with one voice at all times on every issue. God forbid!

On the contrary, I mean that the home and the school and the Church should complement each other: that the opening of the minds of the young, and their growth in wisdom and grace needs to be fostered in careful cooperation. And this applies equally to faith and to culture. An integrated system of education must be characterised by unity without unnecessary uniformity, and by mutual respect for different traditions and loyalties....

On the cultural level, even pilot schemes would need to be preceded by very careful planning (with an openness to ideas from across the 'divide') and firm guarantees from those in authority. On the religious level proper, there is a genuine problem of theology, or perhaps rather ecclesiology, which has to be tackled. It is related to that which lies at the heart of the debate on inter-church marriage.

．．．

To over-simplify this would be far from helpful, but two things need to be said. First, rightly or wrongly, one has the impression that what is really feared on the Catholic side is not so much Protestantism as, at best, 'indifferentism', at worst, neo-paganism.

One of the nastiest results of the post-Reformation divide is (or was, until very recently) that, while men of goodwill on one side might respect certain moral attributes (real or imagined) on the other, these were not seen as related to faith, prayer or sacrament. Extreme 'evangelical' Protestantism is still reluctant to regard Papists as Christians, and while mainstream Anglicans, Presbyterians and Methodists would deprecate this attitude, it has its mirror image among those to whom the 'non-Catholic' is beyond the pale of grace. To such, the mixed school, like the mixed marriage, can only mean a sell-out.

As against such deeply-felt, but I believe, wrong-headed and retrograde views one must declare for the ecumenical objective. But – and this is my second point – there is a strange kind of double-talk, and presumably double-think, in the 'official' Church, which, while extolling Christian unity as a long-term aim, and even recognising it as an evangelical imperative, casts, at the same time, a very cold eye on any word or action that might bring the day of unity nearer than may be institutionally convenient.

The progress towards the great goal is visualised as very slow (although, in theory, sure), and anyone who stands up and rocks the barque of Peter by proposing an ecumenical act beyond the permitted limits must take the consequences of unseasonable and untimely prophecy. 'Leave it to the Holy Spirit' seems to be the watchword.

But, 'God has ordained help: *d'ordaigh Dia cúnamh,*' and we can be certain that a passive though pious stance towards unity will not recommend itself to the Advocate, at a time when a riven world is hungry for a positive lead. It is the kind of stance which has tended to strangle the infant ecumenical movement, and, in the name of prudence, is dominated by fear. Catholics above all should have the courage of their sacramental convictions. If we really believe what we say about Baptism, then we must accept all who share it as being in a special relationship, not, of course, against the world but for the world. Our common missionary vocation, as a sign of God's Kingdom, is surely our most fundamental Christian obligation and the things that divide us should never be allowed to obscure that sign. Above all we must do all in our power to ensure that our sin of disunity is not carried forward to future generations.

(April 1981, vol. 31, no. 4, pp. 243-247)

The 'pro-life' amendment

In as much as abortion involves the taking of innocent human life, it is always, I believe, 'ontically' evil, and usually, I suppose, morally culpable. But with great respect for those whose initiative has brought the proposal forward, the idea of an 'absolute' anti-abortion amendment to the Irish Constitution[1] strikes me as deeply ill-advised.

In so far as constitutions concern themselves with matters of human and civil rights, they should, I believe, be confined to the adumbration of general principles and stop short of detailed directives, these being, I would hold, more appropriate to statute law. Experience in this country has gone to show that such directives, especially when expressed as rigid prohibitions (based on dogmatic assertion), have not always served the security and protection of the human person. Thus it can be argued that the generally admirable thrust of Article 41 of the Constitution

1. The Eighth Amendment of the Constitution, eventually put to the People in a referendum held on 7 September 1983.

(which guarantees the rights of the Family) is hindered rather than helped by the negative effect of subsections 2 and 3 of Section 2, preventing divorce legislation.

On the other hand, I can see difficulties of quite a different kind arising from Section 2 (subsection 2) of the already amended Article 44, in which 'the State guarantees not to endow any religion'.

My point is that such constitutional directives pre-empt the functions of parliament and of the judiciary. They are also to be deprecated, I believe, for practical reasons: how on earth is one to draft an 'anti-abortion' clause which will take due account of all gynaecological possibilities, not to speak of such developments in our understanding of biology as future study may bring? Should we bind ourselves and our children within the confines of our present perceptions?: surely one of the great functions and virtues of positive law is that it can provide for changing circumstances, while remaining faithful to basic values and concerns.

Furthermore, the debate preceding a referendum on the proposed Constitutional amendment would, I fear, generate more heat than light, and serve to polarise the community in a manner to be deplored. The organisers of the initiative have already canvassed the leadership of the main political parties who are certainly unwilling to allow the question to become an election issue: indeed the Taoiseach [Charles J. Haughey] has promised to introduce appropriate legislation, and the support of the other main parties seems assured. Such opposition as may be offered will no doubt come from elements of the women's movement, and some fringe left-wing groups whose views are already suspect. The whole affair is likely to become a crusade, with the 'pro-life' forces damning all dissenters as child-murderers. And to me 'crusade' is a dirty work.

It is in no polemic spirit that I dispute the right of such a movement to appropriate the 'pro-life' title. The great weakness of the case which all of us – Christians and others – who oppose abortion put forward, is that our concern for life seems, once again, selective. Logically a 'pro-life' amendment to the constitution should outlaw all killing – whether in self-defence, as capital punishment, or on military service – and make it impossible to legislate for any of these. I am of course far from suggesting such a move: rather should we depend on the resources of our ordinary legal system and political structures for the implementation of what our Christian conscience and our sense of common humanity may urge.

We must all of course be deeply distressed by the frightening erosion of that humanity which we have witnessed in our time. Certain Irish 'revisionist' historians have pointed to a cult of death as an element in our nationalist tradition, and certainly *troscadh* (fasting) has an ancient and indeed honourable pedigree as a form of social pressure. But in a world where assassination, terrorism and torture are the common currency of 'civilised' countries, and where genocide as practised first by Turkey and then on a more massive scale by Germany was accepted as a method of solving racial problems, our own particularly sickening blend of pseudo-patriotism and vicious trivialisation of life is remarkable only because it seems to be in some way linked to religious faith and conflict. As such it demands the urgent and continuing concern of Christians at home and abroad.

Trivialisation is perhaps the word which best characterises the movement for 'abortion on demand': as if the life or death of the foetus should be a matter of personal convenience or whim. And yet we know that behind the movement are sources far from trivial: the compassion of women (and some men) for their sisters, victims of male exploitation and aggressive sexuality, and a brave and patient, if in this matter misguided, struggle for their liberation. The rhetoric which characterises such a struggle of such people as simply 'anti-life' is not alone unfair, but can only harden hearts. And if ever a softening of hearts and attitudes was needed, it is surely now, not the softening of sentimentality but of compassion....

(June-July 1981, vol. 31, no. 6, pp. 375-376)

Christians and Jews

This year's Ecumenical Conference at Glenstal was generally voted a success, both in the matter and manner of the principal papers and discussions (the theme was 'Conversion') and in the never-failing hospitality of the Benedictines, which extends far beyond material caring.

The meeting was also notable for the presence and contribution of two distinguished guests: the Moderator of the General Assembly, an Ulsterman who by tradition and conviction stands firmly at the 'evangelical' end of the Irish Presbyterian spectrum

– his address impressed all who heard him, in its sincerity and charity – and also the Chief Rabbi of Ireland. It was the first time, I believe, that the holder of either office had come to the Conference and only the second occasion of formal Jewish participation. (Professor Weingreen had been a previous lecturer.)

Chief Rabbi Rosen was most generous of his time and talked openly and at length on many aspects of Judeo-Christian relations, both formally and informally. His main subject was Conversion in the Hebrew Scriptures, and one important effect of his remarks was to preclude any facile identification of Christian and Jewish 'readings' of the seminal texts. The danger of such an unwarranted short-cut to mutual understanding, or even exploratory dialogue, had been already emphasised at a seminar held in Dublin, shortly before Glenstal, under the auspices of the Irish School of Ecumenics, at which the Chief Rabbis both of Ireland and of the British Commonwealth were joined by Christian scholars and specialists in the field.

The inspiration and insights of the road to Emmaus are certainly not to be achieved by any instant over-simplification of the very real differences in the approach of the two great religions to their common heritage. Indeed the adherence to common texts, and the partial use of a common vocabulary, can themselves be stumbling-blocks, raising false hopes and assumptions unlikely to stand the test of serious study and discussion.

The road ahead must then be a long and difficult one for those intent on dialogue, leading not alone to understanding but even cooperation. Which is not to say that the journey should not be undertaken and persevered in. And so we welcome most heartily the establishment of a Council of Christians and Jews in Ireland, which was set up in June and whose membership includes leaders of the four main Churches as well as the Chief Rabbi. One can only wish that such a body had existed at a time when overtly anti-semitic attitudes were all too common among the majority here – even though, to be fair, the more virulent forms of discrimination and bigotry were happily rare.

All forms of prejudice against minorities is of course deplorable: when exercised from a religious or pseudo-religious 'base' it is particularly nasty. Explicitly 'Christian' anti-semitism is an abomination and is itself profoundly un-Christian and indeed anti-Christian. Since our faith cannot allow us to use the past tense about the humanity of Jesus Christ, we must proclaim the continuing reality of his Jewishness. This is not an optional extra, but of the very essence of our incarnational faith.

(August-September 1981, vol. 31, no. 7, pp. 441-442)

Constitutional crusades

Pluralism is one of the key-words of Taoiseach Garret FitzGerald's Crusade manifesto(s), delivered on a Sunday radio programme and later in a speech to Seanad Éireann, the 'upper' house of the Republic's parliament.

Dr FitzGerald's concern is the 'desirability of creating conditions favourable to unity, and of undertaking a constitutional and legislative review towards that end'. As to seeking unity by persuasion and consent, few who reject violence will demur: changing the Constitution as an earnest of goodwill is a different matter. Such a change could, in any event, come about only by referendum, but this would be the final act in a process of discussion, popular as well as parliamentary. This process the Taoiseach has initiated, and the words 'Great Debate' are already current.

The argument is seen to centre on two discrete constitutional elements. One, enshrined in Articles 2 and 3 relates to All-Ireland aspirations and claims: this is clearly of great relevance, but I do not propose to discuss it here at this stage. The other is of specifically Christian concern: it is, in fact, that articulation of 'Catholic social principles' which at the time of its enactment in 1937 caused the Constitution to be hailed as a model of its kind.

Ironically this aspect of the document was at the time subjected to criticism from the Right: Catholic integralists found it 'tainted by liberalism'. Now, words like 'sectarian', 'confessional' and even 'theocratic' have been used to condemn what a calmer voice from the Church of Ireland, Bishop Walton Empey, has recently reminded us 'in by far the greatest part of it, embodies principles which are shared by all Christians'. Bishop Empey went on to hope that any changes seen to be necessary 'would be made *because they are right and true and for no other reason*' (my italics). He said it would be 'a sad mistake to use any change as a means of wooing the Northern Unionist. That would be an insult to his intelligence and he will not be slow in seeing through it'. This was not to 'pour cold water on the courageous initiative of the Taoiseach'.

Quite a few other participants in the debate have spoken of the positive values of the Constitution, and the Taoiseach himself has praised it as proving to be in many respects 'a strong and enduring charter of the rights of the people' and 'a foundation for stability and social order'. In this connection it is good to recall the noble contribution of the late Cearbhall Ó Dálaigh, when on the bench and later as President, in his sensitive pointing to the Constitution as a touchstone of our liberties.

Is there then a need for change? This the people must decide. But now that the debate is on, one would hope to hear the considered views of canonists, and especially theologians, on some of the issues involved, particularly on that provision which precludes any legislation for divorce and remarriage.

When all is said and done, this is the point at which reform would seem most urgently needed. Personally I regard the 'bar' as unnecessary and counter-productive, as well as being a positive cause of distress and injustice to many innocent people, caught up in intolerable situations. And, for reasons which I have previously outlined, when discussing the proposed 'anti-abortion' amendment, I believe that such provisions have no place in a Constitution, whatever the merits of the particular question....

But I do feel that Roman Catholic thinking since Vatican II could make a useful contribution to the Great Debate. What we do not need, at this stage, is the guillotine of an episcopal directive (which is not to deny that for bishops too there is a time to speak!).

For the moment Bishop Empey's plea for only such changes as are 'right and true' deserves our attention. The ulterior motive of 'wooing' the North is beset by ambiguities, as all, including the Taoiseach, will recognise, and in the long run no Constitutional change will cure the sickness of disunity and alienation whether over the Border or across it.

(November 1981, vol. 31, no. 9, pp. 582-584)

The Pope and the Jesuits

Tiresome though the reminder may be, we must always remember that, of all people, Christians have a special obligation to avoid the cryptic, the ambiguous, the arcane. The Church is meant to be the light of the World and must not allow its brightness to be obscured by bushels. Not alone we, but the Gospel and the faith we hold, are rightly judged by what we say and do. We ought always try to make the Message plain.

It is in this context that I feel constrained to make reference to the papal intervention in the government of the Society of Jesus following the illness of the General, Fr Arrupe. The Pope's appointment of Fr Paolo Dezza, an eighty year-old former Assistant-General and Rector of the Gregorian University, as his 'personal delegate' to rule the Society (pending the holding of the next General Congregation) has caused widespread concern. It has been regarded with particular anxiety in that it appears to overrule Fr Arrupe's own appointment of his Senior Assistant, the American Fr Vincent O'Keeffe, to act as his vicar....

It is, I suppose, impossible to avoid utterly the Vatican version of Kremlinological journalism. But, surely its incidence could be considerably minimised by reducing the need for it. Open decisions (with open discussion of the reasons for them); due process; justice not only done but seen to be done – all these things are desirable surely, not for 'political' reasons, or for 'public relations', but precisely because the Church should be seen so to stand before the world....

(December 1981, vol. 31, no. 10, pp. 661-662)

Tackling poverty

It is a wry comment on our society that the establishment of a National Poverty Agency should be greeted as a sign of great social concern. One should regard it, I feel, with some regret, as when one reads of the building of bigger and better prisons. Cure, if cure it be, must always come second best to prevention.

In fairness it should be said that Taoiseach Garret FitzGerald has made it clear that the new Agency is not to be seen merely, or even principally, as an institution of relief. It is, he said, to have an input into policy-making, so that the eradication of the disease itself may be close to the central aims of future social and economic planning. And with Sister Stanislaus Kennedy in charge, I cannot see this or any government easily welching on its commitment.

(December 1981, vol. 31, no. 10, p. 662)

1982

Defending life

There is a real danger that our cowardice and stupidity on the contraception issue have helped to create a climate of moral muddle, indifference and desperation, in which we are ill-prepared to tackle the darker problems which are around the corner. To try to remedy this situation is probably our most urgent Christian task.

It is quite appalling that a phrase like 'the pro-life lobby' has become a term of abuse in progressive circles in Britain. (And one has heard it here in Ireland, though not cried so loudly.) It is equally disturbing that the labelling of Christians as 'pro-life' should be regarded as a damning indictment. It is, in fact, rather the society that produces such phrases that is itself indicted.

But to say this does not get us very much further. Of course it is not just a sign of social sickness, but of something close to madness, when words like 'peace', and now 'life' itself are regarded as dangerous or reactionary. But hand-wringing won't help. The sickness, the madness, need to be diagnosed, their cause discovered, and a cure found.

Now if we as Christians want really to earn the 'pro-life' label, and be proud of it, and if we presume to offer leadership in tackling the problem just stated, we must first examine our own consciences and our own record. For I'm afraid that individually, and ecclesially, our defence of life has been selective and half-hearted, and that we have all sinned and continue to sin in this regard, not least by omission.

For it has to be said again and again that life (like peace) is indivisible. To be anti-abortion and pro-hanging is just as inconsistent as to be against nuclear armament but in favour of the mercy killing of handicapped babies. And malnutrition or genocide in the Third World cannot be ignored just because we are preoccupied by sectarian murder in Ireland, or by the threats to life in our affluent society provided by alcoholism, or drug-addiction, or drunken driving.

I am not saying that we need not discriminate from situation to situation, that we must follow every flag-waving enthusiast, that there are not hierarchies of urgency and value. On the contrary, action for life must be preceded by thought and discussion. And that implies listening to the other side.

We will get nowhere unless we begin by presuming good faith. If we are shocked by cries for 'abortion on demand' or for letting 'unwanted' children die, we must not assume that we are confronted by a new race of Herods, but rather by ordinary men and women who, however wrong-headed, are often motivated by deep feelings of compassion and justice. And, again, we must ask ourselves to what extent distortions of the Christian ethic have pushed reformers into what we see to be tragically mistaken courses.

That having been said, we must hold firm to what we believe to be fundamental moral imperatives – not to inflexible moral positions, while remaining blind and deaf to changing circumstances and the pressure of events. Church teaching does not pre-empt conscience, does not relieve us of the duty of specific moral decision: the Gospel is not the *I Ching*.

(January 1982, vol. 32, no. 1, pp. 51-52)

Experts and witnesses

I would argue against the growing trend 'to leave it to the expert', medical or otherwise. I have observed a similar tendency among conservative Christians when it comes to discussing nuclear war. The discreet suggestion is that the issues are far too complex for the layman, that these things are best decided by those who know all the facts, that security would be better preserved by avoiding public debate, etc, etc … The awful fact that it's our lives, and our world, that are at stake is something which (one gathers) it would be in bad taste to mention.

Whatever the issue, there is a very strong argument for not leaving it to the 'expert' and the more complex the issue the stronger the argument. This does not imply disrespect for specialist knowledge.

The trouble is that the specialist *qua* specialist too often has tunnel vision. In his ordinary life outside his job – i.e. in the areas where he is a layman – his interests and sympathies, his opinions and insights, may be wide and far-reaching. But in his academic discipline or profession or trade, his very distinction may lie in the narrowness and depth of his particular field.

And however honest, he will have a vested interest. The fact that this may be quite legitimate is beside the point. Remember what Shaw said: 'It may be necessary to hang a man or pull down a house. But we take good care not to make the hangman and the house-breaker the judges of that.'

'If we did,' he added, 'no man's neck would be safe and no man's house stable.' God forbid I should suggest that either the doctor or the nuclear expert has a vested interest in death. But they have an interest in using their authority and resources.

(January 1982, vol. 32, no. 1, pp. 53-54)

Politics of discomfort

For a long time now, Ireland, north and south, has been a pretty comfortable place, politically and socially for most of us. (Yes! even in the North). Minorities, small and large, may have suffered, may still suffer, but, to misuse a famous phrase, there has been little to disturb the tranquillity of our Christian lives.

Murder there has been, and maiming and knee-capping, and castrating. But only a minority have suffered. Exploitation there has also been, and discrimination: a whole range of violations from baby-battering to malnutrition. But, again, under each heading, only a minority. Robberies and redundancies, sexual assault and sexual privation, legal 'fiddles' and illegal profiteerings. Yet when all is said and done the visible, respectable, articulate majority have had it reasonably good.

Or so it would appear. Mind you, when all the minorities are added up the figures may be a bit disquieting. We're lucky they haven't got together, aren't we?

But maybe they are beginning to get together, and maybe this is the beginning of the end of the comfortable time, of having it reasonably good. All those minorities together could really form a most powerful force, and perhaps this realisation is beginning to dawn on them. Just like individuals, alone they're helpless: together they can hope and work for redress.

They're a motley crew these uncomfortable minorities of ours: battered wives and small town homosexuals, the raped and the redundant, the physically handicapped, lonely widows and single parents, the over-stressed and the underpaid. And then there's a whole raft of cultural minorities, from the Gaeltacht to the inner-city ghetto.

And what of the Church? It would be hard to deny that, in recent times at least, it has lived on easy terms with the comfort-

able consensus, and has rarely been distinguished for its concern
for minorities. By 'Church' I mean both the leadership and the
rest of us: in fact, insofar as Christian necks have struck out at all
they have been probably more often 'theirs' than ours. (Certain
fringe-groups like the Simon Community are of course a more
than honourable exception).

True to the tradition of 'interest-group' politics, there has
been little interference with what was seen to be the Church's
proper role in the areas of education, 'private' and family
morality, marriage legislation and the like. A desire not to rock
this particular boat has been common to all sides, and accorded
with the profoundest maxims of the conventional wisdom. As a
solemn warning the burned fingers of Noel Browne were open
to inspection.

(April 1982, vol. 32, no. 4, pp. 242-243)

Ecumenics and moral consensus

Church Unity – 'No Cause for Alarm' was the heart warming
headline in a Dublin evening paper shortly before Easter: it
purported to convey the substance of an article in a Church of
Ireland publication regarding the last ARCIC report. One thought
nostalgically of a famous reassurance from another quarter that
Vatican II would not disturb 'the tranquillity of our Christian
lives' ...

It is of course depressing that change and movement, even
movement towards unity, should be regarded askance by Christian leaders. But the quite unedifying attempts to explain away,
and even denigrate, the solid if far from final achievements of the
Anglican-Roman Catholic Commission are, I'm afraid, not to be
wondered at. They are an inevitable result of the comfortable
tribalisms in which we have all allowed our Christian faith to be
encased, so that unity must seem like exile: leaving a familiar
island home for a vast ill-charted mainland.

...

Perhaps – and this is my own feeling – the real crunch is going to
come not in matters of faith and worship, but in the field of
morality. How do we behave, how should we behave, as disciples
of Christ in the light of his gospel? The outlines of our answering
are predictable, and, whatever our differences of language, will
hardly lead to any serious disagreement. Confrontation, if it is to

occur, will be about the particular: and most likely in relation to human sexuality, birth, marriage, sickness – mental as well as physical – and death.

Also – and, for my present purpose, this is the vital point – the lines of such confrontation will be drawn along the contours of doctrinal difference. And, if there is any real 'danger' of practical moves towards unity or even inter-communion, I believe that this moral confrontation will be urged. A wide gap in our ethical approach, the lack of a common '*lex peccandi*', will be seen to imply that there is no common *lex credendi*, no real community of faith.

I am far from suggesting that the difficulty need be without substance, that we could all be led into stalemate by the deliberate act of those whose interest is vested in the *status quo*. Even as things stand, I can see real problems about, say, artificial insemination – to leave aside for a moment even more obvious questions! And, if and when the long promised (threatened?) new Code of Canon Law arrives, matters could be more difficult still.

...

If I am right so far in my forecast of where unity moves may get bogged down, I am not saying that this 'morality-faith' obstacle need be irremovable. Nor do I suggest that we can ignore what would manifestly create a massive crisis of conscience for believers everywhere. But I think that the way forward must commit us to a more demanding pluralism than we have, up to now, envisaged as tolerable.

Much would appear to hinge on the word 'doctrine', that body of teaching which, it must be remembered, is a series of statements about the Faith but is not itself the object of faith. We all profess to subscribe to the triadic maxim about unity, liberty and charity: the time may well be coming when we will have to take a harder look at the distinction between things necessary and things doubtful in any post-credal formulation of our common beliefs. We may then find that some of our moral imperatives are not as firmly rooted as we thought, that there may be room for another option, an alternative way, and that moreover such alternatives can claim the sanction of a well-established praxis in another tradition.

What I am suggesting can of course be dismissed as an attempt to 'soft-pedal the truth', to bend God's law so as to cater for an adulterous generation. On the contrary, I believe that in his providence, the healing of the wounds of disunity provides an opportunity for looking again at our way, and rule, of life.

It is highly unlikely that in a restored unity all the benefits would flow from 'us' to 'them'. Learning from each other should bring a greater discernment, making us less certain about the doubtful, less absolute about the relative. And if we could hope for this from an Anglican - Roman Catholic reunion, how much more should we stand to gain in a wider restoration of fellowship: I suspect our hierarchy of moral values might suffer some drastic revision.

This is not to subscribe to the myths which stereotype the Christian Churches and traditions in contrasting moral stance and posture. Not all Catholics are drunken but chaste, some Quakers are guilty of sharp practice, one has even met drunken Presbyterians! But the lived experience of each must needs have led to insights worth sharing, and to the recognition of priorities, personal and social, which demand the respect if not the assent of all.

...

Mention of a wider unity, at least including the main post-Reformation Churches, reminds us that one of the objections or reservations which ARCIC has evoked is the suggestion that the Agreements, especially over papal primacy, while acceptable to the 'Catholic' wing of Anglicanism would alienate the 'Evangelicals', and the other Protestant bodies. And one does not need to be a Paisleyite to see that, to some, any recognition of Rome must seem to be a betrayal of what the Reformation stood for and what the Protestant martyrs died for.

Let me say two things which I believe to be relevant. One is that I see the historical role of the Church of England over the past century and a half as deriving precisely from her claim to be both Catholic and Protestant: without her the gulf between the Catholic Church and the 'free' Churches might never have come within sight of being bridged.

If only for this reason, we should deplore anything that would seem to do violence to Protestant pieties or sensitivities. But, in fact, our own ecumenical concern must wish to embrace the Protestant tradition, whether Presbyterian, Reformed, Methodist or whatever. And our new-found appreciation of the Anglican communion must not close our minds to those others who profess to be of the Holy Catholic Church.

So ecumenism, to be true to its vocation, must be multilateral in approach: to change old exclusivisms for new would be a sad parody of the vision of unity. The structures of dialogue set up by the Vatican Secretariat for the Promotion of Christian Unity were in fact designed on a multilateral basis, and other inter-church conversations have been similarly shaped. At home there has been some progress within the Irish Council of Churches, and also outside to some small extent.

I fear that the Irish situation offers a classic example of the dominance of non-theological factors. These are too painfully familiar to need rehearsal: as I said earlier, they extend from politics to sport. But precisely because of this, and because, on the Protestant side at least, the symbols of religion carry political significance, and vice-versa, the 'Papal' proposals of ARCIC must be a red flag to a Tory.

So the pace and tempo of the movement to unity can hardly be forecast, still less can we plot the stages along the way. All we can say for certain is that, at the end of the tunnel, the light is clear and bright: the call too is clear, and there can be no going back. In the meantime, we must be grateful to all those whose devoted labour has cut away so much of the theological overgrowth, and notably the ARCIC team. We are indeed proud of the distin-guished leadership provided by the Church of Ireland in the person of Archbishop McAdoo of Dublin.

(May-June 1982, vol. 32, no. 5, pp. 311-316)

A pope for all seasons

Everybody, or almost everybody, has hailed the visit of Pope John Paul II to Britain as a great success. Indeed only a 'begrudger' would wish to belittle the enthusiasm which greeted the Pope everywhere he went. From Westminster to the North, it was a triumph – without triumphalism.

The Scots, and the Welsh too, welcomed the Pope in their own way, and he showed great tact and awareness of the fact that his visit was to three different nations, three different local Churches. Even in England he responded to the differing tones of the crowds' greeting: the sight and sound of Liverpool were in strong contrast to the Canterbury walkabout.

But even there, in the mother-church of the Anglican Com-munion, unprecedented applause broke through the solemn ceremony of reconciliation, giving flesh to the spirit of unity.

This was a great and noble moment when Pope and Archbishop embraced as brothers, followed by the veneration of Martyrs of today and by the moving pause for prayer at the tomb of Canterbury's own martyr, St Thomas.

Then, throughout the visit, there was the Pope's ministry to the sick in mind and body. This ministry was sacramentally, and collegially, celebrated in Southwark Cathedral, but the care and concern which he continued to show especially for the handicapped everywhere he went was, in Britain as elsewhere, rightly seen as a true apostolic sign. This, and a similar care and concern for the young, from babies in arms to those in their teens and early twenties – always marvellously expressed in face and hand and voice – are, without doubt, gifts of the Spirit, justifying for once the word 'charisma'.

'Charismatic', in a rather different and not altogether approving sense, was the word I heard used more than once about the reaction of the young people themselves at some of the events specially arranged for them. Once upon a time the word might have been 'enthusiastic', used with similar disapproval.

. . .

And so the note of criticism filters in, mostly among Catholics (nearly all television viewers). The vast majority of Protestants and agnostics seemed to think it all a good thing. To a ventured suggestion that 'the kids went overboard a bit' the reply was 'No harm in that! He's a good man. Not like these pop-stars and politicians'.

One takes the point. Even without damning all of the two categories named, there was something refreshing in the sheer joy that shone through the young singing faces, and the young swaying bodies who came to see and hear a man of prayer and peace and love, a man who spoke of decency and fidelity and caring, a man standing for social justice, for family life and for the brotherhood and sisterhood of all. A man with no axe to grind, not selling anything … not giving anything away.

It is, I believe, beside the point to say that, if John Paul II is such a man, so was Paul VI, but that the kids wouldn't throng to hear *him*, let alone cheer and sing after every sentence he spoke. The fact that John Paul has, as well as the gifts of the Spirit we spoke of, other gifts of personality and performance, of speech and gesture and timing – this does not take from the authenticity of his mission: indeed we may regard these gifts as of the Spirit also.

There can be no doubt that this pope is reaching more people, of his own flock and outside it, than any pope in history. He does it directly as well as by television and radio: he has, as someone said, turned pilgrimage upside down – he now brings Rome to the whole world ...

Yet, the deeper question, to what extent frequent papal journeyings are of the *bene esse* of the modern Church can and perhaps should be a matter of serious discussion. It is in fact a very timely and relevant question just now when the Pope's ministry is close to the centre of ecumenical development.

It might be argued that the essence of the Bishop of Rome's function in the Church Catholic is a certain *stabilitas*, offering a 'still centre' which is the very focus of catholicity and the lodestar of unity: and that a peripatetic Papacy does little to serve this end. As against this it could be cogently held that in coming in person to the local Churches the idea of *servus servorum* is powerfully enacted and the Petrine mission of confirming the brethren splendidly realised in a way never before possible.

There remain such practical problems as the fear that too frequent absences from Rome could mean 'leaving too much to the Curia', thereby giving a new lease of life to that kind of quasi-anonymous rule by decree to which we had hoped to see an end. Similarly 'authoritative Vatican views' can be all too easily expressed and promulgated with apparently little or no papal input or assessment: an all too recent example of this kind of thing was the response to the final ARCIC report by the Sacred Congregation for the Doctrine of the Faith. It can hardly have reflected fairly the mind of Pope John Paul on the subjects in question: his own recent statements have been very much more positive. Nor does it even appear to have been commissioned or requested by him.

Meanwhile there may be a certain unease about what might be identified in some journalistic circles as a 'personality cult'. The phrase would not be apposite: nothing could be further from the truth than any suggestion of an orchestrated concentration on the Pope's admittedly strong personality. Rather the problem, if there is one, lies in the danger that the immediacy of the papal presence on his visits to different communities could give a new significance to the idea and practice of direct jurisdiction, diminishing the role and authority of the local Church.

It must of course be said immediately that if this happened it would be in spite of the Pope's own scrupulously fraternal respect for, and indeed deference to local bishops. Anyway distortion of the true balance would rather be in popular reaction to an unusual stimulus.

On the other hand it has to be said that on the central and crucial issue of peace and war the Pope's utterly independent statements contrast at times in a very salutary way with those of hierarchies themselves inevitably conditioned if not influenced by the political and cultural particularities. Here the danger is rather that all of us might regard such papal pronouncements as ritual expressions of principle, to be treated with all due deference and respect, while we continue to opt for the familiar compromises ...

One thing is certain. Whether we like it or not, Church and papacy have entered a new age.

(July-August 1982, vol. 32, no. 7, pp. 385-388)

Sins and systems

That violent crime in the North is at least partly caused, or at least conditioned, by the political and economic situation there is a commonplace. Much of it is professedly a protest against that situation. To reject the legitimacy of the protest is not to deny the moral bankruptcy of such structures as can be said to exist, nor to absolve successive British governments for allowing the situation to deteriorate as it has.

In the same way, if not to quite the same degree, the structures of authority in the Republic must be seen as less than morally adequate to their task of upholding the values which, according to the Constitution, they should serve. The word 'structure' is, of course, itself ambiguous, inasmuch as institutional theory comes alive only when put into practice: inadequacy then is as much a matter of politicians as of politics.

It can hardly be denied that, in recent years, a new kind of cynicism has tended to colour public opinion in this State. What I mean is that – shades of the North! – old-fashioned patriotism, however thin a veneer, just doesn't figure any more: the gaining and retention of power are in themselves sufficient political objectives, and seen to be such by the plain people of Ireland (as de Valera used to call us).

To ask what power is for is a question not often posited. Indeed one might be forgiven for believing that anything beyond good 'housekeeping' is to be regarded as a romantic indulgence: so far have we erected the pragmatic as an end in itself. The apparent failure of so many lofty plans has led to the tacit abandonment of what used to be called 'national aims'.

But it still remains true that without a vision the people perish, and in politics, as in all the business of living, bread alone is not enough. For the failed ideals of a nation's adolescence, which have become the broken idols of a sad 'maturity', less worthy or more 'realistic' substitutes are always on offer. And in the face of moral and cultural agnosticism on the part of our political leaders, these must be able to count on more than a few takers, and not only among the deprived and unschooled.

We are in sore need of fresh socio-cultural thinking and leadership of a kind to inspire, and in its turn to be nourished by, the response of a popular national movement – such as the Gaelic League provided in the early years of this century. The genius of Douglas Hyde was the unlikely catalyst at a time at least as barren of hope as our own, and (in his own words) by steering clear of 'politics' the League became the most potent political force in the land.

It is now idle to speculate what the course of our history might have been had the movement not turned away from Hyde in 1915 and gone 'political'. All was 'changed utterly' and there is no going back ... Nor should we look to the kind of leadership or the kind of movement which should seek to transcend the structures and processes of parliamentary democracy, for these, however imperfect, and however in need of reform, are still the surest guarantee of our democratic liberties.

(December 1982, vol. 32, no. 10, pp. 629-630)

1983

Art for God's sake?

I might put it in political terms by saying that while Art may not be a sovereign independent state, it is at least an autonomous region. And the integrity of that autonomy should at all times be respected. It has its own laws and disciplines, its own language and traditions, its own logic and ethic and metaphysic.

The artist must, of course, relate to the society in which he lives. He may react against it, even violently, but he cannot ignore it. Nor can the artist who is also a Christian ignore the Christian community, however much he may be at odds with the institutional Church. In return, both Church and State should take account of the artist, and as I have said, respect his autonomy.

Put like that, it may all sound simple and reasonable. In fact the record shows that artist and community – secular and Christian – are as often as not in a state of tension.

This is not in itself a bad thing. Where there is tension there is life. Tensions can be positive and indeed fruitful, but they can also lead to conflict, prejudice, and a reluctance to listen or learn. And societies which are totalitarian, or tend that way, may seek to resolve the situation by demanding an obedient conformism, to which the alternative is ostracism – or persecution. We have seen this in our own time as well as in history.

Much is sometimes made of the enlightened patronage which the Church has, at different periods, given to artists. This has to be qualified by suggesting that, in some of this patronage, individual popes and prelates were acting as enlightened princes rather than as pastors. One must also concede that there have been periods of neglect, not to say philistinism, and these have been closer and more familiar to most of us. There has been a modest revival in recent years for which we may be grateful. (Incidentally the revival in this country owes much to the pioneer work of the editor of this journal [Austin Flannery, O.P.], and of the late J.G. McGarry of *The Furrow*.)

It needs to be added that painters, sculptors and architects have been the main beneficiaries of such patronage (or have suffered from the lack of it). Poets, novelists, playwrights and

other literary artists have usually kept their distance, neither
asking nor expecting the Church's bounty. Music and its practi-
tioners have occupied a midway position: the composers of the
classic settings of the liturgy have at times been commissioned,
but, as often, have used, say, the Mass-form as they might use
symphonic form – executant musicians on the other hand have
often been in the direct employ of the Church. But poets,
novelists, playwrights and other literary artists have usually kept
their distance, neither asking nor expecting the Church's bounty.
Journalism, pamphleteering and other forms of written propaganda are quite a different matter, and do not concern us here.
Or should not.

The line between art and propaganda is however not always
clearly drawn: and indeed there is often a strong propaganda
element in perfectly authentic works of art. So we have had the
vexed problem of the 'Catholic writer' – notably the 'Catholic
novelist' – often derided by the critics as a purveyor of honeyed
tracts, while being denounced by the Church authorities as
disloyal, irreverent or obscene.

In all this, time the great healer has been at work, and much
holy water has been salted since a François Mauriac or a Graham
Greene was regarded as 'suspect'. Not many creative writers
today would be happy to bear the label 'Catholic' or even
'Christian' as sufficiently descriptive of their purpose, however
deep their own personal commitment. Still, every so often, a
work appears which can be seen to have an unmistakably propa-
gandist – not to say evangelical – quality, however consciously
intended, however obliquely realised …

In communicating the Transcendent, which is the business of
both Art and Church, each uses a language of symbol. These
languages are separate and distinct and it would be a grave
mistake to try to impose one on the other. And the Christian's
faith in Christ as Sacrament makes him see the Church and her
symbols as sacramental: that is, as making present what they
signify. He accepts this on the authority of God's revealed Word.

No such revelation guarantees the reality of the artist's use of
symbol. But whether he works in words or music, paint or stone
or metal, his ministry is a sacred service, both to the Mystery he
strives to communicate, and to the community to which he
relates. And so at a deeper level than the 'political', the autonomy
of this ministry deserves to be recognised, not least by the

ministry of the sacramental community.

(January 1983, vol. 33, no. 1, pp. 48-50)

Poet of Theology

Prophets are notoriously difficult people: the great exception has to be Edward Schillebeeckx. His amiability seems to be endless: even as he firmly distinguishes between the overlapping assertions of a muddled interlocutor there appears no hint of impatience, let alone of tired authority....

Not all prophets are also scholars. The combination is in Schillebeeckx a formidable one. Insight and vision are all the more impressive when backed by a support structure of chapter and verse, of precedent and relevant quotation. While pointing a detail he can hold the whole picture in steady focus. And, without any apparent effort of will, he can be enthusiastic and judicious at the same time.

What I find almost impossible to understand is that anyone could doubt this man's orthodoxy. I remember once in Rome, several years ago, how bewildered he was when he became aware that the Holy Office goon squad were on his trail – sitting, like comic detectives in a French farce, at the back of the hall whenever he lectured. He did a very wise thing: he sought and was granted an audience of the Pope.

He returned from the encounter a happy man. Paul VI had reassured him, and spoke to him warmly about his work, calling him the Poet of Theology ...

Rumours of new stupidities preceded Fr Edward on his recent visit to Dublin. It appears that *Ministry – a case for change* has given particular offence. In arguing the Christian community's 'right to leadership' and its right to eucharistic celebration, he cites Tertullian's famous suggestion that in cases of necessity 'you the laity must celebrate the Eucharist and baptize; in that case you are your own priest ... '

How then, say the Inquisitors (or so rumour has it), how can this be reconciled with the teaching of Trent and Vatican I? ... And Fr Schillebeeckx meekly suggests they should ask Tertullian!

(April 1983, vol. 33, no. 4, p. 239)

Ad cathedram

Professional journeys brought Oisín to two of the great cathedrals of Europe on two of the Sundays of Lent. Both are places of enormous tourist resort as well as of pious pilgrimage, but it must be said at once that neither has allowed its primary function to be interfered with. However, I did find a considerable difference between the two.

In St Mark's in Venice substantial congregations seemed to attend for worship, in spite of the multiplicity of other Churches in the area. The capitular Mass was sung decently but without – it seemed to me – either a sense of classic ceremonial, or of pastoral outreach. But that may be an unfair judgement.

Notre-Dame was a different matter. The morning liturgy which I attended is, as I know from previous visits, only one of three solemn Eucharists celebrated in different styles, each with a large congregation. The day's horarium also includes solemn vespers in the afternoon, and a major organ recital.

What impressed me most was the way that this great cathedral, the very type and symbol of the medieval Church, whose high and soaring gothic is itself a prayer from another age, has been made to serve the living worship of our time. And this has been achieved without any apparent force or straining, though what prodigies of effort have gone into the liturgy itself I can only guess at. Lauds, sung in French, was alive and fresh; a true morning sacrifice of praise. The Mass which followed was unforgettable.

It was first of all a miracle of style, a splendid fusion of Latin and French, new chants and old, discipline and freedom of stance and movement. Secondly, there was a tactful and welcoming involvement which seemed to make sanctuary of all the church and ministers of all who stood there. Thirdly, word and sacrament were subsumed in an act of prayer, which transcended tradition and language, class and culture.

(May-June 1983, vol. 33, no. 5, pp. 313-314)

Left! Right!

Pardoning sins we are inclined to, while damning those we have no mind to is a sickness long endemic in the Christian community. And as often as not, the inclination or mind is political. When Oisín was a teenage anticlerical it was held as an axiom that the Church was notoriously indulgent to right-wing excesses while frowning on the slightest peccadillo of the left. Nowadays his conservative juniors complain that the villain/hero roles have been reversed and that the Right is always in the wrong.

The allegation is indeed given more than a little colour by a fairly steady stream of newspaper headlines. Events in El Salvador, Chile and other parts of Central and South America; the progressively antinuclear stance of the American bishops; a generally critical view of Western economic policies towards the Third World – culminating, *mirabile dictu*, in a fortright denunciation of the capitalist system by an Irish bishop: all seems to point to a notable change in the climate of opinion.

Of course the suggestion (sometimes heard on the dottier Right) that the Church has 'gone soft' on Communism, and entered into a covert alliance with the Soviet bloc, is quite absurd; such a development is hardly likely during the present Pope's reign! Partial accommodations with individual Marxist governments, or the patient pursuit of such accommodation, are no greater evidence of a 'sell-out' than were any one of a thousand precedents involving non-Catholic and even non-Christian regimes in the past.

Nor does the existence of a dialogue between Christians and Marxists presage an ideological synthesis, any more than do similar encounters with Islam or with Hindu or Buddhist thinkers. (Interestingly enough, latter-day syncretists seem to be commonly right-wingers. The most notorious example is the so-called 'Unification Church', less reverently known as the 'Moonies': but there are others in the field – though not nearly as successful in the recruitment and exploitation of the gullible).

It can, however, be maintained that since John XXIII addressed himself to all men of goodwill, dialogue and détente have led to an *apertura a sinistra*, far broader and deeper than that achieved (or even envisaged) in the political context in which the phrase was first used. On one level, cooperation with Marxists, however cautious or partial, became possible in a number of enterprises, while philosophically – and, even theologically – the new situation bore fruit not so much in an acceptance of Marxist insights and values, but in a welcome and long-delayed liberation from categories of thought and expression which we had long suffered, like a kind of compulsory though obsolete armour – or a heavy overcoat on a warm day. I'm not just referring to the fact that Marx (like Freud) has affected the thinking of millions who never read a line of his work. What I want to stress is the belated realism of Christians, and especially Catholics, who have come to recognise that fact, and so come to terms with the real world.

On a practical level, though, any left-ward détente has been less important than the new critical stance in regard to right-wing policies and their execution. Of this there are so many examples in recent years that one would find it hard to know where to begin. In Ireland, however, we can be particularly conscious of the witness of our *oilithrigh* who went to preach Christ in Latin America and have found him in the poor and persecuted people there. Friars and nuns, doctors and social workers, they have all, indeed, 'witnessed' on two levels: by their solidarity with their people they have proclaimed the Gospel before the tyrant, and, by telling the story to their parent Church they have helped to identify the tyranny, and make it known to the world.

And the Irish are, of course, only one note in that united Christian voice which alone can speak for so many of the world's oppressed today from Central America to South Africa.

...

Now the objection is made that criticism of the Right, and of the admitted crimes of the Right, is selective, unfair and a 'soft option' when not balanced by similar criticism of the left. And this view does deserve an answer.

It could be argued that the balance of, say, torture statistics available to us – or, in a quite different context, the treatment of the sick poor – places the nastier Latin American regimes on a far more deplorable level than the Soviet Union or China. As against that, the perversion of psychiatric practice as a way of repressing dissent and legitimate protest is probably unparalleled in the West. But such comparisons are beside the point.

The plain unpalatable fact is that campaigns of criticism against injustice on the Right are more likely to succeed than similar campaigns directed against the Left. This is not because neo-fascist regimes are more amenable than Communists, but because most of them are to some degree clients of, or dependent on, the West.

Even the Republic of South Africa which is one of the world's wealthiest countries is not indifferent to the West's goodwill. And even the more prosperous of the Latin-Americans look to the Western powers and especially to the United States for military aid. In the last analysis, in one way or another, the US is patron or paymaster to nearly every 'free' country where human rights are violated – either through economic and social inequity, malnutrition, inadequate housing, illiteracy, slave labour, and the like, or where these are compounded by institutionalised

violence, cruelty, torture and legalised murder. I do not say that
'socialist' countries are utterly free from any or all of these evils
– though most of them are incomparably better – but, cynical
though it may seem to say it, the others can be 'got at' through
the United States. So the short-term aim of protest is to conscientise
the Americans and to make them force Washington to apply the
necessary pressure.

This is not in itself the easiest of tasks, particularly at present.
To many of us the presidency of Ronald Reagan has been an
unmitigated disaster not alone for his own country but for the
world. Not the least of his sins has been a quite heartless attitude
to the oppressed – except, in theory, those in 'Communist
Thralldom'. And he has succeeded in making his policies a focus
for all the sad frustrations of blue-collar Americans whose striving for white-collar status has been thwarted by recession.

In this populist atmosphere, outreach to the Third World is
hardly likely to commend itself as a policy, especially if it involves
letting down 'allies' who are helping to preserve the American
continent against the Red Menace. It is indeed a bitter irony that
expenditure which if directed to development in, say, Nicaragua,
would cause an outcry, can be hailed when spent as military aid
to Honduras.

But bleak as the picture is, there are signs of hope. Congress
has become more and more wary of the kind of blanket 'defence'
expenditure which has been used to prop up wicked and corrupt
regimes: slowly but surely the tide may be seen to be turning. If
this is so, and there are good reasons for believing it, I would
suggest that no small credit is due to the American Catholic
Church. And while 'Church' here, as always, must include those
who have been working for justice and peace in lay organisations,
as private individuals, and in associations of religious men and
women, an unusually strong role has been played by the Church
leadership.

In a word, what the US bishops have done, especially over the
past year, has been to shift the balance of Catholic influence,
dramatically and unambiguously. The shift has been from docile
acceptance of Establishment policies on war and peace to an
articulate, critical Christian stance …

…

It is of course ironic that questioning of the wisdom of the present
policy of mutual nuclear deterrence is regarded generally in the

West as suspiciously leftist, while the advocacy of unilateral disarmament is equated with a sell-out to the Soviets. So, in Europe as well as in America, the intervention of the Churches, as well as individual Christians, in this area has been of considerable importance.

The British Campaign for Nuclear Disarmament has indeed had a strong Christian presence, both in its earlier 'Aldermaston' days and in its recent revival. But although in this, as in other unpopular causes of the 1960s, the late great Archbishop Tommy Roberts was the still, small, and puckish voice of the Catholic conscience, the main Christian accent was Anglican, embodied particularly in the person of John Collins, Canon of St Paul's, and a peace-fighter if there ever was one.

The emergence of Monsignor Bruce Kent as the prophet and leader of latter-day unilateralism in Britain, has been paralleled by strong Catholic action in other countries, notably the Netherlands. The unbelievable remarks of the egregious Archbishop Heim (the ultimate Envoy Extraordinary) have if anything strengthened Kent's position: even the indefatigable Catholic Tory lobby will hardly be able to have their way with Cardinal Hume this time (and will have to content themselves with more snarling at their other *bête noire*, the Catholic Primate of All Ireland).

It would certainly be unfair to suggest that all who oppose CND, or who deplore Church involvement in such movements are either bloodthirsty, or unaware of the appalling dangers of the nuclear threat. And they may well have a point that unilateralists are – though in good faith – 'playing the Soviet game'.

The very word 'peace' is suspect, because of Soviet exploitation of many Western organisations and individuals whose names may be useful. It is noteworthy also that a discreet campaign for disarmament in East Germany has been received with no great enthusiasm by the authorities there. But none of this can take from the urgency of the present situation: what is at stake is nothing less than human survival, and it has been truly said that there is no moral issue remotely as important.

So once again if we must have recourse to a cynical argument, so be it. Democratic régimes, are in the last analysis, open to persuasion and moral pressure. At times elements within these régimes, notably the 'defense' establishments may appear intractable and intransigent, but as long as the sovereignty of the ballot-box is maintained there is always hope. And this is why Christians must continue to campaign especially on those issues and in those areas where there is some hope of success ...

...

Of course words like 'right' and 'left' are themselves full of ambiguities. No one, on the one hand, would wish to equate the régime of say General Pinochet, with the monetary austerities of Mrs Thatcher. Nor would many of the dissident left agree that the Soviet Union is a Communist or Socialist state, true to the ideas of Marx or even Lenin.

But with all due regard to the dangers of labelling, the shifts and moves of which I have been writing are very much part of the present situation in the Church and the world. And that the 'harvest' I have just referred to is a living reality will be attested to by a thousand young men and women who are labouring to save it, all over the Third World – and indeed, in parts of our own First World, as well. Mission is a *currach* on the great sea, driven by the mighty wind of Pentecost.

(July-August 1983, vol. 33, no. 7, pp. 358-363)

Word and world

'Communications and community in Ireland' is the subject of a series of broadcasts on Irish radio to mark World Communications Year. The title was hardly devised just for euphony, for it points not only to the end and object of all communication but also to the framework and context within which communications must work.

The fact that communication is the very stuff of community, that you can't have one without the other, is a truism but its implications are all too often ignored. And not least by the Church. An all too typical example of this comes to my attention as I write: the failure of the Synod of Bishops in Rome to publish the sixty-three Propositions which were the fruit of their deliberations. Those reporting on the Synod were issued with a paper which purported to provide a précis of these propositions: but the text of the English version, at least, was opaque to the point of making it impossible to glean anything but the most general impression of what they contained.

It may be considered unlikely that this was due to a deliberate desire to mystify. But misinformation due to incompetence is hardly more pardonable. There comes a point when inefficiency becomes criminal, and that point has long been passed in the Vatican's relations with the media.

It will of course be argued that Synodal Propositions are for submission to the Pope, not for promulgation. Agreed: but even this unsatisfactory proceeding need not be compounded by bungling attempts at the preservation of a 'secrecy' which is neither justifiable in theory nor possible of attainment. Leaks there always are and always will be, so why not release the basic documents anyway, with good, clear, reliable translations? Or what preposterous notion of the relationship between the Pope and his fellow-bishops demands what can only be a ritual conceal-ment, temporary and ineffective? Confidential advice has its place in the Church, as in any society, but that place is not a parliament of a couple of hundred members.

During the Second Vatican Council the determined efforts of a number of journalists from many countries succeeded in gaining legitimate access to information without which they believed they could not do their job. (Unlawful access was always available – at a price). The story has been told too often to warrant repetition here, but two points about it are worth remembering. Firstly, the journalists' fight was supported by a minority of Council fathers, but only a minority. And, secondly: the victory was only partial, and, it appears, temporary. In many respects we appear to be back to square one.

It is ironic to recall that one of the present Pope's most promising initiatives was to call that great communicator, Fr Agnellus Andrew, O.F.M., out of his BBC retirement to become effective head of the Vatican's Commission for the Media. It is an open secret that he returned to Britain this year in what in a less Christian man would be despair.

...

I think, however, that it would be a mistake to regard this as anything more than the tip of the iceberg. In fact, the Church as a whole has always been weak on communication, both internally and with the world 'outside'. Or to put it another way, her failures have always been failures of communication. For a strong and healthy community is one where communication flows free and clear, unimpeded by those blockages and muddyings that make for social misunderstanding, leading either to dictatorship, anar-chy or disintegration.

One may well say indeed that the Church's failures in this are inherent in the *condition humaine,* the fruit of original sin, or whatever origin to which the alienation of humankind may be attributed. And we are bitterly aware today that a general availability and sophistication of the means of communication do not make for the will and power to communicate.

And so is the Church to be blamed for sharing in this vastly common failing, this universal inability to 'connect'? Well, yes! In fact, she is. We are. For in a very profound sense, communication is the Church's business – to the glory of God, *et pour encourager les autres.*

Which is only another way of saying that the Church's task is a missionary one, to preach God's Word; that the Church is a sign, and signs are for communication; that the Church is, above all, Christ's Sacrament – and a Sacrament is a special kind of sign; that the Church must proclaim the good news that men and women are no longer alienated from God or from each other, that Christ has broken through once and for all of us ...

(December 1983, vol. 33, no. 10, pp. 618-619)

1984

Forum Romanum!

All of us in Ireland regard the public session of the New Ireland Forum, held in Dublin Castle on February 9th, as a unique historic occasion. For this was the first time that an official delegation of the Roman Catholic Church in Ireland met in open discussion with senior Irish legislators. The three main political parties in the Republic were represented and were joined by representatives of the main Northern minority party; the chairman of the Forum is a distinguished academic.

This was the last public session of a body whose achievements so far have been widely greeted as exceeding anything that could have been reasonably hoped for when set up last year, to explore and pursue policies and projects which might lead to 'lasting peace and stability in a new Ireland through the democratic process'. It would be open to all parties 'who reject violence', with members elected to either the Parliament of the Republic or the Northern Assembly.

In the event, only the (Catholic) Social Democratic and Labour Party responded from the North, their representatives joining those from Dáil and Seanad Éireann, forming a total of twenty-seven members of the Forum (with provision for alternates). At the outset, the new animal was seen as a bit of a non-starter – either as a committee-camel or a lame dog. But against all the odds, once the Forum got going, the mood changed fairly rapidly. The party leaders were impressively dedicated to making it work – and unusually united in their approach. The chairman, Dr Colm Ó hEocha (president of University College, Galway), struck, from the start, a note of urgency and clarity. And, less obviously to the naked eye, the new body was blessed by a remarkably committed secretariat.

The great break-through was undoubtedly in the response to a second line of invitations issued to all 'who agree with the Forum's purpose and reject violence' to submit their views in the form of written evidence. Over 250 submissions were received in a very short time – a third from north of the Border ...

At the time of writing the final Report is being drafted. It is on this document, and whatever developments it may lead to, that the whole project will ultimately be judged. Much depends on the degree of consensus achieved, but as much, if not more, on the response from the North, and from Westminster.

At this stage we can only hope for the best. But let this be said: as far as Church-State relations in the Republic are concerned, nothing can ever be the same again. February 9th was a milestone.

Its importance was all the greater for that it came as a very welcome sequel to what was generally agreed to be a rather depressing confrontation, in the form of the written submission received from the Bishops' Conference, early in the new year. This document (or, rather, series of documents) was, I think not unfairly, generally regarded as hard-line, pedantic, and generally lacking in 'outreach'. The unfortunate misunderstanding which followed, about a supporting oral presentation, had the effect of creating a minor but quite unpleasant tension, not precisely between Church and State, but, apparently, between the Church leadership and nearly everybody else. The news that there would be a 'personal appearance' at the Forum, after all, was received with quite remarkable relief, and this was confidently looked forward to as likely to redeem the situation.

In the meantime there was a second unfortunate development. I refer to the reaction to Cardinal Ó Fiaich's refusal (in the course of a wide-ranging radio interview) to issue a blanket condemnation of all Catholics who voted for Sinn Féin. He was clearly making a distinction between objective immorality and personal motive, but this was too subtle a distinction for his enemies – or even for quite a few of his friends. Even Taoiseach FitzGerald felt moved to issue a rebuke! So, what with one thing and another, fence-mending became something of a priority.

I have no doubt that this was done, and done handsomely, at the Forum. And, while it might be argued that this was more a matter of style than of substance, the very fact that an appropriate style was indeed achieved is no small matter. For style is of the essence of communication, and communication is what we're about – and what the bishops were about.

One might go further and say that an absence of style has been one reason, perhaps the main reason, for the lack of communication between Church and State in the past – indeed as recently as in the case of the written submission of January last. If the word 'style' seems frivolous, you can substitute 'language'; it will surely be agreed that finding a language to address the world has been one of the great needs and tasks of the Church in our time, and that the problem has so far been only partly solved, if at all. It would be too much to hope that it has been solved overnight by the Irish bishops, but they have certainly got off to a good start.

The first thing to note, by the way, is that they did not monopolise the situation. The seven-member delegation included – as well as Bishops Cahal Daly, Edward Daly, Joseph Cassidy and Dermot O'Mahony – Professor Mary McAleese of Trinity College, Dublin, Professor Michael Ledwith of Maynooth, and Mr Matthew Salter of Queen's University, Belfast.

So, from the outset, the point was very clearly, not to say dramatically, made that the 'Church' does not mean just the 'Hierarchy'. And, of course, this very fact added another dimension to the encounter – or rather reminded us of a dimension which might be forgotten (though not for very long!). I mean that of overlap – since most Irish legislators, north and south, would claim to be Christians, and to be members of one or another of the Christian Churches. In this particular instance, nearly all those present were Roman Catholics: and this inevitably gave added significance to what had to be said about the differing roles of Church and State, bishops and legislators!

To return for a moment to the matter of style, the whole episode, as an essay in communication, lost nothing by the presence of television cameras. The session was not transmitted live, but even had it been, its public impact would hardly have been as strong as the subsequent replay undoubtedly achieved – if only because this was transmitted on a Sunday afternoon, a far better time for an audience than the morning of a working day. (Not to mention that the performers too could watch, and learn!)

The camera may not lie, but it can flatter: one of the bishops was especially favoured on this occasion. But camera and microphone together can be ruthlessly revealing, and neither sentiment nor case-making nor sheer evasiveness can, in the long run, withstand them. Of course it 'takes two to tango', and in an encounter of this kind the quality and performance of the interlocutor is as important as that of his witness.

The star performer here was, undoubtedly, Deputy John M. Kelly. His approach and manner could have taught many a professional interviewer the often forgotten lesson that one can press a question, hard and persistently, without impertinence or discourtesy. But then I suppose he is a professional, being a member of the bar as well as of parliament ...

...

I suppose the highlight of the whole encounter occurred when John Kelly raised the 'mixed marriage' issue with a particular reference to the Bishops' Directory of last year, and to the fact that the Church of Ireland had found this 'profoundly disappointing'. He asked 'would there not be a case, in the interest of community reconciliation, for seeking a special régime tailored to Irish conditions, which would leave the Protestant partners in a mixed marriage on a footing of absolute equality with the Catholic partner in relation to the upbringing of children?'

To nearly everyone's surprise, Bishop Cassidy revealed that the bishops had indeed considered just that idea, and considered it very seriously indeed – to the point that they thought of asking Rome for a 'derogation'. The reason that they decided against this course was, he refreshingly added, that they thought it didn't stand a chance! ...

So far, so good. But something more has to be said, and said honestly, if the total picture is not to be distorted. For at the end of the session there remained an area of ambiguity, of some doubt as to the Church's attitudes and intentions. It centred on the question of minority rights in the Republic, and emerged especially from those parts of the discussion led by Senator Mary Robinson and, again by Deputy Kelly.

For it might appear that while the rights and liberties of 'Northern Ireland Protestants' would be persistently defended by the Catholic bishops in any new constitutional arrangement, the full extension of such rights and liberties to Protestants in the Republic – or indeed to other dissident minorities here – would not necessarily be so championed. In this the question of divorce legislation in the Republic could be regarded as crucial ...

In the long run, it comes down to a question of mutual trust. Without this we cannot possibly go forward together – and this applies to Church and State as much as it does to Catholics and Protestants, believers and agnostics, Republicans and Unionists. It also applies to public men (be they bishops or politicians) and their constituents ...

What I find lacking is any suggestion that dialogue between

the Churches on such issues might be fruitful in establishing, if not an immediate consensus on moral questions, at least a clearer picture of where we agree and disagree. For I have little doubt that there is no real disagreement on fundamentals: that the difficulties arise in specifics relating to situations, exceptions and the like. And, as a Roman Catholic, I find it, to say the least, unhelpful that we should proclaim *our* reading of the law of Christ as self-evidently and in all circumstances correct.

The irony is that moves towards convergence on matters doctrinal are now accepted on all sides. Surely we can sit down in charity and humility to see whether some of our entrenched attitudes on moral questions might not bear inspection in the light of what our brethren of other traditions may, painfully and prayerfully, have come to practise and to preach. It would be tragic if we hesitated to do this for reasons of misplaced loyalty.

(March 1984, vol. 34, no. 3, pp. 137-144)

Sede vacante

Archbishop Dermot Ryan, as he leaves [9 April 1984] to take up his appointment as Pro-Prefect of the Congregation for the Evangelisation of Peoples, will bring with him to Rome the good wishes of the people of the See of Dublin, and indeed of the whole Irish Church. It is perhaps historically appropriate that this first Irish appointment to a senior position in the modern Roman Curia should be to the successor congregation of the old Propaganda Fidei which was so long responsible for Irish affairs. The new Pro-Prefect may well be the first of his countrymen to have free access to an archive which must include many documents of great interest (not to use a stronger word!)

Today, of course, the Congregation has no function in regard to 'domestic' affairs here, ecclesiastical or political. However the Irish presence in many younger Churches throughout the world must ensure that the new challenges and problems facing Dr Ryan will, in all their multicultural complexity, include some very familiar ingredients. A little over a year ago, at the Holy Thursday Mass of the Chrism in Dublin's Pro-Cathedral, the Archbishop paid a warm tribute to two of the concelebrants, recently banished from El Salvador for their alleged 'political' activities. And since then other Irish priests have been in trouble both in Central America and, notoriously, in the Philippines. There is little likelihood that the trend will be arrested in the foreseeable future. One hopes that the Church militant, irritant, turbulent, 'protestant' – whether in an Irish accent or not – may find in Archbishop Ryan a strong defender, as well as a wise counsellor.

Apart from all this, the Archbishop's new responsibilities will hardly cause him to lose interest in his home Church. And his voice in this regard is likely to be given an attentive hearing, at all appropriate times, in the highest quarter. Indeed it has been very reasonably suggested that his advice, along with that of the Nuncio to Ireland, and of Cardinal Ó Fiaich, may well be crucial in the selection of his successor in Dublin.

There will, of course, be wide local consultations, among priests and (to a lesser extent and less directly) people. Such a consultative process occurred over twelve years ago when the succession to Archbishop McQuaid was being canvassed, and in fact, Dr Ryan was known at the time to be a strong favourite. But a retiring prelate must have a powerful voice in the final decision-making, as, no doubt, Archbishop McQuaid had then.

Nor would I regard it as evidence of local *folie de grandeur* to suggest that the Metropolitan See of Dublin is of sufficient importance within the universal Church to warrant a strong interest, or even personal intervention, by the Pope himself in the process of selection.

Apart from more closely ecclesial considerations there exists the 'political' questions of the primacies, which though at purely medieval origin, relate, if only geographically (and with some overlap), to our 'north-south' political divisions. The Archbishop of Dublin is Primate of Ireland, his brother of Armagh, Primate of All-Ireland (with an archdiocese part of which lies south of the Republic-Northern Ireland border). This pre-Reformation arrangement, by the way, also remains in the (Anglican) Church of Ireland.

It might be argued, then, that a certain balance between the two Primates is necessary or, at least, desirable. (Although even the most skilled of pundits might find it hard to say in what such a balance should consist or how to achieve it!) In any case, one would agree that any appointment to the Dublin See must take account of a number of important dimensions – social, political and demographic ...

I am aware that by the time these *Laylines* appear, an appointment may well have been made. But I believe that there is a strong case for postponement, pending consideration of a fundamental and, as I would hold, urgent question: should not the Metropolitan Church of Dublin be broken up into several dioceses, each with its suffragan bishop, with the Archbishop in a presidential role?

To quote from the 1984 Dublin Diocesan Directory: 'The Archdiocese of Dublin includes the city and county of Dublin, nearly all of county Wicklow, and portions of counties Kildare, Carlow, Wexford and Laois. At the most recent estimate the population of the diocese was 1,150,000, of whom 1,050,000 were Catholics'.

It seems to me that the figures quoted make a formidable demographic case for change. For I cannot see how any one man can be bishop, father in God, in any meaningful way, to so many people. To say this is in no way to underestimate the pastoral zeal of Archbishop Ryan, or of any other bishop in a similar situation elsewhere. Nor am I ignoring or discounting the work and function of auxiliary bishops – there are six in Dublin, though one of these has retired from active ministry.

Indeed, each of the other five has devolved responsibility for the care of some 200,000 souls – far greater, as Dr Ryan himself pointed out recently, than of any other Irish bishop, save those of Down and Connor and Cork. So that, even if the Archdiocese were to be divided between them, their work-load would still be very large, not least in comparison with that of their fellow-suffragans of the Dublin province (Ferns, Ossory, Kildare and Leighlin).

Not, of course, that such comparisons are the point, nor indeed the 'work-load' as such. If one were thinking only in terms of administrative capacity, organisational flair, coping with awkward logistics, then mere size could be seen as a challenge and an opportunity, rather than as a serious problem. In fact, it could be argued that larger units of population – with any sort of adequate resources and facilities – offer the creative administrator, in the Church as elsewhere, options for development which would be unthinkable in narrower contexts.

A corollary to this argument has indeed been attributed to Archbishop Ryan himself in alleged rebuttal of proposals for archdiocese devolution. He is said to believe that, far from being a popular move among the faithful, it would be (rightly) seen by many Dublin Catholics as leading to a loss of those advantages which central planning for disparate areas of high population density can achieve. And while I would agree that there is a great deal in this, I would respectfully submit (with Kai-Lung): not everything!

One is not so stupid as to belittle the importance of administration, or to underestimate the difficulties of maintaining a viable infrastructure for diocesan life. And as far as finances are concerned, the hard facts of inflation and recession cannot be brushed aside. The bishop cannot avoid ultimate responsibility for hard decisions about the material, as well as the spiritual, structures of the local Church.

But I would stress the word 'ultimate'. For I do not believe that it should normally be part of the daily labour of a bishop to involve himself in the implementation of those basic decisions. This must be left to deputies, assistants, specialist associates – preferably not in holy orders! – if far more important aspects of *episkopé* are not to be neglected. And diocesan structures must be turned and tuned to the service of these essential elements.

I mean the growth of effective sacramentality in the community; of unity in service, involving bishop, presbyterate and people; of outreach to those alienated by faith or culture; of leadership in mission and witness, free from self-regarding concern. I do not indeed suggest that, where the emphasis is on 'practical' administration, this is intended otherwise than to serve the same needs. But the unpalatable truth has to be faced that such highly well-conceived practicality can and often does choke the life of the spirit.

'Pastoral' and 'administrative' can, and should be, complementary. But it is not only in ecclesiastical affairs that a wholly creditable concern for nuts and bolts (or bricks and mortar) can take up so much time and energy and talent that larger issues may be neglected. Worse still it can result in practices, and even policies, continuing to be pursued unquestioningly and uncritically, long after their relevance or usefulness may be in doubt.

I do not want to labour the point. I would only add this: preoccupation with management can turn leaders into mere managers, and cause them to lose credibility, as well as contact. Whatever about 'business' enterprises (of the narrower commercial kind), this can only have very serious effects in social or political organisations. In the church it must be disastrous. For a bishop to be remote from his people, or for what he says to seem

or sound remote, is surely to strike at the very heart of his
vocation and his office ...

(May-June 1984, vol. 34, no. 5, pp. 277-280)

President Reagan's visit

Bishop Jeremiah Newman of Limerick has vigorously denied
that the Roman Catholic Church in Ireland has 'turned to the
left.' And, lest anyone gained such an impression from the
absence of any Irish bishop from the State ceremonies held to
welcome President Ronald Reagan on his recent visit here, he
emphasised that this was not due to any 'concerted arrangement'. It just happened that all the bishops had previous engagements ...

Now the really interesting thing about Dr Newman's statement is that he found it necessary to make it. The Catholic Press
and Information Office made it clear that he was 'not speaking
on behalf of the hierarchy', but it is not necessary to assume that
he was or is alone in his views. Nor need one doubt his accuracy
in saying that there was no 'concerted arrangement' made by or
among the bishops to stay away from official receptions in Dublin
and elsewhere. Those 'previous engagements' were undoubtedly genuine.

But, that having been said, it would be silly to deny that the
absence of episcopal purple was to many of us the most striking
aspect of the whole visit on the 'official' side – more so even than
the non-attendance of certain deputies and senators when the
President addressed Parliament, or the boycott by a sizeable
proportion of academics of the ceremony in which he was
awarded an honorary degree by the National University. Unoffi-
cially, of course, there were some equally striking expressions of
popular sentiment, all – or nearly all (for Ballyporeen, which was
deemed to be the Reagan hearth and home, was an exception)
– sharply critical of presidential policies. These demonstrations
were peaceful, orderly and, in the main, good-humoured and
free from lumpen xenophobia, although there was one unpleasant incident in which an American flag was burned. And those
taking part came from a wide social and political spectrum.

Prominent among them were priests and religious – notably
women. And, while a cynic might suggest that this development
was merely an expression of vocational solidarity with colleagues
under pressure in Central America, the Philippines and else-

where, such a reading would, I believe, be very superficial. If the expression of a much wider and deeper solidarity with the poor and the suffering, victims of oppression, discrimination and blind privilege, in countries within the American sphere of influence – if this means the Church has 'turned left' then She undoubtedly has. I would rather suggest that She has finally woken-up to the sins committed in her Founder's name as well as to those perpetrated by those who deny Him.

However I do not propose to rehearse here again the facts and figures, or even the rights and wrongs, behind this specifically Christian criticism of American policies. The matter was very adequately dealt with by Bishop Eamon Casey of Galway, a man whose leadership and moral passion have been an inspiration, especially to young people here.

(July-August 1984, vol. 34, no. 6, pp. 342-343)

Pilgrims' progress

Last month Ireland played host to the Anglican-Orthodox Joint Doctrinal Commission, one of the key structures in the quest for Christian unity, and impressively representative of the wide range of theological thought in these two great communions. The proceedings were naturally held in private, but they ended with a celebration of Sunday Evensong in Saint Patrick's Cathedral, Dublin, the national cathedral of the Church of Ireland, at which the preacher was the Anglican co-chairman of the Commission, Bishop Hill. And on the previous evening we were invited to meet the participants in the conversations at an informal gathering, preceded by Orthodox Vespers, and followed by a lecture on Saint Patrick by the distinguished Anglican scholar, Bishop Richard Hanson. This event took place in the Convent of Our Lady of Sion in County Meath, where the conversations had been held ...

The Sisters of Our Lady of Sion are indeed something special; proceeding from their original vocation and concern for our Jewish brethren, they have cast their ecumenical net wide and caught many a reluctant fish. Their sensitive hospitality is well-known, and they have pioneered more than a few delicate projects with just the right balance of boldness and prudence. Their name stands high, along with the monks of Glenstal, the Corrymeela and Glencree communities, and most recently the Columbanus Community, as well as a few other witnesses to unity.

But in general attitudes and stance the Irish Catholic Church has come much further forward ecumenically than it is usually given credit for. Even on the subject of inter-church marriages, notoriously one of the most painful issues bedevilling relations between ourselves and other Christians, there has been very considerable movement in recent years. The continuing inter-communal tragedy in the North persists, it is fair to say, in spite of official Church attitudes on every side. That is not to say that Christian leadership could not have done more, or indeed that it has been blameless in the past, but despite certain 'evangelical' reservations of conscience – and, of course, the Paisleyite fringe – the main thrust of preaching and teaching today is towards reconciliation and, indeed, unity. This has been at least as strong on the Catholic side as among mainstream Protestants, nor has it merely been a matter of comfortable words; there has been a great deal of unobtrusively solid work on the ground, involving unsung heroes on all sides.

One could of course be more closely critical, and not alone in relation to occasional lapses into tribalism, sad but inevitable. In so far as the 'Protestant interest' is still the dominant political and social strain in the North there is a tendency among Protestant church spokesmen to identify with that interest, and perhaps to regard its dominance as in the natural order of things. This emerges in a number of ways, tangential but significant: the commonest being an almost automatic support for those 'security forces' who to the Catholic minority, may represent (rightly or wrongly) not security but oppression. Recent events involving the R.U.C. have cast a rather bleak light on this.

On the other side of the picture, however, certain presuppositions and assumptions give more than a little substance to allegations of a Catholic neo-triumphalism as authoritatively self-assured (if less arrogantly articulated) as the older pre-Conciliar variety. It appeals not to the unique authority of the One True Church but to the inviolability of God's Word (as we interpret it!).

(September 1984, vol. 34, no. 7, pp. 405-406)

1985

What majority?

I fear Christians, and even Church leaders, are often no clearer-sighted than anybody else in cutting through the clouds of prejudice, cultural conditioning, fashion, or even fear, which may obscure the facts. An example of what I have in mind relates to our 'Northern problem' and to Christian approaches to a solution ...

Let me put it this way. Here in the Republic we used to talk about the 'crime of partition': we saw the problem as centring on the 'unnatural' division of the country and, for this, we squarely placed the blame on Britain. This is, I believe, a not unfair description of the prevailing view held on the popular level, and generally expressed by politicians, until the 1960s. The emphasis changed to the need for unity, of people rather than of territory, and this has become the national orthodoxy in spite of (or perhaps partly because of) some fifteen years of violent conflict in the North itself. And while the unity of all, north and south, remains a national ideal, a more immediately urgent goal is the achievement of some form of unity between the two Northern communities, if only that to be looked for among neighbours ...

It would be wrong, if understandable, to regard the problem as altogether one of unity of people(s), either in the North or in the island as a whole. For although we don't go on about it as much as one used to, there is another side to the problem: a long-standing frontier dispute between Britain and Ireland, or if you prefer, between the United Kingdom and the Irish Republic.

The point is far from academic, and touches very closely on views expressed by the British Prime Minister after the British-Irish summit last November. She dismissed the three options envisaged by the New Ireland Forum (and did so in a manner generally regarded here as grossly offensive; but this point need not detain us now): her main argument appeared to be their unacceptability to Northern Unionists, whose constitutional status would never be changed by Britain against their will ...

But, I am convinced that in any consideration of the problem, the very existence of 'Northern Ireland' and the delimitation of its boundaries need to be called into question, if only for the following two reasons.

Firstly, because only by maintaining the Republic's constitutional position, and indeed asserting, gently but firmly, that there is unfinished business between us and the U.K., can we ensure that the whole problem could, one day, if necessary be discussed in an international forum, and possibly referred to international arbitration or even peace-keeping. Britain could otherwise successfully claim that the question of Northern Ireland is entirely an internal one for the U.K.

My second reason for raising the matter of jurisdiction and territory is that to omit it would be a serious and dangerous *suppressio veri*. Serious, because consciously or subconsciously, and with very varying degrees of commitment and sophistication it is an essential part of the historical/cultural/emotional baggage of every Northern nationalist. And this is true even if he protests to the contrary, and claims that all he's interested in is a job and to be left in peace by the R.U.C. and the U.D.R. He can no more shed his nationalist 'identity' than he can his Catholic culture, however 'lapsed' he be.

And to ignore this would be doubly dangerous, not only because such suppressions, far from reducing the infective influence of the men of violence, rather provide them with a spurious status as sole preservers of the national conscience, but also because they are, in a very real sense, unjust to the 'Northern majority' itself.

I know that even to suggest that Northern Ireland's frontiers and territory could be anything but stable and copper-fastened, legally and morally, would be commonly regarded as an aggravation of majority alienation from the minority, a cruel reawakening of deep-rooted 'Protestant fears', and an irresponsible blow to the already shaky security of ordinary Protestants, not least in those areas nearest to the Republic where the majority are of the 'minority'.

As against this, I would hold that only by facing the problem, and taking it into consideration in every reassessment of the 'matter of Ulster', can any ultimate stability be hoped for. 'Cruel' is indeed the word I would use for pretending it didn't exist – that 'internal' peace and justice in the Six Counties area is the only concern of the Republic and of Northern nationalists, or that problems of minority alienation and 'identity' can be met by purely 'internal' arrangements ...

(January 1985, vol. 35, no. 1, pp. 49-52)

Cosmography of the spiritual

I believe that in our time, and especially over the past twenty-five years or so, there has been a radical shift of perception in the popular Catholic idea of the supernatural. It is possible to describe this in purely cultural terms, it is certainly closely related to the traumatic cultural transformations which have so deeply affected the twentieth century human experience. In any event, 'inherited spirituality' has dramatically declined to the point of disappearance in most of the Catholic west – and perhaps elsewhere – along with the devotional 'network' which, as I have argued, both sustained and gave it expression.

Am I then suggesting that we should set about 'inventing' or 'creating' a new spirituality to fill the vacuum? Clearly, to speak in such terms would be to misunderstand the meaning of spirituality which is, on the deepest level, the life of the Spirit within us. Again, the deepest articulation of that life is to be found in the gift-virtues of faith, hope and love: its indispensable nourishment in Word and Sacrament. This is common ground for every age and every tradition.

But since the Spirit is incarnate in humankind, in human cultures, spirituality tends to come in different human shapes, even if it may keep these shapes consistently in given times and places. And so, on the human level, we may indeed have the opportunity, and, I would suggest, in our time the duty, of assisting in the shaping of our own spirituality – of forging a contemporary language for the Word, and providing for the widest outreach of sacramental encounter.

It is to this end that we can call, first of all, on past experience, and on the insights and illuminations contained in the spiritual documents and monuments of the Christian centuries, recent and remote. And I would once again emphasise the necessity for a critically selective approach: so much of real value has become encrusted with accretions of dubious merit. In the Irish context there are indeed great riches to be appropriated from the distant past as well as from more recent years.

A splendid example of what I have in mind is the *Lúireach Phádraig*, St Patrick's Breastplate, which has, over the past hundred or years or so, gradually become one of the seminal prayer-formulas of Christians in Ireland, Britain, Africa and elsewhere – but, how much more than this, a veritable 'spine' of spiritual growth not alone for tired veterans of the night-battle but for young newcomers to the Gospel who have seized eagerly on its invitation at once Christocentric and deeply human.

Another source for Catholics in search of guidelines for spiritual growth is to be found in those other Christian traditions from which we have become so disastrously separated – to the point that we have inclined to the opinion that their spiritual content was either attenuated (in the case of Anglicans and Protestants), or fossilised (Eastern Churches)! In all this, our ignorance has not been altogether due to smug self-satisfaction but to a failure of imagination. Our spiritual life was so bound up with that 'network' of devotional practices that we found it almost impossible to imagine other ways.

The ecumenical enlightenment of recent years has helped us to see what other traditions may have to offer although it has to be admitted that any appreciation of these, beyond the most superficial, is still confined to an already interested minority. I would urge that minority then to try to spread the message, and to make the West aware that the Christian East has more to offer than a vague mysticism, and that post-Reformation Christianity is not the cold affair some of us think it to be ...

What we must always do is to test what these other traditions have to offer by the touchstone of faith, and to engage them in our understanding of the Word and enriching our sacramental life. As to the former, we Catholics are all too aware how slight has been our consciousness of Scripture, how small a part have, say, the Psalms played in our prayer-life, how little of the thought of Saint Paul (or Peter or James) has gone into the articulation of our faith. In all this surely we can gain a great deal from studying the spiritual testament of those Christians to whom the Bible, in their own language, was all.

Of course, Word without Sacrament can provide only a poor spiritual diet for most of us, and it could be argued that the decline evident in many Protestant Churches was due to this one-sided emphasis. And while 'evangelical' revivalism both in its older and more modern forms continues to attract converts, and would claim to reassert the primacy of the spiritual in a secularised age, it may be doubted whether alone it provides an enduring base for spiritual growth.

On the other hand, the deeply liturgical spiritualities of the East can be criticised for their lack of evangelical cutting-edge. (It can be seen for instance how in Russia Baptist near-fundamentalism offers an unlikely but acceptable alternative). But for us surely there is a very great richness to draw upon, a profound awareness of, for example, the mystery of the Trinity as experienced reality, not just as a theological formula – and above all the sacramental presence and power of the Holy Spirit.

One immense benefit to be derived from the kind of serious and selective ecumenical 'exploration' that I have suggested is that it so often leads to a rediscovery of hidden and forgotten dimensions in one's own tradition. This is of course inevitable when one considers the common origin of our divided ways, but also the cross-cultural currents which have in history left their mark in unexpected places. Early contacts between Eastern Christians and the Celtic Church are a case in point, and one not without significance for our own present quest.

In working towards any objective it is occasionally useful to pause and ask: What is it for? What is spirituality 'for'? One short answer might be: to enable us to pray. For if ever there was a generation 'standing in the need of prayer' surely it is ours. Prayer for and with the living and the dead, implying an awareness of the communion of saints as a living reality.

But, let me once more insist, this cannot be done in terms of a spiritual 'cosmography' which no longer has meaning save for a rapidly disappearing few. To articulate the life of the Spirit we must seize on the eternal Word in a new idiom, but, like the householder in the Gospel, drawing from the storeroom old things as well as new (Mt 13).

(March 1985, vol. 35, no. 3, pp. 167-170)

Requiescat

The word 'shock' has been degraded by misuse and over-use in so much popular journalism, as has the word 'tragedy'. Neither is inappropriate to the death [21 February 1985] of Archbishop Dermot Ryan, apparently in the fullness of health and vigour, and at the very moment when he seemed set to lead the Missionary Church into a new age of challenge and renewal. Indeed, God does dispose.

From Pope John Paul to Taoiseach Garret FitzGerald there have been many tributes to his abilities and human qualities.

Many of these qualities were known only to a few: but these loved him, and mourn him, as a warm and generous friend.

Unfortunately to most of his flock in Dublin, where he had ruled for just twelve years, he was a respected but rather remote figure: not cold, and certainly not 'pontifical' in the old, grand manner, but rarely seen or met save at a distance. And I do not believe that this was due to any 'academic' aloofness. He was indeed a distinguished scholar and teacher of the Semitic languages, but his wider and perhaps more profound involvement in scripture and scripture scholarship gave him a passionate enthusiasm for 'dividing the Word'.

I am convinced that administration, not scholarship, erected what barriers there were between the Archbishop and his people. He seemed to see his pastoral task as most urgently and most usefully to be served in the reorganisation of the archdiocese, in the erection of structures adequate to the many pressing needs of Dublin in the seventies, and especially in the setting-up of new parishes.

In all of this he showed gifts of a practical and imaginative kind not always to be found among the academically inclined. But perhaps his own deepest inclinations were pastoral: he often said that his first and continuing ambition was to be a parish priest. It is then sad and ironic that his immense work-load, and his caring labours for the parishes of Dublin brought him all too seldom into the parishes. Only occasionally, as in Holy Week, could he be seen where a bishop is most clearly a bishop, at the head of the eucharistic assembly; or heard, speaking at close range, as he could so well, about the riches of God's word.

I say this not from any naïve idealisation of *episkopé*, still less, I hope, in a spirit of brash and uninformed criticism. I am only sorry that the Catholic people of Dublin did not get to know their Archbishop as he, with his great insights, may well have known them.

The question remains of course whether in fact the Archdiocese of Dublin has become too large to be regarded as a unit, a single Church with a single Ordinary. I am strongly convinced that it has, as have indeed many other urban dioceses not half as large in population, and I do not regard the moderate measure of decentralisation (with auxiliary bishops who are still assistants to the Ordinary) which has been achieved there, as elsewhere, as being at all an adequate answer to the problem. And, however it may make good administrative sense, a system of 'permanent' auxiliaries is, I believe, quite at odds with the intrinsic 'character' of the episcopal order. The problem is perhaps the most basic of those facing Archbishop Ryan's successor in Dublin, and one of those facing the Church throughout the world in conurbations great and small.

It could in fact have been one to engage the attention of the Pro-Prefect of the Congregation for the Evangelisation of Peoples as he looked to the future in, for instance, the cities of Latin America and elsewhere in the Third World. The movement towards 'basic communities' could be seen, and has been seen, as a movement away from the institutional Church of diocesan and even parochial structures. But such a 'centrifugal' tendency need not lead to fragmentation, nor would it, precisely if *episkopé* were seen to be a closely present reality, not a remote pillar of power.

Such matters must now await the attention of whoever succeeds the gifted and energetic Irishman who was ready to tackle them with mature concern and boyish enthusiasm – although not without a certain homesickness ... *Requiescat in Patria.*

(April 1985, vol. 35, no. 4, pp. 235-236)

Welsh prophet

Saunders Lewis, who died last month, was arguably the greatest Welshman of the century: certainly the only contender for the title would be David Lloyd George, a deeply ambiguous figure, whose star has, to say the least of it, gone down somewhat in recent years. Indeed there could hardly be a greater contrast than that between the two men. Lloyd George, a born politician, if ever there was one, could turn even his weakness to advantage – his unremitting deviousness, for instance, sustained him in office against all the odds, and his bland disloyalties enabled him to be all things to most men at the time (not to speak of quite a few women!). His devotion to Wales and the Welsh language and tradition was real but basically sentimental, and did not prevent his finding the resolution of his ambitions in leading the Imperial establishment. His brand of nonconformist youth was an aspect of that devotion and seemed, to the outsider at least, just as sentimental.

The adjective was one that could never be applied to Saunders Lewis, even though he might be not unfairly accused of a somewhat romantic view of the Middle Ages. In this he was no more or less wise than many of his contemporaries to whom conversion to Catholicism brought with it a discovery of the medieval roots of European culture. But, unlike, say, a Charles Maurras who saw the Church merely as the great guarantee of a *religio* which kept its adherents firmly in their place as subject-citizens, to Lewis faith and Church were living realities engaging his total commitment.

That commitment was undoubtedly a major stumbling-block in his abortive career as an active political leader. Not that he ever tried to proselytise, and his criticisms of some aspects of the Welsh culture of his earlier years, of which the non-conformist chapels were an essential part, did not blind him to the positive values of the dissenting tradition.

But something like a 'Home Rule – Rome Rule' *canard* was one of the factors which militated against the 'infant' Welsh National Party which he founded in the mid-twenties and left it so long in swaddling clothes. But the time was not propitious and the years of the Great Depression saw the rise in Wales of the Labour Party as 'the voice of the hungry' as one veteran of those grim days said to me. Social policies owing more to *Rerum Novarum* and *Quadragesimo Anno* than to Karl Marx and Keir Hardie were not likely to find favour, and, anyway, nationalism as such was considered irrelevant if not positively inimical to the welfare of the worker and the unemployed. That the party should survive at all might seem remarkable, but that *Plaid Cymru* is today a force to be reckoned with in Welsh political life, while due to several factors – including the wise leadership of Gwynfor Evans in the post-war years – may, not unfancifully, be traced back to a unique act of militancy in which Lewis played an essential and leading role. I refer to the burning down of the R.A.F. bombing school near Pwllheli in 1936.

The motivation was at once practical and symbolic. The school was situated in the heart of Welsh Wales, in an area where the ancient language and culture still flourished, and it was seen as a very real threat, the desecration of a national heartland. Since all petitions and pressures to have it removed elsewhere were ignored, the nationalist leadership decided on direct action, of a kind unprecedented in modern Welsh history. But to Lewis and his collaborators – D.J. Williams, a teacher, and Lewis Valentine, a minister – it had a significance wider than that of its immediate purpose: they saw it as a call to the sleeping Welsh conscience to test itself in defence of its God-given heritage. The date was the fourth centenary of the Union with England.

Scrupulous care was taken to ensure that no human life was endangered, and after the burning, the three gave themselves up to the police. A trial followed and the Welsh jury disagreed: at a further hearing in London they were sent to gaol, despite (or perhaps because of) Lewis's magnificent speech from the dock. On their release and return home there was some enthusiasm, but the Welsh conscience quickly went back to sleep. Lewis lost his job as a university lecturer and remained in the wilderness for twenty-five years.

Although he gave up active politics for good, he continued to evangelise in a long stream of newspaper articles, and more indirectly in his plays. His influence continued to grow and in 1962 a radio lecture which he gave on 'The Fate of Language' inspired a whole new movement, mainly among the younger generation, which by vigorous not to say militant methods, has probably 'saved' the Welsh language and, some would say, the Welsh soul. So the bombing-school fires were not extinguished.

I would suggest that Saunders Lewis should be of considerable interest to Christians and especially to his fellow Catholics. He was *par excellence* a prophetic figure and on a heroic level. His vision was firmly rooted in the values of the New Testament and transcended those accidentals of exaggeration to which his generation of Catholic converts were sometimes subject. And while, as a national leader, he could be written off as a failure, history may well see him as a great European.

And so he was, but in a way the historian might not recognise. For while as a Welshman he was an enthusiastic European, as a European, he was a committed Welshman. In a word, he knew that 'national' and 'international' are complementary not opposing terms, and that the real enemy is the rootless cosmopolitanism which knows neither where it comes from nor where it is going. In this, long before Vatican II, he laid hold of a cultural truth which informs some at least of the best conciliar thinking, but which is only slowly being recognised – in liturgy, in attitudes towards the younger Churches, in an acknowledgement that not all positive values belong to the 'traditional' mainstream, in a clear differentiation between unity and its caricature, uniformity.

I have referred to Lewis's regard for the good things in non-conformist Christianity. Here again he was before his time: an ecumenically-minded convert who celebrated Welsh Calvinist spirituality and saw its place in the Great Tradition. His Requiem was appropriate: Latin and Welsh: a moving sermon by an Irish-born, Welsh-speaking Bishop: lessons read by a Presbyterian: the Anglican Archbishop in the sanctuary: a congregation which was all Welsh, singing classic Welsh hymns and one by Lewis's old companion-in-arms Lewis Valentine.

At the grave-side Bishop Mullins was joined by a Canon of Canterbury and a Calvinist minister. The ground was slippery and to keep from falling they had to join hands ...

(October 1985, vol. 35, no. 8, pp. 443-445)

New hope

The reaction of the Irish bishops to the Anglo-Irish Agreement of November 15 – as expressed by their Standing Committee – is best described as cautiously positive. This has caused little surprise: in fact it had been widely anticipated that they might well refrain from all comment, at least until such time as the Agreement was seen to be working. This would, in all the circumstances, have been highly understandable.

The negotiations leading to the Agreement were surrounded by controversy, and it was unlikely that the Agreement itself would be given an unanimous welcome on the Irish side. Unionist opposition was practically certain, as was that of the Provisional I.R.A., and their front-organisation Sinn Féin. It was also feared that what has become known as the 'republican' or 'green' wing of the Social Democratic and Labour Party, which represents majority nationalist opinion in the North, might withhold support.

In the event, S.D.L.P. support has been solid, if soberly lacking in any great enthusiasm. What the negotiators have achieved is seen as a *modus vivendi*, or at least making this a possibility: and it is emphasised all round that the proof of the pudding must wait on hard work in the kitchen before anything really edible is put on the table.

But even such a modest welcome has found no echo in the leadership of the Republic's main opposition party. Mr Charles J. Haughey has been as negative in his attitude as has Dr Ian Paisley – though arguing from very different premises. Indeed 'argument' seems too cerebral a description of the way in which the Agreement has been rejected both by the Unionist hardliners and by Mr Haughey, and such of his supporters as have so far expressed an opinion. (I write in the week after the signing.) In fact neither side has given us much more than the reiteration of diehard 'principles', accusations of betrayal, and prophecies of doom.

But as long as the matter remains one of major disagreement even among their own flock, one can understand the bishops' discretion. The last thing they want is to get embroiled in a re-run of the kind of national fission, which gave us the Civil War of the early nineteen-twenties and the long years of disillusion which followed. Not that the Agreement is likely to provoke violent action, in the Republic at any rate: although we cannot discount the possibility of a blood struggle in the North, of sectarian murder on a renewed scale, or even of cross-border overspill. But another 'split' in the social fabric of the Republic would be disastrous, and any political leader who by word or action brings one about will have a lot to answer for. It could only lead to a weakening of national will, a wastage of social effort, and yet another regression into a never-never land of delusion and myth.

The bishops are indeed exercising prudence by standing aloof, if benevolently so. One might well wish that they had done the same on other occasions of national debate: presumably they do not see the present issue as of any great moral consequence, requiring their guidance or leadership.

And yet – those of us who are never happy, whatever our fathers in God may do, must surely experience a tinge of regret that the Church's voice was not heard on an occasion which history may come to judge as of great and continuing significance. It could indeed mark the beginning of the end of the long agony which has darkened life in our northern province for well over three hundred years. It could also be foundation on which a new relationship of trust and solidarity could be built between the peoples of Ireland and Britain ...

(December 1985, vol. 35, no. 10, pp. 561-562)

1986

Roman candour

I suppose that, to all who know Rome even moderately well, the admiration and excitement – even love – that the city evokes, is diluted with a healthy measure of exasperation. As one fairly frequent visitor/pilgrim said to me: 'I need to go every year or so to keep my disillusions intact'.

These mixed feelings are hardly confined to those of us to whom Rome is in a very real sense our capital: they infect all true lovers of the city however severely 'secular' their interests. But I believe they are strongest among Roman Catholics, precisely because we are: we have in fact the same kind of attitude to Rome, and perhaps especially to the Vatican, that critical Cork and Derry folk have to Dublin. And though they have the effect of keeping some of us away at a safe distance – remember Ronald Knox's advice to travellers in the barque of Peter: 'keep away from the engine-room' – still more of us are regularly and relentlessly drawn back to this wonderful, maddening place. Old Roman hands will know what I mean when I say that the first glass of Frascati, and the first mouthful of *pasta*, on the evening of arrival are like a sacrament of home-coming: surely a foretaste of the *convivium sempiternum*.

But the crazy traffic, the dreadful bread, the cattle-trucks masquerading as buses, the eternal *subito* which is Rome's answer to *mañana* (and far less honest), the sons of the affluent in their fast cars – all this and much more soon take the shine out of that first rapture. And in the centre-city area the noise can be quite enraging, and inescapable: even the quietest bars no longer offer sanctuary since muzak has taken over everywhere. (Sanctuary of a more traditional kind is alas! too often unavailable since the churches are closed for a considerable part of the day).

In spite of all, we are enchanted again and again by the old magic. My own two favourite parts of the city are Trastevere and Vecchia Roma, where there are houses, still lived in, built when the Middle Ages were modern times. And where that deep wayward *umanitá* which is Rome's most priceless treasure, flourishes in all its vibrant variety.

Trastevere, though not noted for its church-goers, is nevertheless a must for the Christian pilgrim, if only so that he can feast his eyes on the facade of Santa Maria in Trastevere, where one of the triumphs of early Christian art presides over a piazza which is my own favourite of all. In fact, the last time I saw it, I was moved to say that I wouldn't exchange it for all the baroque in Rome. But of course the real point is that, whatever your vision of beauty, you can find it realized in one or another of those churches, *palazzi* or public sculptures which the genius of Christian artists has contrived. And if you want to see Roman Christian history, back to its origins, in one extraordinary vertical kaleidoscope, go to the Basilica of San Clemente, and rejoice in the inspiration of Joseph Mulooley, the Irish Dominican who, a hundred and thirty years ago, initiated the archaeological adventure which revealed it all.

Indeed, for the Irish pilgrim there's a good deal to 'keep for pride', both in those foundations where there has been an Irish presence for over three hundred years, and in places like Via degli Ibernesi and, especially, the Church of San Pietro in Montorio which holds the tombs of Ó Néill and Ó Domhnaill ... But enough of that! Oisín is not in the guidebook business.

Rather, resuming my role of exasperated pilgrim, let me mention two matters which continue to surprise – unpleasantly. One is the survival of what in Dublin we used to call 'Short Twelve' – a 'low' Mass celebrated at a side-altar while the Solemn Celebration proceeds at the high altar. Where, you ask, can this abuse be maintained? Where else but in St Peter's itself!

More personally distressing is the way in which pilgrims and indeed all lay people are denied Holy Communion in the hand. No one denies the right of the Italian Episcopal Conference to rule for their flocks – although this particular decision is hard to understand.

But one might have expected that pilgrims might not have to be so rudely refused what has now become second nature, and touches the very core of the sacramental life. The grace of God is, after all, in courtesy ... And there are occasions when more than courtesy is at stake, gatherings of the Church Universal where our unity should not at this most sacred moment be forced into an imposed uniformity.

(January 1986, vol. 36, no. 1, pp. 35-36)

School at risk

Floreat ut pereat is the motto on the crest of the Irish School of Ecumenics. Since its foundation in 1970 by the indefatigable Michael Hurley, S.J. – who has since gone to work in another part of the ecumenical battleground in Belfast – it has, indeed, swiftly and impressively come to flower. And now there seems a very real danger that *floruit* may, all too soon, be followed by *periit*: the School is, at the time of writing, in grave financial difficulties.

It would be tragic if it had to close its doors, and especially in these most difficult times, when, perhaps most of all in Ireland, the healing of Christian disunity is so urgently needed as a sign and light of hope to a divided society. And when society's divisions are, at least in part, the bitter fruit of that Christian disunity, the urgency is that of a terrible obligation.

In this work of healing the place of the School is very special. As they say themselves:

> We work towards a reconciliation between those of different religious traditions, so that each of us can accept others for what they are and not just for what we think they are.
>
> We work towards a world where our place of worship is no longer a cause for division but a source for unity.
>
> We look forward to a time when an organisation such as ours is no longer necessary....

It has of course to be admitted that the School's present predicament is rooted in its own character and integrity. It jealously guards its academic autonomy, not for its own sake, but in service to all the Churches – while, therefore, remaining independent (one might say inevitably so) of any Church or ecclesial grouping.

This academic autonomy is enhanced rather than limited by links with two Irish universities: with Dublin University (Trinity College), for courses leading to the M.Phil. (Ecum.) and Diploma in Ecumenics, and with the University of Ulster, for a Certificate in Ecumenics course. The School's standing is high internationally, both academically and because of the independence I have referred to, and which is rare enough in institutions of its kind ... Their modest claim is that they are giving an essential service to the Churches and communities in Ireland – and of many countries. And this is undeniable.

I know of no other meeting-place where Christians of all

traditions can live and study and work together for a common Christian end. The opportunities for teaching, research and shared experience are pretty well unique. And this is clearly appreciated in an ever-increasing number of countries, who are sending students to the School year by year. In return, the graduates are going out to preach and live reconciliation wherever they go.

In the School, the students share not only in the process of learning but in worship and social life. There is a small residential hostel in Dublin, but fieldwork brings these young people into real-life situations, enabling them to become familiar with the lives of communities other than their own. So you'll often find Protestant ministers staying in a monastery – or Catholic nuns working in a manse or rectory.

The international dimension to all this is quite significant, not least because of the remarkable breadth of study undertaken by the School. For it goes far beyond inter-church dialogue ('Christian' ecumenism), extending to inter-faith dialogue (involving world religions), and Justice and Peace, with particular reference to the 'sociological, political and theological implications of the search for justice and peace in an age of injustice and of the threat of nuclear war'.

This last area of concern indeed brings us back to the more domestic importance of the School, since the Department of Peace Studies has in fact provided a unique forum for discussion on Ireland's place in the nuclear age. Frank and penetrating exchanges of views on subjects like neutrality, and pacifism, and European defence have taken place, unhindered by political and ideological prejudices and inhibitions ...

(February 1986, vol. 36, no. 2, pp. 99-101)

Man of the people

I was surprised and saddened recently to read that Archbishop Tom Morris 'has been granted a coadjutor'. In response to his own request for 'someone to assist and to succeed him'. Surprised, until I was forced to realise that the Archbishop has reached an age when retirement begins to concentrate the mind: saddened at the further realisation that none of us is as young as we were!

Among the Irish bishops who attended the Second Vatican Council very few survive in office, and certainly Cashel is the only one of the four metropolitan sees still occupied by the same archbishop. Indeed he was present at all four sessions, and was outstanding in his concern for post-conciliar renewal at home, especially in the area of liturgy.

In this he found ready allies in the Abbot and Community of Glenstal Abbey, which lies in his suffragan diocese of Emly. At that time Dom Joseph Dowdall was the youngest abbot in the Benedictine world, and along with Dom Placid Murray, Dom Paul McDonnell and others, gave informed and dedicated leadership at a crucial time. His premature death came as an enormous blow.

Another link with Glenstal came through the late Dom Winoc Mertens (one of the original community from Maredsous in Belgium), and Dom Bernard O'Dea who is now working in Africa with Dom Augustine O'Sullivan, bringing a new Benedictine dimension to the Irish presence there. Both were associated with Tom Morris when, as a young priest, he was the strong right arm of Father John Hayes, founder of Muintir na Tíre, and social apostle of rural Ireland in the thirties and forties.

His own social concern has continued over the years both on national and local levels. But one feels that he has always had a special care for that Tipperary-Limerick heartland, centred on the fertile Golden Vale, which has been very much 'his own place' by birth and rearing, and later, happily, by appointment to the ancient see of Cashel.

If ever one had a sense of the local Church it is surely here. The Rock and its noble ruins, dominating the rich flat lands of the *machaire méith*, and attesting its Patrician origins; the snug parishes, some of them a witness to Penal survival; the great Abbey of Holy Cross whose restoration is perhaps the most splendid witness of all. This restoration was inspired and brought to fruition by Archbishop Morris: he must be allowed a pardonable pride in what will always be his monument, *i gceartlár a dhaoine*.

(February 1986, vol. 36, no. 2, pp. 101-102)

School mistress

Not the least significant feature of what has become known as the 'Carysfort Affair' is that it shows how far we've come in 'Church-State relations' since the mid-century. The famous 'Mother-and-Child' confrontation in 1951 seems to have been long ago, and in another country.

But perhaps a word of explanation is needed for overseas readers. The 1951 reference is to a public health scheme which fell foul of the bishops, who urged its withdrawal as not in accord with 'Catholic social teaching': the government yielded, and the minister concerned resigned. Actually the government itself fell in the aftermath. (I have simplified the story but, I believe, not unduly.)

Carysfort College of Education, in south Dublin, whose closure was announced by abrupt ministerial *fiat* at the beginning of February, was one of three major institutions devoted to the academic training of primary school teachers. All three were historically under the direction of religious congregations, but with – in recent years – the status of 'recognised' colleges of the National University of Ireland, and financed from public funds.

The tripartite involvement of State, university, and independent administration (in this case the religious Sisters of Mercy) might seem to guarantee an admirable balance in the running of the college's affairs, and a safeguard against hasty or partisan action from any side. The utterly unexpected closure of Carysfort must put paid to any such illusion.

Perhaps indeed 'closure' is not the accurate word: presumably the college premises and facilities might continue to be used for academic purposes, and the university might in principle be prepared to award degrees and diplomas to the alumni. But public funds would no longer be forthcoming. And even if a fairy godmother came to the rescue, the Department of Education might well refuse to accept graduates in schools wholly or partly under its control. It appears then that a hundred years of teacher training in Carysfort have come to an end.

A declining birth rate – after a near decade of remarkable growth – and other socio-economic factors have been adduced by the Minister of Education [Gemma Hussey] in defence of the decision. But her case has, to say the least of it, so far failed to convince an unusually united body of opposition, led by representatives of all sections of the country's educational life – and linked, incidentally, to other expressions of vigorous disaffection by the teachers' union (for quite separate reasons).

The college principal and staff pointed to projects and plans for diversification presented to the department in recent years but mainly ignored. And all involved – not least the student body – are understandably concerned about their future: details of redeployment seem vague and uncertain. In any event, an institution such as Carysfort develops a moral identity and personality over the years, and even the most rational and generous arrangements for the redisposal of resources, human and otherwise, can hardly compensate for its extinction.

But what everybody, or nearly everybody, except those who made the decision, is agreed upon is this: however necessary the closure may have been, it should have been presented in the context of a clearly more satisfactory restructuring of the educational area concerned, with full details of compensatory arrangements – and, perhaps some expression of regret, appreciation, gratitude, sympathy, the common human feelings which the occasion might reasonably be expected to evoke. At the very least, it is universally felt that those most nearly concerned should have been given some reasonable notice.

In the event, the minister confined herself to a letter (described as 'terse') addressed to Archbishop Kevin McNamara as 'manager' of the college a few hours before the government's action was made public. The college principal, Sister Regina, was treated in an even more summary fashion. As somebody remarked, nobody was left in doubt as to 'who was master or, rather, mistress ... '

...

We have come a long way since the days when a prime minister bowed before the crozier, and apparently neither he nor a majority of his ministers saw anything wrong with this. Opinion in the country was however far from giving universal approval to his action, although for the most part support for Dr Noel Browne (the offending Minister for Health) and his scheme was expressed in fairly cautious terms. Few dared to challenge, at least openly, the bishops' right to effectively veto the scheme. But, within a very few years, the widespread though latent feeling that this sort of thing must now stop, and the government should govern, came to the surface with increasing clarity.

And the new openness of the 60s dealt a final blow to the 'mind you, I've said nothing' attitude, especially since even loyal Catholics could cite Vatican II in support of their sharpened view of the separate autonomies of Church and State.

In retrospect, the Mother-and-Child affair does seem to mark the beginning of the end, not so much of episcopal intervention in affairs of state, as of general acceptance of such intervention by government. One should of course acknowledge that even before that, Church pressures were almost certainly resisted more than once, at least during the de Valera years – one thinks of the Spanish Civil War period, when the government's steadfast refusal to recognise Franco, while the Republican Government still continued to fight, gave great displeasure. But such confrontations as there were remained discretely behind closed doors: there were no open challenges on either side.

It is of course also true that the late 'fifties and subsequent decades did not see an end to strong and determined urgings of episcopal opinion on matters of public morality – or of private morality with a social dimension. One need go back no further than recent debates on the availability of contraceptives, or, notoriously, the constitutional amendment on abortion.

But what did change was the nature of public response on the part of those engaged in the political process, whether in government or opposition. No longer was acquiescence to be taken for granted, or disagreement necessarily suppressed or at least veiled. (And one could point to a change of style on the part of the bishops as well: the emphasis was now on their duty to state their view – or that of the Church – on a given issue, without any desire to dictate legislation or obtrude on the function of the legislators).

The new attitude is particularly evident in the areas of public health and education, in both of which the Church was traditionally seen to have a special role and voice. And while in the former this was usually confined to a range of 'ethical' matters, the whole educational process was regarded as a proper ecclesiastical concern. Indeed the orthodox Catholic view was that the function and rights of the Church came second only to those of the parent – leaving the State a bad third, merely as a 'facilitator'.

One would never believe it from the treatment meted out to the Archbishop and to the principal in the present case. I may however take leave to doubt that this was a deliberate expression of anticlerical policy or attitude. Rather does it appear to be just a particularly egregious example of bureaucratic heavy-handedness, of a kind with which less exalted persons will be all too familiar. The discourtesy seems to derive from insensitivity rather than from deliberation.

But however one may regret the immediate consequences of the closure – for the Carysfort community, lay and religious, academic as well as administrative; for the whole field of primary education; and even for the neighbourhood which had been a beneficiary of the college's presence for over a century – the way it was done, deplorable in most respects, may, in the long run, be 'good' for the Church. For, unpleasant though it may be in the short term, anything that dissociates the institution – and especially the hierarchy – from the socio-political establishment is to be welcomed.

It is indeed arguable that such association as still exists, or is popularly perceived to exist, has the effect of blunting the impact of the Church's voice, not least on social issues. And this applies not alone to what may be regarded as 'conservative' pronouncements, rooted in 'outworn' dogmas and traditions: statements on national and international issues, which are by any standard 'progressive', not to say radical, may be ignored or overlooked as coming from a predictably 'safe' source.

I remarked – after the ill-starred visit to Ireland of President Reagan – that the absence of bishops from the scene was to be welcomed, not just as reflecting reservations about U.S. foreign policies, but because it showed that such events could proceed without an episcopal presence. Just as the Church does not seek a 'special position' in our society, neither should Church leaders be given the status or dignity of officers of state. Neither should they or we look for any privileges whatever. Our rights as citizens are enough.

(March 1986, vol. 36, no. 3, pp. 145-148)

Beginner's mind

In my last *Laylines* – written before the result of the Referendum [on removing the constitutional ban on divorce, 26 June, 1986] was known – I ventured the opinion that, whether or not that result changed our legal situation with regard to provision for civil divorce, sooner or later such a change was inevitable. I argued that the law must eventually respond to the 'deep and rapid' transformation in our *mores*, and that the Church too would have to make its own response.

I cannot see that the actual result [rejecting the proposed amendment] should alter my judgement in this matter. At the heart of the transformation to which I have referred is the fact that what the Church teaches or prescribes is rapidly losing its dominant, not to say decisive, role in the determination of personal or social behaviour. We may deplore this, we may differ as to the speed with which it is taking place in different areas of our society, but we cannot deny it. In a word, secularisation is taking over, and I, for one, cannot see the process being reversed.

Now it needs to be said at once that secularisation is not necessarily the dreadful evil, the final victory of the enemy, that some of us make it out to be. In itself it is nothing more than a cultural shift, a new phase in humanity's long march – as was the European renaissance of four or five hundred years ago, and as were many other moves out of 'religious' epochs of civilisation. Such a development may well be regarded as a liberation – and indeed Christianity itself has, from time to time, been a notable agent in the freeing of peoples from theocratic thought processes and tabus. But while only a fool or a philistine would undervalue the achievements of Christian civilisation, or welcome its destruction, it would be tragically wrong to identify it with Christ's Kingdom. Nor are what have come to be known as 'Christian values' always those of the Gospel, and indeed the New Testament message may be just as subversive of 'Christian' institutions and structures as of those which are avowedly secular.

To say that secularisation is not to be confused with secularism is no mere playing with words. For while the first is, as I have suggested, a natural and perhaps inevitable cultural process, the second is a closed system which would seek to exclude the spiritual, the transcendent, the numinous: to deny the possibility of God's existence; and hence of any divine influence or function in the physical universe and human life.

A secularised society need not be secularist: far from it, it may well offer, especially to the Christian, new and exciting opportunities for the proclamation and grateful recognition of God's presence. I say especially 'to the Christian' because, in the preaching and practice of the Good News, freed from the conventions and preconceptions and accretions of an inherited 'religion', the triple dynamic of Creator, Redeemer and Spirit can be seen at work in truth and love. It is a literally God-given opportunity to begin again, to bring Pentecost to the people ...

(September 1986, vol. 36, no. 7, pp. 376-377)

Siobhán

The death [16 November 1986] of Siobhán McKenna, first lady of the Irish theatre, was the occasion last month of national mourning in a sense far deeper than the common ceremonial implication of that phrase. Born in Belfast of a Cork father and an Ulster mother, most of her youth was spent in Galway – it was there she served her theatrical apprenticeship, in time snatched and stolen from a quite remarkable academic novitiate combining science and humanities: and it was in and from Dublin, especially in and from the Abbey Theatre, that her great gifts as an actress came to flower. She was known and admired for her stage and screen appearances in London, New York and elsewhere, but her art was deeply rooted in Ireland and in her own Irish experience. Ireland made her. This she knew and was grateful for it, and Ireland knew that she knew and was grateful in return.

The honours paid her by Church and State at her Dublin Requiem and her burying in Galway, and the great cross-section of Irishry that came in sad solidarity to say farewell, were for once no belated tribute to a neglected artist. The consistent recognition of her high talent throughout the years was a rare and happy exception to the way we usually value such gifts. And that her last performance in Tom Murphy's dark comedy *Bailegangáire* was hailed on all sides as one of her greatest was no sentimental salute to one whose course was clearly run. It was rather a delighted welcome to a new and exciting development in the work of an artist at the height of her powers, and a collaboration of great potential with a brilliant young director. The sudden and (mercifully) brief illness which has left us so cruelly bereft has served only to enhance her name and fame.

It should also be said that Siobhán McKenna was one of those rare people whose Irishness made them more, not less, conscious of wider cultural horizons: in the theatre the late Mícheál Mac Liammóir was another such. Thus, to both of them, the Irish language was at the very heart of the matter, and went to shape their thought and enrich the texture of their art. But they were also very much aware of and open to what the living variety of Europe and world had to offer. Their patriotism was never parochial. They deserved the honour in which they were held ...

(December 1986, vol. 36, no. 10, pp. 536)

1987

The Year of the Laity

Writing as 1986 nears its last gasp, I can see it all looming over the horizon, and, only too clearly, hear the magic words: Role of the Laity, Mission of the Laity, Vocation of the Laity, climaxing in The Synod of (sorry! – on) the Laity ...

A long series of papal and episcopal pronouncements and exhortations, leading up to the dogmatic and pastoral enactments of Vatican II, have stressed the dignity of lay Christians and the nature of their role in and for the Church. And if lay initiatives have not always, or immediately, been welcomed with open arms by the institution (the work of Frank Duff is an instructive case in point), it should also be admitted that pastoral invitations and even pleas for lay cooperation have too often fallen on deaf ears. Still there have been advances on both sides, and, in this country, some very impressive developments in areas of social concern, peace and justice and so on.

On another level, the involvement of women and of unordained men in liturgical celebration has been remarkable, and by the generally accepted standards of twenty-five years ago, quite startling. The ministry of reading appears to be firmly and widely established ... But the real break-through is surely in the engagement of the unordained as 'Ministers of the Eucharist'. I'm not all that happy about the title, but the development itself is, I am sure, one of great significance and potential. I am also convinced that if it had been proposed and discussed publicly in advance, the proposal would have encountered widespread opposition – and by no means only among the clergy. The suggestion that women should be involved would have come under particular attack.

In the event it all happened unawares – or nearly so. For all I know, there may be a few diehards here and there who avoid taking the Host at Communion from female hands, just as one has heard of white communicants in the United States objecting to black ministers. But as far as one can see the new (restored?) practice is accepted, wherever it obtains, without comment or reserve. It is not so very long since the handling of even an empty chalice, paten or monstrance was generally regarded as taboo to the unordained: that any of us might bring Host or laden Cup to communicants was something we thought could never happen. But is has happened and is happening every day ...

One pleasing aspect of the matter is that there is no attempt to 'clericalise' either readers or Communion assistants by dressing them up in surplices or the like. (I have in fact seen a curious cloak-like garment, more suited I would have thought to the stage than the sanctuary, worn by both men and women in one area which charity forbids me to name.) But I would hope that this welcome diffusion of *diakonia*, in cult as in common service, might not be used as an argument against the possible ordination as deacons, where desirable, of say married men or, please God, women.

Those who oppose any ordination of women not on theological grounds (which they would find it hard to adduce), but for socio-psychological reasons – 'the people would never accept it' – might find it hard to maintain their position now the sanctuary taboo is broken. And the same considerations could be seen to apply in the case of married men.

All this is very welcome as far as it goes. But there is a real sense in which the words 'lay' and 'laity' should have no place in the discourse of the People of God, or at least as descriptive of any part thereof. Certainly they may properly be used in reference to theology and theologians as to any art or science: as the title of this column suggests Oisín is a layman in this area, not because he has not been ordained but because he has no academic or professional qualification in religious affairs.

It is this use of 'lay' as implying 'non-professional' which is, I hold, utterly unsuitable to the Christian community as such. For our common vocation, the 'universal call to holiness' (*Lumen Gentium*) rules out any such distinction. To regard those who practice the three-fold ministry of bishop, presbyter and deacon as the professional minority in a Church the vast majority of whom are amateurs is surely close to blasphemy.

It is particularly and ironically unfortunate that the original Greek word *laos* means all the people. And here again we have an incongruity (to say the least of it) in the relegation of the people to the status of *plebs*: 'those to whom things are done and who themselves do only what they are commanded to do.' An opposite process distorted the word 'Church', commonly arrogated to those who do the commanding. And in spite of Vatican II – and, indeed, of age-old traditional teaching – the distortion lives on, even among those who should and do know better. There remains at least an ambiguity of meaning.

Another ambiguity in the use of the word 'clerical' in its secular and ecclesiastical senses, has failed to dislodge it from its place of privilege in Church order – I nearly said its 'sacred' status. One more irony: for it could be argued that the growth of a clerical class in the Church, its recognition as a 'state' higher than that of the ordinary laity, and its ultimate near-identification with ministry, was the first and most enduring fruit of secularisation!

(January 1987, vol. 37, no. 1, pp. 35-37)

Mulier fortis

In his *Apologia pro Mediis Suis* (*Doctrine and Life*, December 1986), Louis McRedmond gave a very proper wigging to those conspiracy theorists whose view of our national press and broadcasting services borders on the demonic. The word *media* itself has been subject to a kind of reification, making it, as it were an anti-idol: those caught up in the cult may well be beyond the reach of argument, even when delivered with all Mr McRedmond's sober but stylish cogency.

Perhaps though one might have recourse to an *argumentum* not *ad hominem* but *a muliere*. For the life and work of Áine McEvoy who died, seventy years young, at the year's turn, must surely give pause to the denouncers and generalisers. In the long run the media, anywhere, are no better and no worse than the men and women who work in and for and through them. And Áine McEvoy was one of these.

To say she was untypical is to beg the question. Personally I would find it hard to define or describe the typical 'media person' ... and indeed the more I think of it the less possible it appears. They are such a mixed bunch, in background and education and beliefs and tastes, as in their jobs and the way they do them, that no identikit portrait could be anything but a vague blur.

Áine was a communicator in two media: print and radio. Print came first, for she had been writing in the religious press before she joined the broadcasting service, just thirty years ago, and continued to do so until her final illness. Her radio work was initially (in the Cork region and afterwards in Dublin) not in the religious area: when she eventually did become a producer in that department, she brought to the job considerable experience and understanding of broadcasting in general. Always her own woman, and by no means uncritical of the organisation in which she worked, she was quick to refute what she saw as unjustified attacks – no matter how eminent the attackers.

Since her death, more than one friend has applied to Áine the phrase she loved to quote from J.G. McGarry's encomium of 'a woman of great holiness, utterly uncorrupted by piety'. Piety in the primal sense of loyal devotion she certainly had in plenty, but from what in Ireland we call 'piosity' she was certainly free.

As to holiness, I suppose in the long run only God knows. From a few, a very few, it seems to shine, and in some others we can surely detect it. With Áine, again the primal meaning applies: a wholeness of humanity which was very attractive in its sanity, its unfussy but determined sense of mission, its commitment to what she saw as her job in life.

Her own early illness, and that of her husband, whose untimely death left her a widow in her prime, gave her a remarkable awareness of the needs and concerns of the sick and disabled and she identified her vocation with theirs. That vocation she fulfilled in her work in the media.

An earlier call to convent life had to be abandoned through ill-health. She retained the friendship of nuns and priests alike, and indeed could count at least one bishop in her circle, but hers was essentially a lay ministry. Her pleasure on being awarded a papal honour was genuine, but she never allowed that real piety of hers to cloud her judgement or her sense of justice: no more than her keen sense of suffering took from her enjoyment of life's comforts.

She lived fully to the very end. Formal retirement was merely a ripple in her professional life, and her Christian ministry. *Bhí Dia buíoch di.*

(February 1987, vol. 37, no. 2, pp. 94-95)

The Hunthausen affair

News of the full rehabilitation in office of the Archbishop of Seattle has been widely welcomed. Few Vatican blunders in recent times have aroused such reaction; the patent injustice done to a good man both angered and saddened people of goodwill all over America, and indeed all over the Catholic world...

One might then be tempted to say 'all's well that ends well' and leave it at that. But it would, I believe, be a pity not to recognise in the whole affair certain elements of real and even urgent significance to all local Churches in their relationship with the Church universal and especially the See of Rome.

On the occasion of the *ad limina* visit of the bishops of Switzerland (March 1987), Pope John Paul took the opportunity of reiterating the emphasis laid by the Constitution *Lumen gentium* on their role, not as 'vicars of the Roman pontiff' but as heads of their several local Churches. He went on to quote the Constitution as pointing out that far from 'effacing' their power, the papal role must confirm, strengthen and defend it. And, perhaps more importantly, he insisted that the relation between bishops and papacy was no mere 'administrative' matter, but belonged to the basic *communio* at the heart of the mystery of the Church.

It is then, one must say, quite deplorable that an authority which appears to be purely administrative, should – invoking, of course, the papal name – be in a position to ride roughshod over episcopal rights and prerogatives, which, unlike those of a bureaucracy, however exalted, are of sacramental origin and character. I do not of course suggest that a bishop may never be criticised, even impeached, even removed from office: far from it, for, if he seriously betrays his trust or even becomes incapable of performing his duties, his flock will need another pastor. But any necessary measure should be taken after due process has been fulfilled – and, if at all possible, without harming the weak and innocent, proceedings should be conducted openly ...

What I have said should, of course, apply not only to bishops, but to all whose work in and for the Church leaves them open to criticism, serious or trivial, informed or uninformed, well-intentioned or malicious. It can involve parish priests and parish clerks, teachers and theologians, choirmasters and collectors and confessors. In all cases, the old, and maybe boring, maxim must obtain: 'Let justice be done and be seen to be done.'

...

While we must regret that in the case of Archbishop Hunthausen justice was so long and so painfully and humiliatingly delayed, we must also be under no illusions as to how it was finally achieved.

I think we can identify four factors.

First, and all-important, the Archbishop's own strong, dignified, courteous refusal to back down from what in conscience he knew to be the rightness of his stand. One can only guess at the pressures brought to bear on him to yield and, indeed, he could have been forgiven if he had withdrawn quietly through the escape-hatch of retirement. But he did not.

Second, the declared support of the great majority of both priests and people of the Church of Seattle. The firm statement issued in the crucial final weeks must have been especially valuable, as it provided a strong underpinning for the third factor: the fraternal solidarity of a core group within the U.S. episcopal conference, without whose efforts the process of rehabilitation would never have got off the ground.

Finally, of course, we must give due credit to that formidable if sometimes wayward lady, public opinion. The issue was kept alive in the pages of the *National Catholic Reporter*, and a few other journals, as well as by a number of loyal and determined individuals. Their efforts have been admirably justified. Indeed, I can recall no similarly successful campaign, mounted on such a scale, to have a wrong righted within the institutional Church – and not very many in civil society either, at home or abroad. I need only mention the 'Birmingham Six' to recall what a long, frustrating business such a campaign can be.

So the Seattle affair may yet be seen in retrospect as a turning-point in the struggle for justice in the Church – which is of course a *sine qua non* for the credibility, not to say efficacy, of the Church's own admirable, and at times, heroic struggle for justice in the world. It may go to show that the cliché argument 'the Church is not a democracy' is, at best, a half-truth and it may, just possibly, mean that the idea of a 'loyal opposition' could be recognised not only as permissible but even valuable.

At the very least, Seattle proves that a just cause can be won by determination, intelligence, organisation and perseverance. It proves that the Vatican is not necessarily impervious to the clearly expressed convictions of local Churches – especially when pastors and people are of one mind. What remains to be seen, though, is this: can the authentic voice of a local Church prevent a contemplated injustice or simple blunder before the damage is done?

(July-August 1987, vol. 37, no. 6, pp. 360-362)

Sing Jubilee: Sunday, October 11

On this morning, twenty-five years ago, Pope John XXIII of happy memory, presided at the opening of the Second Vatican Council. Those of us who were there – as Council Fathers, *periti*, or mere journalists and allied riff-raff, are now getting thin on the ground, and not quite as young as we used to be.

There were, I imagine, a few moist eyes in St Peter's this morning among those at the commemorative Mass. And not a few ghosts. Two of them were remembered by name in the Roman Canon – John himself, and his great successor Paul VI – and, of all the others who were not named, each of us was thinking of the special ones we loved and worked with and argued against. And as we sang *Kyrie eleison* our prayer was for them, for us all ...

Not that my own 'dispositions' on that October morning 1962, the feast of the Motherhood of Mary in the old calendar, were altogether appropriate to the occasion. For one thing we had to be in St Peter's at the crack of dawn, hours before anything happened – whether this was Vatican bloody-mindedness, or anxiety or for the good of our souls, I never found out. Nor why the 'tribune' that was supposed to accommodate journalists was three-quarters occupied by nuns – a variety of them dressed in voluminous habits that are now probably museum pieces. By sheer brute force and ignorance and refusing to take lip from the 'black' aristocracy who patrolled the Basilica (one learns quickly in Rome), I eventually squeezed into a corner which I shared sardine-like with, as I recall, the *Daily Express* (a devout Anglican), the *News of the World* (an old Downside boy) – both alas! no longer with us – and dear Molly McGee, then representing *The People*, who still flourishes, and I am sure remembers Cardinal Newman as a small boy. Lest I should be completely anglicised by contiguity, I turned my eyes to another loftier tribune where among the foreign delegations I could just glimpse the Irish, led, as I seem to remember, by the then Taoiseach, Seán Lemass.

But that was little help to a man with a hangover and no breakfast, nor indeed was the 'warm-up' by the Sistine Choir, members of whom, I could not help recalling, had got stuck, with their conductor Bertolucci in a lift in the Shelbourne Hotel a couple of years before, while the old Theatre Royal, packed to its 4,000-seater capacity waited and waited – and this unfortunate commentator waffled and waffled into a microphone. (It all ended reasonably well ...)

And then at long last the great procession entered the basilica, over two thousand strong, and, like all such processions, part impressive, part (because of all those bobbing mitres) slightly comic. My own memories of the beginning of the Liturgy are, as they say, fitful, but I do remember the beloved face of John as he sat in Peter's chair, like a mother hen with her chickens, as he looked with evident delight at the circle of guests who sat in places of high honour, and especially the Observers from other Churches, of the East and of the West, whose presence was the tangible sign of a new Christian era and the fulfillment of John's own ardent hope.

The pontifical liturgy continued in its stately Tridentine way. If my memory serves me right, Pope John was not the celebrant – 'presiding' without celebrating was quite common in those days. And, of course, only the celebrant (Cardinal Tisserant, I think, as Dean of the College of Cardinals) took Holy Communion. This would, thank God, be unthinkable now – at today's Mass everyone in the basilica, I imagine, took part (also in the singing and the prayers) even though I have to say the method of bringing Communion to the people left much to be desired.

I have to confess that St Peter's is not my favourite place of worship. Like the Church of the Holy Sepulchre in Jerusalem, Notre-Dame in Paris, St Patrick's in Dublin, it attracts tourists who, with the best will in the world, can hardly be called pilgrims – not so much the Church in the world as the world in the Church! (Who is being élitist now?) However it must be said that conciliar reform is triumphantly vindicated on occasions like today, when a Papal Mass is a genuine community celebration, stripped of the accretions of the past – many of them admittedly 'impressive' – and, all in all, a splendid example of that 'noble simplicity' the Council sought ...

But over and over again, memories of that first morning kept crowding in: memories of physical discomfort; an almost reluctant response to the grandeur of the ceremony; a certain scepticism (shared by many) about what it was all going to add up to (it was commonly believed that the proceedings were 'all sewn up in advance' by the Curia) struggling with an inescapable sense of occasion ... and then, suddenly, in the twinkling of an eye, the great, clear trumpet-call from Peter's chair, as John aroused us from our torpor, bade us cast off fear, listen to the lessons of history, stop moaning and condemning, and go out into the world in the hope of the Holy Spirit – into his world and ours, and let our light shine before men.

It was the end of an age, the beginning of an age, a revolution, a leap into the future, a new call to faith and hope and love ...

For what we have failed to do: *Kyrie, eleison.*

(November 1987, vol. 37, no. 9, pp. 534-537)

After Enniskilen

No flattering unctions are on offer for Enniskillen.[1] What happened there is not something we can, with a faintly pleasurable tremor, ascribe to psychopaths, hardened criminals and other outsiders. Psychopaths those responsible may have been, and they may, by now, have grown hard in terrorist cruelty – or again they may not. But whatever and whoever they are, they are not outsiders. They belong to us.

They are, almost certainly, the products of a Good Catholic Education – and I do not mean just Good Catholic Schools, but also Good Catholic Families, not to speak of the Church itself into which they were baptised, and confirmed, the Teaching Church from whose pulpits they have heard of God's Law, of the sin of murder – and, presumably, of love and compassion and our common kinship as children of the one Father ... There is, I think, an urgent need for something like a national examination of conscience among those of us who still profess to be followers of Christ, and more particularly those who belong to the Roman Catholic Communion. For there is something very rotten here.

God knows, Enniskillen is not without precedent. I suppose the most recent comparable atrocity was the Darkley massacre, a slaughter of the Innocents which at the time stunned us so completely that we grasped gratefully at the 'psychopath' solution. Any other explanation would have been intolerable ... But this time we do not have that way out: we must face the fact that an 'organisation' supported – yes, and Sinn Féin votes show it – by a large number of 'Catholics' in the North, and a not inconsiderable minority in the Republic, claimed responsibility for what was, in effect if not intention, an act of genocide. And their 'explanation' of the 'civilian casualties' has been rightly regarded as an obscene insult.

I have used the words 'examination of conscience'. For there

1. The reference is to the I.R.A. bomb at the Cenotaph on Remembrance Sunday.

is far, far more buried in the dark places of our Catholic souls than this one crime, enormous though it be. In our whole attitude to 'political' violence there has been over the past decade and a half a continuing process of self-deception, of hypocrisy, of public double-talk, of sick sentimentality which has warped us so that, it would appear, we hardly know right from wrong. And I do not think it is unfair to say 'we' and 'our'.

We have not all killed or maimed, or placed a bomb – directly or by proxy – where it could kill or maim, or protected those who did, or brainwashed kids into thinking they were part of a glorious army of liberation, or blackmailed or intimidated in Ireland's cause. But too many of us have, by our acquiescence, by our inaction, by our refusal to speak out against the 'lads', given aid and comfort to those who have been doing these things. And this is only one side of the picture.

Because, of course, the crimes of 'republican' violence have not been committed *in vacuo*. This evil has its roots in other evils, some of them perpetrated by those who held the reins of power and privilege in the North for a long time, some by a series of stupid British administrations who just did not want to know, but some again traceable to our failure – and I mean the Catholic majority of this island – to build a decent society.

(December 1987, vol. 37, no. 10, pp. 584-585)

Let-down

Nobody who was in Rome for the Synod [on the laity], either insider or outsider, would be pleased with the outcome. Maybe some of its predecessors have produced equally uninspiring results, but there was so much publicity and activity in advance of this one that even those of us whose 'expectations' were modest and limited felt seriously let down. The first days, while not over-exciting, were marked by several excellent speeches, some of them quite outstanding. It became clear that the 'laity' were most definitely not to be regarded as second-class citizens, and there were even (to me very gratifying) criticisms of the use of 'lay' and its derivatives. The lay-cleric dichotomy, and especially that which sharply differentiated Church and world as fields of ministry and mission, were also questioned, and the whole matter of lay ministry was discussed from a wide range of view-points: from those who considered the very idea as inappropriate, to advocates of the admission of all – women as well as men

– to any and every ministry not requiring ordination. And the 'forbidden' topic of the ordination of women and married men was at least tangentially raised.

Women's role and dignity were discussed in a very positive way – and here particularly there were some particularly perceptive contributions. Other hopeful signs included the frequently reiterated praise of the small or basic community as a vital organ of the local Church – it is now clearly accepted, and 'warnings' about its 'dangers' were very few. And of course there was the deeply impressive, and sometimes deeply moving, account given by bishops from every corner of the earth – including the 'second' and, especially, the 'third' worlds – on the life of the local Church within the Church universal.

And this last is, sadly, the one positive feature of the Synod that continues to enrich the spirit, and shine through all the disappointment of the last days. Once the 'secrecy' blinds came down hearts began to sink. There was a quite pervasive if irrational feeling that the bad old days were back. And the worst disappointment of all was this: that when the blinds were torn aside we saw there was little or nothing to be secretive about.

Except, of course, that everything had turned out flat, neat and tidy as if by some curial smoothing-iron. Archbishop Chiasson of Moncton in Canada spoke for many when he expressed 'deep suffering' at the month-long process, complaining he felt deceived by a Church system that made 'real dialogue' impossible. He described the Synod's Message to the People of God as 'paternalistic and laced with platitudes', and their final submission to the pope as equally vague ... Asked what he and his fellow-bishops from Canada would take home, he answered: 'Nothing ... except perhaps the conviction that the Church is lived at home' ...

One need not go all the way with the archbishop in his understandable depression to echo his words 'the Church is lived at home'. The time has come in Ireland for us to recognise this, and make it something more than an ideal. As well as the change of heart for which we need to pray and work, we need, as a matter of urgency, to explore ways and means of making this Church of ours a living force for love and justice. We need to talk, all of us, men and women, ordained and unordained, married, single, religious – to talk first of all about structures. Then to set them up – and use them.

(December 1987, vol. 37, no. 10, pp. 589-590)

1988

The poor and the private

It would indeed be a poor joke to compare the Irish situation at its worst with that obtaining in a hundred places from Colombia to Kampuchea. But it is far from what it should be or what, with a little help, we could make of it. Although Enniskillen has continued to resonate in words of grief and repentance and reconciliation, still, so far all we have had are words, and, however valuable, these are not enough. As I write, the Birmingham Six appeal is dragging to a close: one awaits the result in hope and in fear. Nor can all this, painfully important though it be, leave us unaware of other concerns, less dramatic but gravely disturbing. These mainly centre on the 'cuts' which present economic policies dictate in some of the most vulnerable areas of our national life, notably health and education. The focus is at present on the latter, and understandably so: the situation creates serious doubts about our young people's future, and that of the country as a whole. And there are other ominous implications in government policies and measures.

I mean that while past domestic errors and ineptitudes, as well as the effects of international recession, have necessitated strict economic self-discipline, the way in which the present government (with the general support of most of the opposition) has set about this leaves much to be desired. Not alone has there been a marked reluctance to tackle the areas of unproductive wealth, while diligently pursuing the most vulnerable, but there has been also an apparently indiscriminate 'thinning-down' of certain centres of intellectual, artistic, scientific and other skills, leading in many cases to emigration of a particularly disastrous kind. Not indeed but that the present wave of general emigration is in itself quite deplorable, at least on the scale which we have come to accept as inevitable. Those of us who remember the 1950s can only regard what is happening now with the deepest foreboding, nor can we easily expect a recurrence of the small economic miracle which lifted us out of the rut in the following decade (and that didn't last very long).

One of the most depressing aspects of the prevailing climate is the all-too-familiar way in which socio-economic 'orthodoxies' are adopted here just when they have nearly run their course elsewhere. Friedman on one level and Mrs Thatcher on another will no doubt still have their Irish devotees when their names have been expunged from the manuals and memories of their original disciples. I don't know how much longer 'privatisation' is likely to survive as an article of economic dogma in post-Socialist or neo-Socialist Britain, but it's still the buzz-word here, and regarded as the panacea for all our social ills. With, of course, a judicious admixture of its lubricant: 'competition'.

They say that hope is ever triumphant over experience, and I can think of no other basis for the childlike confidence that our prevailing wisdom displays in the private sector. Public enterprise in Ireland has had its flops and its failures, but, over the past fifty years or so, its record compares more than well with that achieved by private entrepreneurs – with a very few distinguished exceptions.

The fact that not so many years ago public investment in the Republic was the highest in western Europe was not to be explained in ideological terms. The reasons were strictly pragmatic and realistic, and there is little evidence that a shift of policy now is necessitated by such fundamental changes in the body politic as would lead us to expect that private investment and enterprise can or will provide the industrial initiatives which are so desperately needed to deal with the twin problems of unemployment and emigration.

No less serious, and equally dubious on the social level, is the shift of emphasis to the private sector in the area of public health. The question is too large and too specialised to be dealt with adequately here, but already the gap between what is available to have and have-nots is becoming glaringly obvious, and represents a sad regression in a field where some positive progress had been made in recent years. Here again the voices of Christians need to be raised and heard.

(January 1988, vol. 38, no. 1, pp. 30-31)

Iconic illumination

That gentle, modest, but immensely stimulating Anglican scholar, A. M. Allchin, Canon of Canterbury, now director of an institute for Orthodox studies in Oxford, was in Dublin shortly before Christmas, and, under the joint aegis of the Irish School of

Ecumenics and the Fellowship of Sts Alban and Sergius, he conducted a week-end seminar on icons and iconography in the Eastern Churches, and especially in the Byzantine tradition. His discourse was part theological, part liturgical, part historical, part aesthetic, part devotional – I know I make it sound like a rag-bag, which it certainly wasn't. Allchin's own scholarship and enthusiasm for his subject imposed their own unity on what he had to say, and his wit and utter lack of pretentiousness made him a joy to listen to.

I should add that, for an Irish audience, his central thesis, rooted as it was in Byzantine Orthodoxy (Greek, Russian, Rumanian) was given remarkable clarity and relevance by his frequent reference to Celtic sources: his knowledge here is first-hand, since unlike so many admirers of our tradition he has taken the trouble to learn a Celtic language (Welsh), and is already an acknowledged authority on aspects of post-Reformation Welsh spirituality. He apologizes for not knowing Irish – yet!

The juxtaposing of Celtic and Byzantine however was no mere exercise in eclecticism, nor even an interesting reflection on our own very real debt to eastern sources in the 'dark' ages. For me, at least, its importance was fundamental to Allchin's whole exposition: I mean that iconic art, while uniquely special to the eastern Christian tradition, is of universal significance in precisely that difficult, delicate but exciting area where art and religion meet.

The key, I believe, is to be found in what was one of the central insights of his thesis: that specific does not necessarily mean exclusive. This is a truth which we tend too often to lose sight of, especially in societies and at times which value the polemic more than the eirenic: it prevents the easy absolutes of 'either/or'. It's a truth of great theological resonance: its implications for Christology, not to mention ecclesiology, are enormous. Thank God I don't have to explore them here!

The religious specificity of the icon must impress itself even on the most untutored of us. It says things about the divine, about holiness, about love, about God's ways with men, in a manner that is quite different to any other visual art-form. And as we learn something about the theological and artistic seed-bed from which this extraordinary flowering grew, we begin to recognise how that artistic specificity could only have been born of the spiritual specificity we call Orthodoxy.

But – and this I believe is crucial – neither in its 'artistic' nor in its 'Orthodox' aspects does this specificity imply exclusivity. To take the second first, there is indeed a growing school of artists working in the iconic mode in the west in recent years, but it is not here, nor in the visual genre at all, that I would see the universal significance of iconic art. As, in fact, Canon Allchin suggested himself, the clarity, the purity, the impersonality, as well as the intimate relationship with the revealed Word which we find in the icon, are in, the Christian west, found in the equally strict and ancient art of plainsong. In its expression of the numinous, it is to all other music, as the icon is to all other painting. Again the specificity is clear, and recognised by the least skilled ear: again the artistically specific derives from a unique, and precisely attested, tradition. But, again, neither carries any excluding shield, neither closes any doors.

(February 1988, vol. 38, no. 2, pp. 82-83)

Prophet and pastor

Cardinal Bernard Alfrink was truly one of the great men of the Second Vatican Council and of the first post-conciliar years. Pius XII was still Pope when he became Archbishop of Utrecht and Primate of the Netherlands in 1955: when he retired, just over twenty years later, the Dutch Church was utterly transformed. His enemies – and they are still around – would say 'destroyed', or, at least, so seriously damaged that even the 'remedial' measures introduced by Simonis, Gijsen and other conservative bishops were insufficient to stop the rot.

It's one reading of the situation, but by no means the only one. Indeed a strong case can be made for casting Alfrink as the saviour of Dutch Catholicism at a time of great social and spiritual upheaval, and that his calm, courageous leadership was nothing short of providential.

Of his own great integrity and fidelity there can be no doubt – indeed to suggest otherwise would be supremely stupid as well as impertinent. I can personally recall an incident in the Dutch bishops' information centre in Rome – either in 1965, the last year of the Council, or during the 1967 Synod – when a rather brash journalist saw fit to question his loyalty, indeed his obedience, to the Holy See. His response was masterly. Clearly restraining his anger, not so much with the journalist, as with those for whom he was an obvious and naïve mouthpiece, Alfrink spoke

briefly and with great dignity on the meaning of loyalty and of
obedience, as well as making a trenchant distinction between
Peter and some who presumed to speak in his name

His last years must have had more than their share of sadness.
But, as prophet and pastor, his place is assured in the history of
the twentieth century Church.

(February 1988, vol. 38, no. 2, pp. 87-88)

Christians and the lottery

I remember the late Cardinal Conway telling me how one of his
diocesan priorities was to get rid of the appalling 'Funeral
Offerings', a custom peculiar at the time to the Armagh Province
– and how hard he found it to do so. This led to a somewhat
revealing (to me) discussion on clerical incomes which he was
attempting to rationalise – in several cases to provide local
pastors with something approaching a living wage.

Another conversation (not so well informed) about the general funding of the Irish Churches, the other evening, inspired
the facetious proposal that 'they should all be financed out of the
National Lottery'. After all, the arts, sport, youth activities and
other 'non-essentials' are become increasingly dependent on
those pound notes offered daily not to the God of Abraham, nor
to the Muses Nine, but to the capricious Goddess of Chance. Why
not then put religion along with the rest?

I should not be altogether surprised if that 'why not' were to
be echoed not just by the irreligious and irreverent, but by one
section of very committed Christians. I mean those who, for
conscience sake, have already stood up and been counted as
refusing the material benefits of the Lottery – grants for youth
clubs and the like. Roman Catholics have often tended to smile,
a little impatiently perhaps, at the very rigid anti-gambling
teaching and discipline of some, if not most, Protestants. We
have usually confined ourselves to condemning 'excesses' –
spending the week's wages at the bookmakers, wagering huge
amount at poker games and so on: our concern being mainly
with those suffering as a result.

But while I would not go all the way with those who regard all
'gaming' as wrong in itself, even on the smallest and most clearly
innocuous scale, I do feel uneasy about apparent insensitivity to
the inherent antisocial and depersonalising aspects of the whole
gambling culture – on many levels. It cannot fail to have a

corrosive effect on the minds and hearts of those, of all classes, conditions and incomes, who are involved to the point of addiction. And I am uneasy about its institutionalisation on a national scale as has happened here over the past year or so.

The old Hospitals Sweepstakes were popularly regarded as making a valuable contribution to the care of the sick – though there too, certain 'Protestant' institutions remained aloof. And hindsight, taking a closer look at the whole affair, has raised some awkward questions, as yet not satisfactorily answered. But on a more fundamental level, am I being unreasonably puritanical in taking the view that a society whose care of the sick depended on the partial resources of large-scale gambling is itself very sick indeed? And I would have similar reservations about funding the arts and so on, on the same basis.

Of course if we regard the whole method as desirable generally, why not indeed include the Churches? Put like that, I think the moral objections to lottery-funding become somewhat clearer. Not indeed that Catholics, at least on the parish level, have had any great objections to gambling as a form of Church funding: the most notorious example being bingo, as an on-going parochial activity. And I use the word 'notorious' advisedly: it's one of the things that kindly Christians of other denominations hesitate to mention to us, but which cause somewhat bewildered speculation among themselves. I wonder do we realise how literally shocking the bingo poster in the church porch must appear to them?

Some will ask, robustly, what business is it of theirs? Or, it will be pointed out that the bingo sessions fill a real social need, bringing the lonely and solitary together once or twice a week in a harmless communal activity, which also helps to pay for some of the multifarious expenses of a modern lively, caring parish. Until one is made to feel like a mixture of Scrooge and Cromwell.

And yet and yet ... Whatever can be said for such local events, for small-scale raffles and the like, organised national gambling – backed up by an intense advertising campaign on radio and television and in print, urging us to spend more and more – is very difficult to justify. And at a time of national economic and social crisis, it seems to give encouragement to all the wrong things and ideas: get rich quick; don't invest – gamble; dream about prosperity instead of working for it. I can only see it all as contributing to an already widespread national sleaze, with a

light top-dressing of tinsel. Can or should Christians remain
silent about it?

(April 1988, vol. 38, no. 4, pp. 218-219)

Diakonia

On the Sunday before midsummer day I attended a celebration
of the Eucharist in Dublin's Christ Church Cathedral, at which
Archbishop Donald Caird ordained four new deacons for the
Church of Ireland. What made the occasion special was that one
of the four was a woman, a colleague in journalism and the widow
of another colleague. She is also deeply involved in the ecumenical movement, and those present included the Abbot of Glenstal,
the Director of the Irish School of Ecumenics, and a recent
member of the inter-church Columbanus Community in Belfast.

But, of course, far more deeply significant than these immediate aspects of fellowship is the fact that Irish Anglicans are now
set firmly on a course whose ultimate resolution we can indeed
only guess at, but which could represent a real breakthrough not
only for Anglicans, but for all Christians of the Catholic tradition.
And that perhaps sooner than some of us dare to hope.

I should, I suppose make it clear that I personally can see no
valid theological or even institutional arguments against the
admission of women to any of the three historic ministries. On
the contrary, I do see urgent and compelling reasons why this
should happen for the good of the Church and the preaching of
the Gospel. 'Cultural' arguments and difficulties are often cited,
and these clearly need to be faced: in general, however, I would
suggest that they should not be regarded with awe, as monumen-
tal barriers in the way of our proceeding in a desired direction,
but, at the same time, given due consideration as factors necessarily influencing strategy and timing. Not everything worth
doing needs doing now, but postponements, when seen to be
prudential and perhaps, on the long term, valuable, should not
be made an excuse for inactivity or cowardice: they must be
constantly subject to review and certainly never *sine die*.

The continuing debate on these matters in the Anglican
Communion is of no small importance to us all. While the battle
of the diaconate has been won, presbyterate and episcopacy are
still areas of conflict, at least internationally, and at 'provincial'
level in some instances, including the Church of England itself.
And the arguments *contra*, based on a probable alienation of and

from Orthodoxy as well as Roman Catholicism, while painful to many of us, do represent a very real concern for the unity of Christ's Church on what is seen to be a matter touching the core of Catholic belief and practice. Sadly, this aspect of the debate may seem to be merely 'political' in a strategic sense, as may the counter-argument pointing to the practice of the 'Free' Churches. And it would be too much to expect that division on such an apparently basic question should not lead to entrenched positioning and the growth of mutually hostile factions.

The most useful thing we can do is to pray that the Holy Spirit lead our brothers assembled at Lambeth along a way which will accord with his will for all his Church. To say this is not just to utter a pious aspiration, rather it is an expression of hope for all Christians as we come into the third millennium of the faith. It would of course seem as if both Rome and the Churches of the East were unshakeably opposed to the admission of women to holy orders. But whatever about Orthodoxy, any Catholic who has lived through the 'changes' of the past twenty five years must need to be a little sceptical about unchangeability. And not the least of these changes has been in relation to the place of women in public worship: here we have an example of 'cultural' received wisdom and institutional discipline being turned unceremoniously upside down.

...

The very idea that women should handle the sacred vessels of the liturgy would only a few years ago have seemed deeply shocking, or at the very least improper. That they should actually distribute Holy Communion was quite unthinkable. Indeed, I can remember a discussion in the 1950s when it was rumoured that women were being ordained in a certain Lutheran Church, and when somebody said, as a joke, 'Imagine Peggy here giving you Communion!', the remark was regarded as being in the worst possible taste. The fact that Peggy was herself a devout and regular communicant was beside the point: even the story that St Clare once handled a monstrance was best taken as apocryphal.

Admittedly, similar intrusion by laymen on the role and area of the ordained was as unthinkable – or nearly so. 'In an emergency' maybe it would be possible, because after all a man could be a priest. In those days we didn't talk about Ministers of the Word, because the very concept was outside our experience: or, rather perhaps, the Word itself was subsumed into the total liturgical action as part of the *opus operatum*. But one did hear travellers' tales of lay readers during the Holy Week Offices – 'chanters' might be a better word, as they intoned the Latin texts to a set 'tune', however untuneful … But these were never women: they might sing on sufferance in the choir – provided it wasn't in the sanctuary – although Pius X would prefer they didn't. (Gabriel's aunt had a word to say about this in Joyce's *The Dead*.) In fact the only way women were, as I can recall, admitted inside the 'rails' was for cleaning and decorating purposes, outside the hours of Mass and other services. They needed to know not just their place but their time.

I have rehearsed all this, not to add to a litany of complaints nor to emphasise how badly and stupidly we used to behave, nor yet to congratulate ourselves on how good we are now. I merely want to point out that the Church has changed, and by the Church I mean all of us, pastors and people, men and women. And it has not just been a change of rubrics and regulations, (although the reform of discipline has, of course, been crucial): I am rather concerned with the cultural *bouleversement* that has occurred in an area where it might have seemed less predictable. Not alone are women reading the lesson and sharing the Bread and Cup but their Ministries of Word and Sacrament have been accepted (and, I believe, gladly) by all sorts and conditions of people of both sexes. I know that there are exceptions: individuals who will avoid, if possible, receiving Holy Communion from any hands other than those of the priest – though even this may not always have to do with women but with the lay minister as such.

· · ·

What I am suggesting is that, based on this experience, women would be equally acceptable if their ministry were of orders. I realise that 'acceptability' is not necessarily the ultimate consideration in judging suitability for ordination. By no means. But when the argument is on the 'cultural' level, it is a very important consideration indeed. And further, I have a very strong feeling that it is far more important institutionally than authority may recognise.

As to the diaconate, many if not all of the functions which it involves are already being performed by lay ministers, including women. In this country, they seldom, if ever, preach or read the gospel. But such extensions of their ministry are, I suggest,

unfamiliar mainly because we have so few non-Eucharistic services. Where and when such are common, and especially when
they have to substitute for the Sunday Mass, the practice may be
quite different. As to non-Eucharistic sacramental functions:
again, baptising and presiding at weddings are quite common
where clergy are scarce.

And so, one might ask why bother with ordination? What
would it enable a deacon to do that the lay ministers can't do
already? The answer lies of course in the very salutary reminder
that the preacher in Christ Church provided in his sermon:
ordination relates to sacrament, and is in itself a sign of the
sacramentality of the Church. To say this is not to suggest that the
sacrament is confined to the laying-on of hands: any more than
the sacramentality of marriage is confined to the exchange of
vows. Nor are we to see ordination as a quasi-magical rite giving
the ordained certain 'powers' which he would otherwise not
have. It is an expression of specificity rather than uniqueness. It
does not say: only these men or women are committed to
diakonia. It does say that, in them, the common *diakonia* which
Jesus enjoined on us all is sacramentally manifest.

I do not then agree with those who think that the ordination
of 'permanent' deacons, of either sex, is an unnecessary luxury.
There is of course always a danger of clericalisation, even where
the ministry is being exercised on an auxiliary or part-time basis.
And those who remain unordained must never be made feel
'inferior' to those who are. Above all, such ordinations are not to
be promoted at the cost of narrowing the range of non-ordained
service, not least in the pastoral area.

As to ordination to higher orders, and the admission of
women thereto, the subject is too large for now – although I
would like to return to it one day. But I am convinced that the
development which I regard as desirable and inevitable will come
only in the context of a broader and deeper understanding of
what ministry – and ordination – are about. Towards this fuller
understanding we are moving slowly but, I hope, surely.

(July-August 1988, vol. 38, no. 6, pp. 311-314)

Sign and reality

A few of us were talking last night about Mrs C.F. Alexander who,
as well as making a superb translation of *Lúireach Phádraig*,
Patrick's Breastplate, was inspired, when her husband was Bishop

of Derry, to write the crucifixion hymn *There Is a Green Hill* by the sight of the then green hill of the Creggan! Green today it is not, but I would venture to say that it offers now a setting for crucifixion more painfully immediate. Again last night we talked of Pasolini's film *The Passion according to Matthew* and how Christ's last journey to Calvary had more of the conventionally tragic isolation we're accustomed to: rather is his progress barely noticed as he and his cross and his minders are pushed and jostled by the Passover crowds – after all, what to them was another criminal getting what was coming to him! And the unlikely combination of Creggan and Pasolini set me thinking about the actual context in which our Paschal celebration is set in today's world and today's Ireland. After all we have said about the meaning of celebration, we cannot shut out the bitter question posed by voices both old and, sadly, young: What have we got to celebrate?

What have the unemployed, the kids with no prospect of a job, the desperate unwilling emigrants, to celebrate? What joy and hope does Easter bring to the poor, the marginalised, the oppressed in Dublin's Sherriff Street, or Derry's Creggan – or in the *barrios* of Brazil or the slums of Calcutta? What does Christ's victory mean to the defeated and half-defeated of Chile and Colombia, of Bangladesh and the Sudan? He is risen but they are, at best, on their knees. What price the renewal of the earth's face when we are busy destroying rivers and rain forests? Can we salute light and life and still stand idly by as war and the threat of war bid fair to complete the extinction of thousands of species with that of the human race itself?

Alright, there is rhetoric there and maybe some exaggeration. But most of what I've said might seem an understatement to many, who would see our celebration as a blasphemy against suffering humanity – or, at best a frivolous irrelevance. And let's not fool ourselves, there are many on our own doorstep who would say just that.

Does it matter? Of course it does and they do. I have spoken of our own liturgy in terms of sacrament, and as we know, the essence of sacrament is that it should be an effective sign: and that we, the sacramental community, should also be an effective sign.

For this, the first essential is faith. Unless we believe what we're saying and doing, unless we believe in it, it just won't ring true.

If we see the Easter Vigil as just a holy game, (and it is that, but much, much more), if we don't see the true light shining in each other, we can't be a light to the world.

The second essential is hope. It is hope that enables our celebration to encompass and transcend pain and loss and death itself. It is hope that sustains us through Good Friday, and all the empty Fridays in our lives and the life of the world. It enables us to see evil in perspective, as the negative non-being which it is. It enables us not to turn our back on the Cross but to salute and embrace its wood *in quo salus mundi pependit* and to see the Enniskillen and Gibraltar and Bangladesh and the holocaust in the light of, and in solidarity with, Christ's passion.

To see the daily crucifixion of our brothers and sisters in the light of his crucifixion. To know that Friday will end, and Saturday will end, as we keep vigil in a suffering world which will not suffer for ever, as we await him in sure and certain expectation.

And, of course, hope is the bridge that links faith to love. The sacramental community must be, and be seen to be, a loving community. We will have learned that lesson on Maundy Thursday – if we listen, really listen to John 13, and if the people whose feet are washed are men and women who need our love and our caring. St John's account of the Passion on Good Friday should confirm what we have learned: 'he loved them to the end' and so must we.

(October 1988, vol. 38, no. 8, pp. 413-415)

1989

Liberty, equality, fraternity ...

Beset as we have lately been by anniversaries, national and
international – most recently by the Liffeyside 'millennium' – the
proclamation of yet another Year for Remembering may be more
productive of yawns than of cries of enthusiasm. But there is no
escaping the fact that 1989 is the bicentenary of an event, or
series of events, which, for good or ill, made for a radical
reshaping of the destinies of Europe and of the modern world.

For good and ill. The French Revolution was not all glorious
within or without: like most human endeavours and achievements, it was riddled with ambiguities, deeply scarred by mis-
deeds and mistakes, and destructive not only of much that was
evil but of not a little that was good. Its 'worst excesses' were
indeed such as to chill less tender hearts than Lady Bracknell's,
and its consequences might cause the most sympathetic to ask:
Was it all worth while?

Certainly for a very long time after the fires had died down,
established Christian opinion would have answered that question with an unhesitating and unqualified 'No!' On this at least
nineteenth century Catholics and Protestants, Anglicans and
Lutherans, were at one: only on the dissenting fringes were the
new ideas made welcome, or seen to be reconcilable with Christian thought.

It is hard for us now to realise that for a long time the word
'democracy' was as offensive to pious ears as were later 'socialism'
and 'communism', and that even the more moderate expressions of post-revolutionary political and social thought were
deemed anathema. In France itself any accommodation with the
'enemy' was seen as the grossest of infidelities and only in this
century, and especially since World War II, have the old *rouge et
noir* lines become seriously blurred. There were indeed, from an
early date, great exceptions on the Catholic side, but it is useful
to recall that in our own time Lefebvre and his bully-boys were
not just opposed to 'liberalism' in the religious sphere.

The sad thing was, and I am afraid to some extent still is, that
not only were the excesses of the Revolution condemned, but

even the very ideas that informed the whole revolutionary movement were uncritically dismissed as at best 'mere humanitarian-
ism' and at worst 'godlessness' or, to use a quaint term of
derogation, 'naturalism'. In all of this it was clearly taken for
granted that the 'new trinity' of Liberty, Equality, Fraternity,
made and left no place for God – just as the Rights of Man were
seen as a tacit denial of, or at least disregard for, the overwhelm-
ingly more important Rights of God.

Indeed, when the late Marshal Pétain established his new *État*
after the Fall of the French Republic in 1940, he deliberately and
ostentatiously proclaimed yet another trinity of ideals to replace
the 'discredited' revolutionary triad. These were, I think, 'Family, Fatherland and Church' – but I cannot quite remember. Does
anyone?

All this was sad, because while the Pétains and the Lavals can
be written off as tragi-comic footnotes to history, the French
Church which, happily, cannot, made the truly sad mistake of not
seeing, through all the blood and mud and cruelty and stupidity,
that something good was happening, something that could be
read in the light of the Gospel – of not hearing in the words
'Liberty, Equality, Fraternity' the teaching of Jesus himself.

...

The law of liberty and the rights of man (or human rights as we
say now) are firmly enshrined in the Vatican II's Constitution on
the Church in the Modern World and Declaration on Religious
Liberty. So firmly, in fact, that at times one might be forgiven for
feeling that they are expected to remain there. I do not have to
explain what I mean – either at home or further afield. But, at
least, there can be no going back to *Mirari Vos* or the *Syllabus* –
whatever the failures in courage or honesty or simple justice,
these are merely failures, not pseudo-virtues. That, if we want
freedom for ourselves, we must (as Lacordaire said) want it 'for
all men and under every sky', is a lesson which is as yet only half-
learned. For, if we seek it only for ourselves 'it will never be
granted ... '

At first sight, we have a better record on equality and fraternity
than on liberty; at least there should be no theoretical or
doctrinal hang-ups. On the contrary, that we are all equally
precious in God's sight, and all children of the one Father, would
seem to be a fundamental of our faith.

We are, however, past masters in the art of qualifying such

splendidly simple concepts, of idealising and spiritualising them so that they soon become empty of any human meaning. 'Equally precious', yes! but not necessarily of equal capacity, talent, social importance ... and, as to being children of the one Father, this is purely a theological idea far more refined and subtle than any talk of a crude and simplistic brotherhood of man – a dangerous notion too often invoked by agitators to subvert the body politic. In such terms do we back away from the clear imperatives of the New Testament.

Indeed, by an upside-down sort of logic, we can misrepresent to ourselves the equality and fraternity of the revolutionary tradition as suspect ideas simply because they are associated with that tradition. And while few of us today would consciously yearn for the old alliance of throne and altar, there remains at least a subconscious hankering for the civil and religious order of a romanticised old régime.

It would, of course, be quite unfair and indeed untrue to pretend that all falling away from the positive values of the Revolution is to be blamed on the Church. A series of 'restorations' (monarchic and otherwise) in France itself provides only one dimension of the decline of these values: the majority of republican régimes there, as elsewhere in Europe, down to 1939, were conservative in temper and bourgeois in governance. The 'popular front' was never a dominant force, except briefly in Spain, and was not allowed to survive very long there.

Undoubtedly the institutional Church and 'Catholic' politicians and pressure groups were among the forces of reaction, but they were by no means the most effective or important of these. Financial and property interests were far more influential, and, in fact, nationally and internationally, they have remained in control, except (till now) in Eastern Europe. And the same could be said *mutatis mutandis* of the Americas, and most of the post-colonial world.

Nevertheless democracy, however imperfectly realised, is by now widely established or at least aspired to. In this the Revolution has won through, and despite serious and notorious reversals in both theory and practice it continues to hold its own. The socio-economic dimension, is, as we have noted, the weakest both in individual societies and internationally: in other words equality and fraternity have not been brought to their logical conclusions. And very recently liberty itself has come under

threat, most notoriously in that society which always prided itself
on having achieved it in law and practice centuries before 1789.

I mean of course the land of *Magna Carta*, the land where a
man is innocent until found guilty, the land where the 'mother
of parliaments' has long been the very temple of democracy. For
the regime of Thatcherite Toryism is now moving from socio-
economic to political *revanchisme* – thus in two easy moves
turning the Welfare State into a National Security State. In other
words, having thrown out equality and fraternity, she is now
locking up liberty.

No one in Ireland, north or south, will need me to spell it out:
the pity is that, despite warning voices, from Neal Ascherson in
the *Observer* to John Harriott in the *Tablet*, the English as a whole
(whatever about the Scots and Welsh) seem to be unaware or
uncaring of what is happening. The series of measures taken to
gag press, publishers, civil servants and even members of the
public, on matters of public interest, is only the tip of the iceberg.
The contempt in which Parliament is clearly held (remember
the report on the Stalker enquiry); the emasculation of the BBC
– to be followed by the planned destruction of the whole fabric
of public service broadcasting; the subordination (one can
hardly chose a milder word) of legal process to 'reasons of state'
(again remember the Denning dictum that justice is less important than the prestige of the police) – all these add up to a very
serious situation indeed. And, worst of all, the parliamentary
opposition (as embodied in that once radical and libertarian
body, the British Labour Party) seems (with honourable exceptions) to have all the resistance of a petrified rabbit. If the price
of liberty is eternal vigilance, it is apparently far too high for the
sleeping beauties of the Left.

...

Which brings us back to our own dear Republic, whose official
voices will no doubt be hoarse with emotion throughout the year,
as they recall how '89 inspired '98 and '48 (and '67?) and, finally
'16. July the fourteenth will be the hoarsest and most emotional
day of all – for wasn't it an Irishman (and a Clareman at that) who
led the attack on the Bastille? Pass the champagne, somebody!

No harm at all in any of that, and perhaps quite a lot of good.
We do well to remember that we are a Republic, and even if we
have inherited more of the respectable pragmatism of the
American model than the confused, raffish and somewhat anar-

chic idealism of the French, the fires that lit up the dark skies of an Ireland emerging from penal stagnation were first kindled in the streets of Paris. The Irish, like the French, have lost or mislaid that first bright vision: even the word 'Republic' has been misused, distorted and robbed of much of its meaning, and we have not always remembered that freedom like peace is indivisible, and not to be sought 'only for ourselves'.

Still, by and large, the Republic of Ireland remains reasonably faithful to the overall idea of liberty, constitutionally and legally – so far. In fact as far as the liberty of the citizen is concerned we have made some modest progress, mainly due to the insights of the late Cearbhall Ó Dálaigh, as Chief Justice and later President, as well as one or two other enlightened members of the judiciary. In this, as in other related matters, the fact that we have a written Constitution has been a considerable advantage.

Developments across the Irish sea, however, should cause real concern inasmuch as our political leaders and what, for want of a better word, may be called 'political thinkers' have an apparently incurable tendency to follow mummy's lead ...

We have, I hasten to admit, not yet gone the full Thatcherite hog in deliberately making the rich richer and the poor poorer. But in our pursuit of 'privatisation' as the sovereign remedy of our economic ills, in the cynical 'tenant purchase' ploy as a form of social engineering, in educational 'policies' which can only harden and deepen existing inequalities, in the abandonment of all pretence of making adequate provision for the sick and disabled, in lip-service to ecological standards while leaving uncaring and inefficient entrepreneurs free to poison and disfigure the environment ... in these and many other examples of 'follow the leader' we are slipping away from our admittedly not very high standards of equality and our 'traditional' sense of fraternity.

So let us make sure we do not lose what we have gained on the freedom front, by following the new bad example across the water. The notion of 'national security' is one which at once covers a multitude of political sins and provides a cast-iron-type excuse for refusing to explain. The day we accept it unquestioningly will be a black one for Irish soci...

...

In view of the fact that our own left-wing political forces, while not as tamed or as tired as their English equivalents, are few in

number, divided in tactics and (mostly) lacking in initiative, I
would make the serious suggestion that it falls to Christians, and
to some extent to the institutional Church, to provide the kind
of leadership we need at this crucial time. Or at least, to enter into
active collaboration with others who realise the need for such
leadership.

I do not mean that the Church should take over the Revolution and throw holy water over the Liberty-Equality-Fraternity
triad. To try to do so would be to invite some little derision to say
the least of it. I am rather thinking of a belated acknowledgment
that Toqueville and Lacordaire were right, and a reminder that
O'Connell was right too, but that in our time we need a new,
sharper and more urgent reassessment of what the three great
values imply in our society.

The time is, I believe, ripe. Already the positive role of the
Church in the present appalling socio-economic situation here
is being recognised in quarters not unduly prejudiced in her
favour. To build on this, not for ecclesiastical advantage, or to
gain favour with any interest groups, but for the sake of the
victims of present policies, is an urgent imperative.

But we must look beyond the immediate needs, compelling
though they are. This Republic is desperately lacking in forward
thinking and planning, in political and social vision, and (apart
from a few studies of 'Europe' after 1992) in any sense of
international direction. Even our thinking about our relationship with the rest of Ireland lacks any kind of vigour. I am
convinced that a re-examination and recultivation of the revolutionary roots of our democracy, brought into focus in the light of
economic realities to be undertaken this year, could be of
enormous value, and that the Church's contribution could be
crucial.

One of the difficulties of the present Irish situation derives
from an uncertainty about the concept 'social'. It has become
fashionable to use the word with little or no reference to economics: it reflects such concerns as the right to legal divorce rather
than problems of unemployment and emigration. On the other
hand, Catholics may be happier to concentrate on these bread-
and-butter issues while preferring to avoid 'dangerous' questions which could lead to confrontation with higher authority.
Sooner or later these questions will have to be faced, but in the
meantime a *modus vivendi*, a 'rainbow coalition' on an agreed

agenda would be a valuable influence for change, and an effective agent of conscientisation. This would both be a splendid way of marking 1989 and the best of all preparations for 1992. For if we are going to be authentic Europeans we need to get our own house in order first – not just by balancing our books.

(January 1989, vol. 39, no. 1, pp. 31-37)

Elevations

Early last month, the Minister for Education Mrs O'Rourke announced the intention of the government to create two new universities in the Republic by 'upgrading' the National Institutes for Higher Education in Limerick and north Dublin. The necessary legislation, she promised, would be introduced as soon as possible: it would be simple and brief in content, and would probably take the form of one or two amendments to existing legislation. The announcement was, as they say, 'widely' (though not quite unanimously) welcomed, and it is probable that the proposed legislation will have a clear run through parliament. Whatever the merits of the case, none of the opposition parties is going to risk political suicide in Limerick by attempting to deny its citizens something that they (or at least their political spokesmen) have long demanded. And if one N.I.H.E. is to be 'elevated' how can the other be left on the floor?

Certainly it seems to be generally accepted that the dual elevation is already, in practice, achieved: and it would take considerable expertise to rebottle the celebratory champagne. But, while not wishing to play the begrudger, one is forced to express certain reservations about the whole proceeding.

First of all, it seems to me quite remarkable that a government minister, with or without cabinet support, can by *fiat* 'create' a university, not perhaps out of thin air, but out of elements which may be less than totally adequate. And, secondly, that there has been not the slightest pretence of providing for a public discussion, examination, debate, such as the importance of the proceeding might appear to warrant.

Since their foundation some years ago, both N.I.H.Es have made a significant and valuable contribution to third level education. Their aim and programme, like those of the regional technical college and other specialised institutions, have been severely practical: the adjective 'applied' can be properly attributed to their academic disciplines. Trade and industry, involving sophisticated economic and technological development, formed the *raison d'etre* of their establishment: an adequate supply of adequately trained young specialists, able to serve the needs of an expanding and rapidly changing economy – not least in the context of European integration – was seen as their end product. If the supply has recently tended to outstrip demand, in certain sectors at least, few authoritative voices would lay the blame at the institutes' doors.

So far, so fairly good. But while giving them all the support they need, and honouring them for what they are, why pretend they're something else? For, by calling them 'universities', a different kind of expectation is surely raised, at least in the mind of anyone who has any idea of what the word has meant since the middle ages.

I don't mean, of course, that nothing has charged since Padua and Oxford and Heidelberg and Cracow and the rest were first founded. Only a fool would suggest that. What I do mean is that all over the world, from Berkeley to Moscow to Tokyo to Melbourne to Durban to Bogota, the university, whose roots are essentially European, has, maintained a remarkable fidelity to certain basic common norms: catholicity of range; a humanist centrality; and a balance between 'pure' and professional scholarship.

Again, admittedly, one has to concede that the copybook has been badly blotted over and over again. 'Purity' of scholarship has been an excuse for ignoring actual needs and for sheer self-indulgence; too often the range has been restricted for lack of resources, or by the indolence or prejudice of academics; worst of all, the high demands of humanism and the humanities, both in ethics and scholarship, have in every generation been somewhere ignored, or ruthlessly brushed aside, in the interests of national or academic politics. The *non serviam* when spoken by brave men and women, refusing to conform, is all the more admirable for its comparative rarity.

But the sins of the university are seen to be such, precisely because they represent a falling away from standards and norms commonly agreed on and upheld, however hypocritically. And these standards and norms, far from being externally imposed, or inherited from out-dated 'tradition' derive from the very nature of the university beast itself.

...

Take the balance between 'pure' and professional. There is, or was, a romantic idea about that, in their heyday, the great European universities were completely dedicated to the pursuit of knowledge as 'its own end' (to use Newman's phrase). This was never the case. The medieval university had this in common with the N.I.H.E.: it had the job of producing a supply of men of sufficient training and education to administer the two great overlapping societies of Church and State (or Empire). These were the ubiquitous *cleri* – a word we may translate as 'clerks' or 'clerics', according to how we see their role. Philosophy and theology were the central disciplines but law and medicine were additional specialisations. A job – or, better, a career – was the common goal of the student body then as now: mostly out in the 'real' world, civil or ecclesiastical, but for some within the university itself, as teachers or what we would now call research fellows.

Which makes my point that some part at least of the university's activity, some part of its role was the pursuit of knowledge and the accumulation of a store or *corpus* of learning, which was not or need not be of any immediate or practical 'use'. It could indeed be argued – in fact it was widely accepted – that the men engaged in this task of 'pure' learning were serving the long-term needs of both Church and society. And down through the centuries this has been the tacit understanding of all societies in which the scholar and his work are honoured and patronised.

With the development of first the physical, and then the social, services as autonomous disciplines, the ultimate value of apparently 'useless theorising' became gradually clearer. And despite occasional tensions, the long-term dependence of technology on pure science is now so apparent that even the most unlikely projects of research are seen to be deserving of support – at least in such scientific areas as can be seen to have some technological implications. (Other sciences may not fare so well).

Now the university is, historically and actually, the major school of speculation, of 'theorising', of scholarly analysis and synthesis – and, not infrequently, the *locus* for those sudden imaginative leaps, the lateral forays, the uncovenanted epiphanies which can in a moment transform a familiar and long-observed intellectual horizon. To say it provides the environment, the right 'atmosphere' for the work of scholarship sounds facile, but it has done and still does, in a hundred different and changing ways. And, oddly enough, what I have called the 'catholicity' of a university's range, is one of the main reasons for this. You might imagine that the wider the variety of concerns and disciplines the less would be the stimulus for what, in the nature of things, must be the highly specialised and ultimately personal business of research. But it has never worked like that: I could suggest a number of explanations, but I won't delay on it now. I would only recall Newman's insistence on that interdependence of the different branches of learning and knowledge, and on the crucial importance of recognising this fact and its implications.

He was of course thinking mainly of the young men who would pass through his ideal university as they learned to be gentlemen if not scholars: at least they would form some idea of the 'geography' of knowledge, of the contours and frontiers on the map of learning. It has to be admitted that the all too common lack of any such idea is both one of the weaknesses and one of the most unfortunate results of the kind of over-specialisation prevalent today. The tunnel vision, the lack of respect (based on ignorance) for other disciplines, the utterly vain quest for solutions to problems which no one discipline can of itself provide – these and related flaws in what purports to be a higher education can and do often have consequences of a kind which may without aggravation be called disastrous. To say this is in no way to dismiss the importance, the necessity, of specialisation – neither scholarship nor high education can proceed without it – but to insist that it needs always to be seen in a wider context.

...

I would further claim that the humanities have a central role to play in this context. One might argue that there should or can be no such role, that no map has a 'centre', or rather that all such centres are subjectively projected. But I believe that in this case one can appeal not just to history – although there the evidence is overwhelming – but what is still held by common consent, or nearly so. We have come a long way from the days of *trivium* – grammar, rhetoric, logic – and *quadrivium* – arithmetic, geography, astronomy and 'music' – which went to make the magic number of seven 'liberal arts'. And today there can be argument as to which subjects and disciplines the 'humanities' include. A core of language, literary studies, philosophy may be expanded to involve law, theology, anthropology – even physical science.

And how about economics, architecture, music? One thing, I would urge, is beyond argument: whatever is included must be independent of any 'applied' dimension. I mean for instance, that a chair or department of German must involve linguistics (synchronic and diachronic), literature, institutions, not just a 'practical' course for scientists or businessmen.

On this crucial issue alone I would say that to call an N.I.H.E. a university is a misnomer. Not that there's anything wrong with 'applied humanities' in themselves, but it is precisely this 'applied' emphasis, along with the absence of certain core studies, which, as it were, proclaims the function of a non-university third level institute.

It might be thought that it's all a matter of custom and convention in nomenclature. After all, why not call all such institutions 'universities': what harm can it do? Quite a lot, I should imagine. For, as the distinction became blurred, so also would the thinking of those responsible for the direction of educational policy. Present trends within certain university establishments are sufficiently alarming to give ground to the fear that in the interests of economy, practicality, modernisation or whatever, the older established universities would be under pressure to conform to new patterns as exemplified by the new arrivals, and to shed outworn activities of little apparent value.

(As far as nomenclature is concerned, the only plausible argument adduced for the 'elevation' of the N.I.H.Es has been that their graduates have had difficulties with their credentials, outside of the Republic, due to the absence of the university cachet. I wonder why graduates of, say, the Massachusetts Institute of Technology, or the London School of Economics, or a certain French institution of stratospheric distinction, don't seem to run into such difficulties!)

If there were to be a public debate on this whole affair, I should expect the epithet 'élitist' to be thrown at those who would argue as I have argued here. I am well aware that at various times, probably more often than not, the university and its advocates have deserved the impeachment, though rarely for the reasons implied. Educational élitism is in fact a socio-economic matter: although there has usually been a place for the poor scholar, and certain societies have made brave efforts to offer access to all, higher education has tended to be the preserve of the rich, or at least, the fairly well-off.

Even the great Newman, whose vision was in many ways so broad, was heavily blinkered in this regard. He certainly did not see his university community as classless – or, if he did, it was to the exclusion of all classes but one. Today we would count ourselves free from the social inhibitions of Newman's generation, but I'm afraid that in practice, the Irish working class can have little hope that their children will proceed beyond, at best, second-level schooling. And rising costs on the one hand, and the widening ranks of the unemployed on the other, can only make the situation worse still in the immediate future.

One thing is certain. The cure is not to be found in populist 'solutions' involving the dilution or impoverishment of what are seen as unnecessary or 'luxury' subjects or departments. Scholars may be élitist; scholarship is not. To put a brake on such academic activities as do not seem to show an immediate return is not just short-sighted but suicidal. The liberal arts, the sciences, and technology are separate species but they have common roots and, in the long run, they depend on each other's vitality.

(February 1989, vol. 39, no. 2, pp. 89-93)

1990

Man of hope

Samuel Beckett was the last of the three twentieth century giants
of Irish writing. By blood, birth and upbringing, he belonged to
the colonial minority — Protestant and Anglocentric — as did W.
B. Yeats. But like Yeats, though in a very different way, he soon
transcended this heritage, and came close to that of his sometime
mentor James Joyce, who was of the mainstream Irish Catholic
tradition. And this, too, was transcended, as they both ultimately
found their fulfilment in exile: internal as much as external,
social, and above all, linguistic.

Still, like Joyce, Beckett remained recognisably, quintessen-
tially Irish — not least in the peculiar quality of his comic genius:
by turn, understated and wildly farcical, but at all times, reflective
of humanity's pilgrim-core, naked and alone.

There is little to lighten the journey, to 'shorten the road',
certainly 'naught for our comfort' — except the only comfort
that counts: A stubborn, persistent indestructible hope. The
hope that urges us, makes it possible for us to go on.

(February 1990, vol. 40, no. 2, pp. 98-99)

Justice indivisible

At Mass in a Dublin working-class suburb, on the Sunday of
Nelson Mandela's release, the celebrant began the bidding
prayers by inviting the congregation to join in thanking God and
praying for the people of South Africa. He was interrupted by the
congregation's applause, which was as loud and fervent as it was
spontaneous: a deeply moving gesture of humanity across the
divide of distance, race and culture. The celebrant was Michael
Paul Gallagher, S.J. ...

I know that Fr Gallagher was very much moved by the reaction
of his congregation to the invitation to prayer for Mandela. And
I would like to suggest that it was also a valuable and authentic
sign of a kind of solidarity on whose existence some of our
mentors would cast doubt. Indeed I have often heard concern for
the victims of apartheid described rather contemptuously as a
'soft option', a fashionable liberal cause with little relevance to

the realities of life nearer home, and even an evasion – a way of ignoring injustices in our own society, both in the North and in the Republic.

To which one may very properly reply that it's not a matter of 'either/or', that justice like peace is indivisible, that while charity begins at home it mustn't stay there. But these sentiments are far more cogent when they are given expression by those who themselves may well be among the underprivileged and disadvantaged of our society. I would be fairly certain that Fr Gallagher's congregation consisted largely of such people – and that their Christianity and humanity was and is wider in its vision than that of many of us.

...

This is not indeed the first time that we have been given evidence of the solidarity of Dublin working people with their brothers and sisters in South Africa: just a couple of years ago ten young women (and one man) put their jobs on the line, by refusing to handle South African products in the supermarket where they worked. They suffered for their courage, and like all who are rash enough to speak, or (more dangerously) act prophetically, they were more honoured in the 'far-off country' than in their own.

However overall grass-roots support for the Irish Anti-Apartheid movement has through the years been quite impressive – especially, perhaps, in Dublin. The city fathers did themselves the honour some time ago of inviting Nelson Mandela to add his name to the roll of Freemen. When, as we hope, he comes to do so in person, he can be certain that the welcome he receives will be no mere formality, but will truly come from the heart of the city and its people.

That 'justice is indivisible' should be seen not just as a moral axiom, but as a fact of political reality whose relevance was never more obvious than now. Thus, it is only proper that developments in South Africa should share the attention of the 'West' with the continuing drama being enacted in Eastern Europe and throughout the Soviet Union. And, in as much as international pressures have contributed to the change of policy if not of heart in Pretoria, it is vital that neither the member of the European Community nor the United States should relax their attitudes – or indeed the economic and other measures which have so far been at least partially successful. I am glad to note that the Irish presidency of the E.C. seems prepared to stand firm on this issue.

But, more immediate problems arising from happenings to the East may unfortunately induce a certain inertia in relation to similarly urgent matters farther away. And with the promise (threat?) of German reunification, the miseries of central America may appear remote and unimportant ...

(March 1990, vol. 40, no. 3, pp. 149-151)

Comharba Phádraig

First there was the shock of the news, then the chorus of voices – nearly all in 'prayer or praise' but with a few sad and bitter notes. Then came the long process of ritual morning and all the liturgy of Christian death: not as it used to be, when 'the climbing agonies' of the *Dies Irae* set the tone, but with the accent all on hope: *Sé an Tiarna m'Aoire* and *Ag Críost an Síol* ... hope and thanksgiving, given their transcendent expression in the Eucharist. Slowly we come back to everyday living and thinking, and begin to realise what we have lost in the sudden death of Cardinal Ó Fiaich [8 May 1990].

And there are uncomfortable thoughts that demand a hearing. Questions like why was this man, whose pastorate was at once intensely local and wide-ranging to the point of universality; who cared for his people and seemed to know them all by name, and also cared deeply for all that concerned the Church Catholic; who seemed unable to refuse any call to service, whatever the time or place, and contrived never to neglect any of the day-to-day duties of a busy diocesan bishop – why was he left so long without assistance? Why was his much-valued auxiliary the late Jim Lennon never replaced?

A heavy responsibility rests on those guilty of this glaring negligence. The arcane mechanisms which regulate such matters in the Roman curia operate, as we know, in the dimmest of 'religious' light, but surely those in charge, however preoccupied with their task of placing safe men in a range of sees from Switzerland to South America, are not so blind that they cannot see simple straightforward pastoral needs – nor the danger of leaving one man, however diligent and uncomplaining, to carry three men's work.

Or did they perhaps wish to foist a 'suitable' coadjutor on him, so that the succession would conform to the king of orthodoxy now in fashion? Not that even the craziest of heresy-hunters could concoct a case against the Cardinal, or make anyone doubt

his loyalty to the Roman See. But then he did express himself
rather robustly on the subject of women's 'rights' in the Church,
even to the point of entertaining the possibility of admitting
them to holy orders!

Well, there was no coadjutor (for which, Thank God!), but
also no auxiliary – an omission which may have been fatal. Still,
Tomás Ó Fiaich would be the last to want us to cry over spilt milk:
rather would he have us drink his peace, and, having prayed for
his soul, laugh and sing over a glass of *sú na heornan* ... And
between the laughter and the singing he would hardly expect us
not to speculate, and ruminate, and even fulminate, as we
consider the possibilities and probabilities of who is to be the
next *Comharba Phádraig* ...

(July-August 1990, vol. 40, no. 6, pp. 284-285)

An open letter

To the Most Reverend Emmanuele Gerada
Titular Archbishop of Nomento
Apostolic Nuncio to Ireland

Excellency,
I presume to address you as a diplomatist, since it is in that
capacity that you, a distinguished Maltese ecclesiastic, find your-
self engaged in the unlikely task of sorting out the Irish, or, so to
express it, of finding a Roman solution to an Irish problem. And
if the tone of this open letter may appear somewhat frivolous, or,
indeed, the very choice of such a mode of communication more
than a little impertinent, I should hope successfully to plead 'not
guilty' to either charge. My intention at least is serious, and I
believe that what I have to say is in fact very pertinent to the
matter in hand, that is, the appointment of a successor to Tomás,
Archbishop of Armagh, and thus ultimately to Patrick. Who is
honoured in our most ancient calender as *ceann creidimh na
nGael:* 'head of the faith of the Irish'.

The title has always had more in it of poetry and *pietas* than of
law or jurisdiction. The Primate of All Ireland has little or no
canonical authority over his suffragans in the province of Armagh, and still less over the archbishops and bishops of the other
three provinces: his role may be regarded as merely presidential.
However the fact that the Irish Conference of Bishops is long
established, and that, unlike more recent creations, its presi-

dency is permanently vested in the senior primate, does give him a considerable moral authority. One may not improperly speak of a leadership role, one which several though not all holders of the office have assumed.

(You will, I trust, bear patiently with what must be to you a tiresome reiteration of familiar facts. But the convention of the 'open letter' demands such rehearsal, for the benefit of those to whom the detail may not be so familiar.)

Today, ecumenical considerations prescribe a certain delicacy of reference to earthly 'heads' of Churches: happily, Patrick is honoured on both sides of the post-Reformation divide, and differing views of the succession no longer lead to acrimony. Indeed, during the primacy of Tomás whom we mourn, a quite exceptional degree of mutual regard, even affection, prevailed. This has been of no small benefit in a situation where the direct pastoral care of both primates spans a political border, and their metropolitan responsibilities cover a wide cultural diversity.

That these matters touch closely on your own dual role is perhaps not widely appreciated. Perhaps even the 'duality' itself is not generally understood. I am uncertain whether your acting both as Papal Legate to an all-Ireland Church and as Nuncio Apostolic to a government and state whose jurisdiction covers under four fifths of the 'national territory' is unique, but it must be very unusual. As is the fact that in much of the Primate's own diocese and province jurisdiction is *de facto* exercised by another government and state, to which the Holy See is also diplomatically accredited.

One may be grateful that the age of investiture by the civil power is, in the Catholic Church, almost entirely a matter of history: such survivals as still linger on are more matters of form than of substance. More serious is the unofficial *agrément* which is sought, for considerations of goodwill and practical politics – very serious indeed in the case of regimes whose attitude to the Church may be, to say the least of it, problematic. Certain Latin American as well as eastern European states have provided painful examples of this in recent years.

In the present case the matter is of some interest and concern: it was an open secret that the last appointment was not best pleasing to the U.K. authorities, nor indeed to certain highly placed English Catholics. It was a matter of considerable satisfaction to many of us that those protesting voices did not carry as far as had been expected, when elevation to the college of cardinal was under discussion!

As to this dimension of the question I am sure we all have complete confidence in the wisdom of the Holy See and its advisers and representatives. We are indebted for the firm and clear response to what might have become a very delicate and difficult problem and can only guess at the advisory role played by your predecessor. And it would be truly impertinent even to reflect on your own wide diplomatic experience, not least in El Salvador and in your native Malta. In the latter case your role had another kind of duality – as coadjutor archbishop, the diploma-tist gave precedence to the pastor ...

...

Though addressing this letter to you in diplomatic form, it is of course as a pastoral question that one is concerned with the Armagh succession. As such it might appear to have much less immediacy for those of us who are not of the archdiocese, than our own several local bishoprics and those who hold them. In one important sense this is certainly true.

But it is equally true on another level that, having regard to that moral authority, that role of leadership mentioned earlier, which the new Primate may come to assume, our concern is very real. It is no exaggeration to say that the leadership exercised by William Cardinal Conway in the immediate post-conciliar period was crucial for the pastoral life of the whole Irish Church, in many ways, and especially in liturgical reform.

Which is not to suggest that Cardinal Conway's primacy was unmarked by negative aspects, any more than was that of his successor. But Cardinal Ó Fiaich too gave providential leader-ship, most enduringly perhaps by setting a tone of authentic Christian fellowship on several levels: ecumenically, both with his fellow prelates, and with all sorts and conditions of men and women of different traditions; with the priests of his archdiocese young and old; and with the plain people of Ireland, who learned to see in him a friend and brother, as he saw in them.

It would be too much to say that Tomás Ó Fiaich 'demythologised' the higher reaches of hierarchy, but certainly anything less like the old image of a 'prince of the Church' it would be hard to imagine. The pomposities of dress and behav-iour which formally tended to characterise anyone of the rank of *monsignor*, and so on up, have, thank God, been seriously eroded in recent years (although they have by no means totally disappeared), and while the credit must be shared with other men of intelligent humility, the leadership was unmistakeable.

Leadership, if it is to be effective, must never go too far ahead of the pack, and neither Conway nor Ó Fiaich could ever be accused of running too far too fast. This was particularly important in leading a body with a strong tradition (at least in this century) of close, not to say tight-lipped, solidarity. But it could result and often has resulted in disappointingly bland, over-cautious statements, giving an unfortunately negative impression.

* * *

It has been said that 'the world sets the agenda for the Church'. It is certainly true that in this century the agenda has been changing with increasing rapidity, at times to a dizzying degree. Gone, happily, are the days when the institutional Church pretended to ignore 'secular' developments, taking its stance as the still centre in a mad whirlpool. Of course the *koinonia* has always reacted to, and often against, the context in which it finds itself, and even the institution, however imperturbable in style, has always been forced, however unwillingly, to face the realities of the temporal. Technology, economics, political change and political violence, radical social change often leading to consequent changes in social *mores,* have however, over the past hundred years, combined to force the Church universal to come to terms with the 'modern world', to scan the new horizons with positive discernment, and to rekindle the flames which make it the *lumen gentium.*

One can trace this process of renewal from Leo XIII's *Rerum Novarum;* through the first reforms of worship instituted by Pius X; through the attempts of Benedict XV and Pius XI to face the complexities of modern politics, in war and peace – and to find a new role for the papacy and the Church in the emerging international community; through the remarkable post-war pronouncements of Pius XII as he sought the proper approach and response to a host of contemporary developments.

Then came John XXIII who, at the outset of his Council, definitively rejected not alone the 'prophets of gloom' and their inherently pessimistic view of the world, but what came to be known as 'Non-historical orthodoxy'. And the conciliar constitution on 'The Church in the Modern World' was only the climax to a whole conciliar process which might well have been so styled, as it undertook the drawing-up of a blueprint for renewal across the whole Christian spectrum – from liturgy and scripture to mission (and 'missions'), to inter-church and inter-faith relations, to religious liberty.

One of the most refreshing and hopeful fruits of Vatican II was the 'rediscovery' of the local Church with its implications for collegiality and 'inculturation', but also for a renewed pastoral consciousness on the local, regional and national levels. This was seen as leading to practical autonomy on a wide range of ecclesial matters – applying within the Church what the Church had often prescribed for secular society: the principle of subsidiarity. We saw this not as weakening or endangering the structures or authority of the universal Church, as centred in the papal primacy. On the contrary, we believed it would strengthen our understanding and practice of catholicity, in which we would see the Church universal not as a kind of religious multi-national, but as a living organic union of local Churches whose catholicity was expressed and activated in the fullness of its communion with the see of Peter. Such was the vision of the years which followed the end of the Council twenty-five years ago.

It was a vision which inspired us to make the Church-in-the-world a reality in our own countries and communities, and to implement the message of *Lumen Gentium*, in the local context, and following the local secular agenda. For the universal search for unity, and the movement to articulate and establish it through and in international institutions, far from presaging an end to local diversities, demands their recognition and cultivation – if only as a defence against a flat, colourless uniformity. Such uniformity is not an expression of unity but its caricature.

The new and urgent counterpoint of local particularity as over against centralising uniformity provides the context within which social and cultural problems and opportunities have to be faced in the local (regional, national) framework. The challenge to the Church which this engenders is even sharper than it was twenty-five years ago. And so the need for a vibrant local Church, strong in *koinonia* and flexible in its structures, is paramount.

...

It is hardly necessary to say that these remarks apply to Ireland with no less force than elsewhere. The years of *aggiornamento* in the Church catholic have been matched by radical changes in

Irish society which amount to nothing less than a cultural revolution. This, you will agree, is a very different Ireland to the country you came to on your first diplomatic mission here in the mid-1950s.

The Irish Church too has changed (as you will also agree). This is right and even necessary: was it not John Henry Newman who wrote that to live is to change, to grow is to change often? And further growth, implying further change, demands 'leadership and moral authority' of a kind primates have given in the past – but more finely tuned to our ever-changing society. Leadership not too far ahead, but clearly not afraid to go forward. Authority mindful of its root meaning and function: to guide and nurture growth.

I know that this is not how all my fellow-Catholics (or fellow-Irishmen) see it; to some, authority implies discipline, the firm hand, the clear-cut command, the judgement in black and white. I would rather suggest that this is precisely what gives authority a bad name, and slowly but surely causes it to erode, in the Church as in society. (I do not, of course, deny the value of discipline and definition when clearly needed, but they do not go to the heart of the matter.)

The erosion of ecclesiastical authority must be a cause of concern in the Church worldwide as it is here. It may, as is so often claimed, be due to a general 'unbiddability' among 'young people', but I doubt it. Forty years ago it was remarked that if bishops declared 'mixed bathing' or dancing after midnight a mortal sin, they were, not unnaturally, ignored when they condemned perjury, violence or even 'political' murder. Could a parallel assimilation of the marginal to the essential cause a similar reaction today?

A heartening development in the Irish Church, pointing the way to leadership through dialogue, is the series of consultations which are at present in train on a wide national level in preparation for a new pastoral letter on social justice to be issued jointly by the conference of bishops. This kind of consultation is something new to us, at least on such a scale. One may be confident that it will bear fruit.

I am sure that consultations of another kind which you will have undertaken as Papal Legate, in relation to the primatial succession, extend beyond the minimum enjoined in canon 377 of the Code. You stand, I know, in little need of advice on your proceedings in this matter. I would only venture to recall that in the Irish situation the number and kind of people actively interested in the question is more extensive than might be imagined, that quite unlikely people may have sound views on the subject, and that it is our custom to deliver such views – and any possible suggestions – in an oblique or seemingly tentative way. He that has ears to hear ...

It is right that the last word in such appointments should rest with the Holy See. But one would wish that it were exercised always in accordance with that admirable principle of subsidiarity which I have already cited. The conciliar vision of the local Church does, I fear, seem to have faded somewhat, and the conciliar insistence that diocesan bishops are not 'to be regarded as vicars of the Roman Pontiff' (*Lumen Gentium,* 27) appears to be less than fully effective – not least in some recent appointment procedures which gave quite the contrary impression.

I know that the results of your consultations, formal and informal, will have provided the material of your submission to Rome. I do not know whether that submission has yet been made, nor when we may expect a decision. Vatican procedures seem to take little account of any difference between proper discretion and obsessional secrecy. So we, the Irish, priests and people, are likely to be kept in the dark until someone 'over there' decides to lift the curtain.

So all we can do is wait and see. And pray. Pray that the considered will and wish of priests and people, if at all clearly expressed, will not be set aside, except for some consideration serious enough to cause subsidiarity to be made yield to central power: any such consideration should be carefully weighed and discussed, and not only in the corridors of the Congregation. Final decisions demand full awareness of the needs of the local Church, in the context of our changing society ...

And pray to that final Authority without whose light and nurture there is no growth.

(September 1990, vol. 40, no. 7, pp. 368-374)

Successions

The month of November 1990 brought to the Republic of Ireland a new President [elected 7 November 1990], and to the primatial see of Armagh a new Archbishop ... Cahal Daly [appointed 6 November 1990] has earned high regard as a scholar as well as a pastor of considerable moral strength and courage: Mary Robinson has had a distinguished legal and academic career, and has been a bonny fighter in several admirable causes. They can both rely on an enormous fund of good will.

What needs to be said at this point relates to the background of the two successions. The process by which a candidate comes to the Presidency is of course very different from that obtaining to the Primacy, but they both bear examination, and both raise questions relating to the future of Church and society in Ireland. I believe that these questions should be faced and discussed, calmly and widely, as a matter of some urgency.

I have written on more than one occasion of the canonical procedure leading to the nomination of diocesan bishops of the Roman Catholic obedience. I have suggested that it leaves much to be desired, both on the prescriptions of the law, and the way in which these may be carried out. The main thrust of my reservations is that the process gives such a central and crucial role to the 'papal legate' leaving to his discretion how widely and deeply he must consult, and take soundings of interested opinion – and insists that 'the definitive judgement on the suitability of the person promoted rests with the Holy See'.

Of course, as a Roman Catholic, I uphold the authority of the See of Rome in this as in other matters. But it is surely consonant with the tradition of the universal Church, as confirmed by the Second Vatican Council, that Rome's 'last word' should be just that: and that judgement on the 'suitability' of an episcopal candidate should normally be made by the local Church, and overruled only for grave reasons of faith and order.

It has to be added that loyalty to the throne of Peter, as well as admiration and affection for its present occupant, should not leave us blind to certain centralising and indeed domineering tendencies which are all too evident in today's Vatican administration. Whether or not these trends are to be ascribed to the dominant role and influence of Cardinal Ratzinger is beside the point: the insights of Vatican II and the fine words in which they were articulated would appear to be jettisoned or forgotten.

. . .

When it became evident that Mary Robinson was going to be the seventh President of Ireland, a friend remarked that even if she turned out to be a disappointment in office at least she would have broken a mould. I remember a similar remark on the

election of one Karol Wojtyla to an even higher position ...
Actually a very large number of people expect the new President
to 'do well' – and this, I believe, includes more than a few who
didn't vote for her ...

(December 1990, vol. 40, no. 10, pp. 534-540)

1991

A 'Catholic's Catholic'

The first Graham Greene novels I read were *It's a Battlefield* (1934) and *A Gun for Sale* (1936) followed closely by *Brighton Rock* (1938). That was just before the Second World War, when I was starting to read 'seriously', and the three were quite unlike anything I'd come across before. They were modern without any of the glitter or glamour that the word usually implied; their 'landscape', human and material, was unfamiliar and a little frightening; they were uncomfortable in their sense of loneliness; and they were utterly readable. *Brighton Rock* made the biggest impact, not alone because of the richness of the characterization and the power of the social observation, but to me, at least, because it dealt with good and evil in terms which a Catholic could accept, and was the first modern reflection on the 'appalling strangeness of the mercy of God ... ' I didn't catch up with *England Made Me* (1935) until the end of the war, by which time I had read not alone such 'entertainments' as *The Confidential Agent* (1939), and *The Ministry of Fear* (1943) but, above all, *The Power and the Glory* (1940).

This was of course the novel which forced Greene on the attention of a Catholic readership, providing an English companion to Bernanos and Mauriac. Not indeed that the story of the Mexican 'whiskey-priest' was universally welcomed or approved by the *bien-pensants*, any more than were the sad and tortured heroes and heroines of the two French novelists. And while the latter might claim honourable literary ancestry in writers like Leon Bloy or even Huysmans, the relatively small and selfregarding English Catholic community could be perhaps forgiven for finding a Pinkie or a Father Lopez improbable and distasteful co-religionists. The whole thing was a far cry from Belloc and Chesterton.

In the event, it was *The Power and the Glory*, of all his early work, that spread Greene's reputation among 'Protestants, Jews, and Presbyterians', as well as the great post-Christian majority in Britain and elsewhere. And, after some initial hesitation, the majority of his fellow-Catholics, especially – but not exclusively –

in English-speaking countries, came to see him as 'their' great writer.

This position became consolidated by the novels of the post-way years from *The Heart of the Matter* (1948), through *The End of the Affair* (1951), down to, say, *A Burnt-Out Case* (1961). Problems of faith and conscience, and the demands of love and moral responsibility were most explicitly addressed in these three, while of course they continued to beset *The Third Man* and *Fallen Idol* (1950), *The Quiet American* (1955) and *Our Man in Havana* (1958). Through this whole middle period Greene's reputation continued to grow, and his name became familiar, even to many who had never read him, through several film versions of his work (although only one of these, *The Third Man*, was wholly successful). And his Catholic faithful continued to be proud of him.

Not that there wasn't competition. His friend and contemporary Evelyn Waugh shared much of his *réclame*. He too had begun by shocking pious eyes, but went on to become a pillar of the Catholic intellectual establishment, and a safely conservative one at that. In contrast to Greene, whose leftist leanings and lack of enthusiasm for the *pax Americana* were beginning to cause a certain unease by the later nineteen-fifties.

Graham Greene's first novel was published when he was twenty-five, and his last followed his eightieth birthday. His output was remarkable by any standard, in quantity as in quality: as well as some twenty-six novels, he published twelve plays and several collections of short stories, and his 'other works' range from screenplays, to children's stories, to essays, to autobiography – and, of course, the incomparable travel books. Both he and Waugh were already accomplished writers in their thirties, each had achieved an individual and immediately recognisable style and thrust, with an equally distinctive approach to characterization. Both developed over the years: *Brideshead Revisited* is as far from *Vile Bodies* as is *The Quiet American* from *England Made Me*. But I think it fair to say that nothing in Waugh matches the late flowering of Greene's last great novels, written in his sixties and seventies. I mean *The Comedians* (1966), *Travels with My Aunt* (1969), *The Honorary Consul* (1973), *The Human Factor* (1978), and *Monsignor Quixote* (1982). I do not include *Doctor Fisher of Geneva* (1980) or the final one, *The Tenth Man* (1985), but five out of seven isn't a bad score.

...

It may perhaps be evident by now that I am to be counted among the Greene faithful ... 'devout' might not be too strong a word. And I am willing to raise my voice, even to shout a little, with those who deplore the begrudging and patronising tone of some of his obituarists, including one or two near to home. I am not so worried about the Nobel: his exclusion reflects more on the Swedish Academy than it does on Greene. But I do think it a pity that some latter-day literary pundits should so ignore his work that a generation may well miss out on it: this sort of thing does happen and has happened – as with writers like Ford Madox Ford and Bernard Shaw and G.K. Chesterton. These are perhaps now being 'rediscovered', but what a shame that it had to happen at all ... though maybe such fallings in and out of fashion or favour are inevitable. I only wish more of the films were as good as *The Third Man*: it is especiallu unfortunate that *The Fugitive* (made by John Ford, of all people) should be such a travesty of *The Power and the Glory*.

As to the Catholic 'label', whatever he may have said or wished or pretended, Graham Greene was not just a Catholic who happened to be a novelist, or *vice-versa*. Culturally, he was not of the same stable as Joyce or Mauriac – or, for that matter, Ó Faoláin or O'Connor: he was not a 'cradle Catholic'. But his conversion and adherence to the 'Roman discipline' went far, far deeper than is sometimes alleged or supposed. He became and remained a man of faith – which is not necessarily to say that he was free of doubt or infidelity – and this faith was his entrée to the culture or cultures of the Catholic community in all its plurality, from the *barrios* of Latin America to the pages of the London *Tablet*. It's ironic that among contemporary English writers his sworn enemy should be Anthony Burgess, a cradle-Catholic, but one who shared so much of his own *pietas*. As another of 'them', Oxford theologian Herbert McCabe, O.P., said to me, Greene was a 'Catholic's Catholic' – only we could understand him, his prejudices and his contradictions ...

I suspect the Irish have always understood him – those of us who came to know him, chiefly of course through the novels, but also in what we've heard of his doings and sayings, particularly in the political arena. His regard for ourselves and what he could learn of our aspirations is a matter of record, and I have sometimes wished that his travels here, many years ago, had produced an Irish novel. Indeed the composition of imaginary extracts from such a work would make an amusing literary competition ...

Greene never saw his Catholicism as demanding that he toe any particular political line, an attitude that should recommend itself to all who refuse to identify Home Rule with Rome Rule. His own left-wing sympathies remained consistent throughout the years, and his personal loyalties were always splendidly stubborn. His errors of judgement came nearly always from the heart rather than the head.

The word 'outrageous' is not inappropriate in relation to another of the late novels, *The Human Factor*, where the sinister underbelly of the British establishment at its most 'clubbable' is subjected to a deservedly cruel knife job. Here the comedy is jet black, with the savage precision of Molière in *Tartuffe* of *L'Avare*, while never allowing the mask of gentlemanly amateurishness to slip. I remember, in a books' programme on television, the outrage expressed by a very cultivated Irish politician at Greene's 'disgraceful calumny' on the governing classes of his country: when I weighed in on Greene's side I also was denounced! ...

But the fullness of his comic genius is, I would hold, most evident in the last great novel, *Monisgnor Quixote*. *Finis coronat opus*. Again, I'm glad to note that it too is one of its author's four favourites. It is short, but by no means lightweight, and most elegantly shaped and styled.

...

I suppose the fact that he has been my literary companion throughout nearly all my adult life has made me especially sensitive to the final flowering of his genius in the last years of creativity. And perhaps what I have come most unexpectedly to realise is that Greene is a great comic writer: *Travels with My Aunt* is one of the finest comic novels in the English language and I am delighted to know that its author placed it among his four favourite works.

I should add here that I mean 'comic' in the fullest sense: not just funny or witty or humorous – although *Travels* is all of these. And from *England Made Me* to *Our Man in Havana* it is possible to find passages that would not disgrace Evelyn Waugh at his funniest. Indeed the whole conception and execution of the vacuum-cleaner ploy in *Our Man* is marvellously, outrageously funny.

And within this elegance there is, once more, fun and wit and humour, but most of all a great humanity, a humanity that lives and moves and is fulfilled in the abiding presence of the God of love. It is nowhere marred by sentimentality or the kind of pious optimism which is too often confused with hope. Of hope indeed there is full and plenty, as always the essential link between faith and love ...

(May-June 1991, vol. 41, no. 5, pp. 255-259)

Charity and justice

Pope John Paul has announced his intention to create several new cardinals, including the Archbishop of Armagh. His nomination was to be expected, and while of little significance in the ordering of Irish Church affairs, it has been widely recognised as a very proper tribute to both the office and the man. Since his accession to the primacy, Cahal Daly has not alone maintained but increased his activity in the public arena with a vitality which many a younger man might envy. The moral authority of his position as senior Irish pastor has been well underpinned by his admirable courage, and by the evenhandedness of his pronouncements on a variety of issues touching on politics, social justice and, of course, violence and the rule of law. Again, he has never faltered in his promotion of the principles and practice of Christian unity in a situation which so often gives little grounds for optimism in this area.

His ecumenical pronouncements and activities do indeed reflect a personality and style very different from that of his predecessor, Tomás Ó Fiaich, but his commitment is equally sincere. Certainly, his views on some issues touching inter-Christian relations on the ground – as, for instance, in the matter of denominational education – will not recommend themselves to all concerned: but it should be recognised that his critics, and supporters, on this question, as on other socio-moral problems, are not all to be seen as denominationally aligned.

But none save the hopelessly bigoted and prejudiced can fail to admire the consistency with which he has insisted on the inseparability of the dual objectives of peace and justice – the two great dimensions of the biblical *Shalom*. It was then singularly appropriate (yet another example of his remarkable vitality) that the launch of his book *The Price of Peace* should be followed a couple of days later by his major keynote address – 'Rerum Novarum 100 Years Later' – to the centenary conference of

Maynooth on 'The Church in Society'.

The latter occasion was of some personal significance for Dr Daly as, in his ordination year of 1941, he and his fellow-ordinands set up the organisation *Christus Rex*, to promote the social teaching contained both in Leo XIII's encyclical, then fifty years old, and Pius XII's *Quadragesimo Anno* (a stripling of ten).

An impressive and wide-ranging series of topics was discussed at the Maynooth conference by an equally impressive and widely-recruited team of speakers and workshop directors, ranging from Denis Faul to Jim Kemmy, from Donal Dorr to Herbert McCabe, from historian Joe Lee to poet Nuala Ní Dhomhnaill. The climax was reached on Sunday June 16th with a session on 'Looking to the Future of Irish Society' with John Hume, Sister Stanislaus, and Garret FitzGerald, and Maurice Hayes (the Northern Ireland Ombudsman) in the chair, in the presence of President Robinson.

It is too early to say whether these deliberations, while obviously useful in themselves, will have any long-term effect or influence on our society and those who shape it. There is a temptation to be sceptical, even cynical, about such proceedings: if conferences could make a new and better Ireland it should have arrived by now! But to take this line is not just unhelpful: it can give comfort only to those who themselves having lost all faith and hope would seek to convince the rest of us that trying to make things better is a lost cause ...

(July-August 1991, vol. 41, no. 6, pp. 319-320)

Christians at war

Over the past twenty years, Ireland has had the unhappy distinction of being the only country in the world where Christians are seen to be in violent, indeed murderous, conflict with each other. Now we have been made to share this distinction with Yugoslavia.

The labels attached to the competing crusaders in Ulster are of course of fairly recent origin: 'Protestant' as opposed to 'Catholic' belongs to post-Reformation terminology – indeed our northern troubles have been seen as an extension of the Thirty Years War (prematurely so called). The roots of the Serb-Croat conflict go much deeper, for, though the two nations share a common Slav culture and language, they stand on opposite sides of the ancient East-West divide in Christendom. The Croats (like the Slovenes) are Latin Catholics in religion, they use the

Latin alphabet, and have historically tended (at least in modern times) to look westward: the Serbs, who belong with their Bulgarian and Russian neighbours, are of Orthodox tradition – witness their rich iconic and musical heritage – and write in Cyrillic characters.

It has been said that to travel from the old city of Belgrade to Zagreb is to move from an oriental market to an eighteenth century drawing-room. A more than slight exaggeration, perhaps, but with a residue of truth: there is a very perceptible cultural divide; which a common spoken language does little to bridge. And while Islam has left its mark on Serbia (as on Bosnia and Herzegovina), the elegance and tolerance of the Austro-Hungarian empire remains a nostalgic memory for many Croats even among those who never knew it. To this must be added the fact that while the Serbs are by far the largest ethnic group in the modern Yugoslav federation, the Croats and especially the Slovenes are more economically advanced, have a higher standard of living and so resented the dominance of the eastern 'backward' republics in federal government and administration.

This resentment pales however in comparison with that of the Serbian minority in Croatia who have a very lively memory of Ustashi atrocities during the Second World War. This minority and their attitudes and grievances (real or imagined) provide one of the most dangerous flashpoints in the present conflict.

Analogies and comparisons in such matters are dangerous, but it is difficult for us here not to think of minority-majority tensions in Northern Ireland and in the country as a whole. And, naturally, the religious factor suggests parallels. It may be claimed that both in the North and in Yugoslavia religion is only marginal to what are political, social and economic divisions, and is in no way responsible for the eruption of these divisions into violent action.

I'm afraid, though, that it is not as easy as that. Certainly the most vehement protagonists of conflict on all sides may be – and, I suppose nowadays, usually are – innocent of any deeply held religious convictions of a positive kind, let alone any religious motivation. That is if by 'religious' we imply credal, spiritual or theological content – or even a simple or simplistic loyalty in faith or devotion. Loyalty there may well be, but usually to the tribe. However we have to recognise that too often religious commitment has been reduced and perverted into the service of the tribe. When that happens, faith degenerates into a kind of mindless, exclusivist ideology – often of the crudest sort – while hope yields to a presumptuous appropriation of 'destiny', and love simply becomes its dreadful opposite.

When this happens, a very heavy responsibility rests on the pastors and religious mentors of those involved. And sadly, this responsibilityis by no means always recognised, nor its implications accepted ... On the large scale, this happened in Hitler's Germany with results we need not rehearse here; and in the Yugoslav context the weight of evidence would seem to indicate that some at least of the Croatian Catholic clergy were involved in acts of appalling savagery. The late Hubert Butler was vilified by many of the *bien-pensant* in this country for presenting part of this evidence: a reluctance to believe the worst was, to some extent, related to a popular Catholic concern for the good name of Cardinal Stepinac, who certainly never countenanced Ustashi crimes but who may have been over-'prudent' in his dealings with the murderous Croat puppet-dictator Pavelich.

Ecclesiastical collusion with terrorism in Northern Ireland is happily almost unknown: the exceptions being confined to a very few individual clergy. But tribal oratory, of a professedly 'peaceful' kind, is by no means unknown, especially on the Protestant side: and on both sides pastoral concern may often shade into sympathy for 'our people', to the apparent exclusion of others – especially and understandably, but none the less regrettably, at the funerals of terrorist victims, or of those, mainly Catholics, killed by trigger-happy security forces.

It can however, I believe, be honestly said that a common attitude to a common evil has developed significantly in the North in recent years, and on the Catholic side, the even-handed approach of Cardinal Daly, both as bishop and now as primate, and (on another level) Fr Denis Faul has been of very great importance in helping to create a general over-all climate of Christian concern. I say this while recognising the sincere and informed dissent of a Fr Des Wilson: he raises many questions that demand answers, and maintains an admirable solidarity with some of our untouchables. But I cannot subscribe fully to his analysis or to his policies.

...

It would of course be very silly for us here in Ireland, or in Western Europe as a whole, to propose 'solutions' to the Yugoslav crisis. In fact the well-meaning efforts of the European Community to establish even a temporary cessation of hostilities were hardly likely to bear much fruit: however simple and 'contained' the situation might appear to be, it is in fact of a complexity more than usually intractable even in the historic 'Balkan' context.

To attempt here a summary of the various stages of what is by now quite an old story would be quite impossible. The original Kingdom of Serbs, Croats and Slovenes was the creation of those who set about redesigning the map of Europe after the First World War (which was trigerred off by an incident on Serbian territory). It survived as well, if no better than other post-Versailles confections, but ancient history and modern politics had combined to plant several time bombs – social, economic, cultural and ethnic – whose moment of explosion came when the 'kingdom' was caught up in the maelstrom of Hitler's war.

Germans and Chetniks, partisans and Ustashi all played their violent roles in a war which merged into a national social revolution, led by the Croat communist known to the world as Tito. And after a number of post-war debts were paid, bloodily and in some cases with great cruelty, injustices righted – or aggravated – the new federation of republics found its feet and a certain guarded, often reluctant acceptance among the nations of Europe and the world. The new Yugoslavia survived a dangerous and decisive breach with Moscow, and made its independent communist way in the world – not without a little help from the United States, accorded on the principle that 'my enemy's enemy is my friend'. Indeed a certain international status was gradually achieved as a leader of the non-aligned, and the ruthless partisan leader and stubbornly nonconforming Marxist, slowly but steadily, achieved a certain elder statesman standing in some quarters – though not all – and as a selfless friend to the Third World.

One thing at least that Tito was given credit for on all sides: he had performed the miracle of bringing Serbs, Croats and Slovenes together to work in a common polity, with the peoples of Bosnia, Herzegovina, and Montenegro, not to speak of Macedonia and considerable Albanian and Hungarian minorities. One heard occasional rumours indeed of 'nationalist trouble-makers' within, and read of irredentist Croat or Serb emigré groups, mainly in America. But in general all seemed to go remarkably well. I can personally vouch for apparently amicable arrangements for participation in international broadcasting conferences and festivals which seemed to provide equitable representation to all. But, of course, the outsider rarely knows.

The outsider today is not, as I have suggested, in any position to judge the situation or what is the best way forward. I have read that *L'Osservatore Romano* in its wisdom warns against contentious 'micro-nationalisms' and the 'violent creation of mini-states'. This view would be held by many European pundits who believe the federation can and must be preserved.

Unfortunate;y, 'micro-nationalisms' have a habit of getting in the way of political planners of a wide and utopian vision – witness developments in Africa and elsewhere in the first post-colonial years. If the Croats and Slovenes decide on independent statehood that's what they'll do their damndest to achieve, and the Croats are unlikely to change their minds just because of their Serb minority, however awkwardly situated. And if the federation or even a looser alliance in its place is no longer an acceptable option to those who comprise it, no amount of high-minded rhetoric from outside will save it.

On the other hand, German intentions reportedly (as I write) coming down heavily on the Croat-Slovene side – with economic concessions – would seem to be dangerously ill-advised. The Christian Democrats have allegedly brought pressure on Chancellor Kohl 'to support the two republics' right of self-determination'.

If this move is an indication of a C.D. desire to incorporate the breakaway states into a new 'Western Christian front' it is to be hoped that saner counsels will prevail. The fact that neo-communist influence is apparently still dominant in Belgrade should not be seen as an argument for discrimination in favour of Zagreb or Ljubljana, and any recrudescence of Cold War attitudes might be fatal to an equitable solution.

Irish interest in Yugoslavia in very recent years has mainly centred on Medjugorje, which had become a flourishing pilgrimage centre before the present crisis. The fact that one of the worst Ustashi wartime atrocities, involving a massacre of Orthodox Serbs, took place not far away should be a salutary warning against easy religious and cultural identification. I hope that pilgrims have been encouraged to pray for the victims, and in reparation for a crime committed in the name of a Catholic people.

(September 1991, vol. 41, no. 7, pp. 372-376)

Visions and revisions

That robust but careful critic of the proceedings of Irish society since 1922, Professor Joe Lee, has not alone offered a less than comforting assesment of our 'performance' over a wide range of issues, but has also suggested that we have lost sight of what were once seen as the objectives of a 'new Ireland'.

Central to these was the idea that the haemorrhage of emigration would be ended, and that our policies would go to provide for a significantly increased population, especially in the rural areas: 'standards of living' were not much talked of in the early years of the century, but it was taken for granted that a decent degree of comfort would be available to all, even if it was only to be the 'frugal comfort' which at a later stage was proposed by Eamon de Valera (in a phrase drawn, I think, from one of the social encyclicals).

It is all too easy to smile at the simplicities of a time 'when the patriot's vision seemed bright': it is equally easy to dismiss later visions (not confined to this country) of full employment, equal opportunities, a minimum wage, and so on. Easy, but hardly productive. Hard economic thinking is essential to the welfare of this or any society. But so is Vision. Without it the people perish.

I have often thought that economics without social purpose is like a building without a design. And more and more in recent years I am forced to think that where public economic policies are concerned, the social dimension is too often seen as an after-thought, an irrelevance or even a dangerous interference. Only slowly has the world of production come around to realise that 'more' does not always or usually mean 'better' – not even on ethically value-free terms. The lessons of pre-war overproduction have, apparently, needed relearning in our sophisticated European Community. And the obscenity of butter- and beef-mountains in a world where famine is still a regular visitant has perhaps served to bring those social and moral values back a millimetre or two from the margins of our minds.

At home the bankruptcy of our social thinking has reached rock-bottom ... Against the background of scandal in high places, record unemployment figures have given added urgency to what seems to be our only hope: the possibility of a new quota of human exports to the American market. And while domestic dreams of fortune centre on our National Lottery, even the emigrant quota depends on the luck of another Draw 'over there'. Meanwhile, public voices reassure us that the 'apparent' increase in the number of workless is due 'only' to the temporary expansion of emigration, due, in turn, on the American and U.K. side, to a temporary recession. Once the magic wheel swings round again, all the horses will find succulent pasture.

The time has surely come to shout: stop! But who will do the shouting? Even if a number of clever and unscrupulous men have been creaming off some of our national wealth, even if 'business ethics' are by common consent in need of reappraisal, the roots of our problems go much deeper. We have, I believe, lost our way, gone very seriously astray, and if recent scandals make us aware of this, and lead us to change course, then good may come of it all.

Ours is a society deeply divided, as between on the one hand, a very prosperous and moderately prosperous majority and, on the other, a significant minority (between 25 and 30 per cent) living below the poverty line. This is not alone unjust, it is a recipe for national disaster.

(November 1991, vol. 41, no. 9, pp. 477-479)

1992

Gaudeamus

While the phrase *'fin de siècle'* has come to suggest a certain decadent listlessness, and would certainly not lead one to expect anything much in the way of energetic enterprise, the recent succession of multi-centenary commemorations seems to belie this as far as the Irish past is concerned. Two such memorials have been claiming our attention in the area of learning and piety, and while not relating to our Golden Age, they might claim to bear witness to a continuing tradition of saints and scholars – though this could be, and often was a matter of sceptical question in individual instances!

I refer to the fourth centenary of the foundation of Trinity College, Dublin, and to the celebration of twice that length of years in St Patrick's Cathedral, Dublin. The close of this latter commemoration on March 17th was marked by an unprecedented ecumenical event, when Cardinal Cahal Daly of Armagh preached to a large and distinguished inter-church congregation at a festival service. The Cardinal, his fellow Primate Archbishop Eames, and other eminent persons had been the recipients of honorary degrees conferred in the Cathedral by the Chancellor of Dublin University (Trinity) a day or two earlier: an event which not alone linked the two centenaries but recalled the medieval *studium* associated with St Patrick's to which the sixteenth century foundation claimed a certain succession.

In the College itself, the School of Hebrew, Biblical and Theological Studies, newly enlarged and revivified under the energetic direction of Professor Seán Freyne, was host to a three-day theological colloquium on 'The Doctrine of the Trinity: the Christian Understanding of God Today' with participation by scholars from Germany, the U.S., Scotland, England and Wales, as well as from within the College itself ...

Nothing that was said might provide the spiritual fuel to enable us to bring conviction to our singing of the Nicene Creed in College Chapel as the colloquium drew to a close. But the experience surely had a serious bearing on this confession of a faith which must always 'seek understanding'. And, for me at

least, it related closely to that learning process which the discipline of Lent enjoins on us, the slow and at times painful business
of 'learning to be Church'.

(April 1992, vol. 42, no. 4, pp. 210-211)

Economics and morality

'Comprehensive "yes" vote heavy blow to anti-abortion lobby...'
This was the main headline on the front page of my favourite
newspaper on the morning after the vote [18 June] on the
Maastricht Treaty. Whoever wrote it didn't seem to have read the
article which appeared under it, which indicated that the 'anti-
abortion forces' were already confidently regrouping to fight
another day. Indeed the article itself was surely somewhat mis-
leading in its report of '69 per cent of the electorate in favour'.
In fact, well over a third of the electorate didn't vote at all.

That having been said, the result was decisive, and clearly
sufficient to reassure those, at home and abroad, whose faith in
the future of European Union had received a nasty jolt from the
Danish referendum. Our role as saviours of Europe was inevitably more than a little overstated, and our claim on a much larger
slice of community cake expressed without undue subtlety. The
Taoiseach [Albert Reynolds] was not undeservedly lauded for
sticking to his guns, and holding the referendum without reference to abortion. His gamble came off: if it hadn't he – and
perhaps his government – might well have been forced to resign.

It might be argued that the issue was never really in doubt, that
our numerous beneficiaries from the Common Agricultural
Policy and other sources of Euro-lolly know on what side of their
bread the *pâté* lies, and that an even larger constituency whose
lives have in some measure been materially enriched, even
indirectly, were unlikely to risk going out into the cold. But as
successive opinion polls showed ever-shrinking margins of support, and canvassing by the asserting parties hardly happened, a
chill feeling descended on even the stoutest hearts. At my own
polling centre there was little or no evidence of any political
presence, and the only posters outside the centre urged 'If you
don't know, vote No!'

This exhortation expressive of an unpleasantly mindless form
of populism, was alas! all too indicative of the low level of debate
which prevailed generally in the weeks before the Referendum.
Indeed, cogent discussion on any level was hardly evident at all

until the immediate run-up to the polling day. I except, of course, the serious arguments adduced by Professor John Maguire, Anthony Coughlan and some others on the intellectual wing of the 'No!' coalition.

(Not that 'coalition' is probably the right word for such a disparate company, ranging as it did from Professor Maguire to Professor Binchy, from Tony Gregory to Des Hanafin, from the Democratic Left to Fr Denis Faul. It reminded me at times of the infinite variety of the first post-war 'inter-party' government, whose members were united only in a common desire to put Fianna Fáil out of office.)

The conspicuous absence of Deputies and Senators from so many polling areas on Referendum day itself has been widely commented upon. One explanation is that they just weren't interested because their seats were not at stake. On the other hand, they may, it is alleged, have seen discretion as the better part of political valour, and hence were reluctant to be seen in conflict with the local guardians of morality, mainly lay, but sometimes clerical as well ... Which brings us to the bishops' statement on Maastricht, and to its implications for the 'distasteful challenges' of the near future in relation to the abortion problem. And to the wider implications for the whole future of Irish society.

...

First of all, to look at the statement itself: it came no doubt as an enormous relief to the government since it did not, as the 'pro-life' lobby would have hoped, urge a 'No' vote on the faithful. In fact this was never really on, but the 'dangers' of an affirmative vote might have been so strongly stressed that, while leaving the decisions to the voter's individual conscience, many – perhaps most committed Catholics – might have found it morally impossible not to say 'no'. We may be grateful that this didn't happen, because, in the long run, it would have done untold damage to the already rather shaky authority of the bishops.

What was said then, on the narrow issue, did provide for a genuinely free choice. Individual pastors may subsequently have seen fit to circumvent this by such tactics as 'You must of course decide for yourselves, but this is what I'm going to do and why ...' But clearly most Catholics – and the vast majority of the Republic's voters still are! – did in fact make up their own minds.

I have written elsewhere of the disappointing failure of the

bishops to reflect in their statement on the substantial issues of
the Treaty, or to offer the 'guidance' to which (in their own
words) the faithful was entitled, on the moral implications of any
of these issues. They appeared to be giving support and comfort
to those promoters of the Treaty (including, regrettably, the
Taoiseach) who insisted that it was 'an economic, not a moral'
question. Do we still in practice believe that morality relates
exclusively to sexual and associated matters? Sadly, it looks like it.

But, as to the future, the bishops indicated their conviction
that the problems relating to abortion can be adequately, dealt
with only by a Referendum ... The bishops are far from being
alone in their view. It is shared not only by those who promoted
the Eighth Amendment in 1983 and were happy with it until the
Supreme Court 'overturned' it, but also by a range of citizens of
a wide spectrum of opinion, who accept that the present position
is unsatisfactory, or even dangerous, and who see a further
Amendment as the way out.

This is, I would hold, a serious misreading of the whole
situation, and indeed of the place and function of the Constitution in our society. I regard it as most unfortunate that the
bishops support this misreading. I believe them to have been
badly advised in the matter, and would hope that they might
reconsider their position. There are serious reasons why recourse to the referendum-amendment process may be seen as
neither necessary nor desirable: it is at the very least an open
question, and that the bishops should cast their authority on one
side is, as I have said, unfortunate.

...

I should like to draw special attention to three considerations.
First: it is inappropriate to overload the Constitution with particularities. Its basic role is descriptive: detailing the extent,
shape and structures of our society and dealing with matters of
jurisdiction, legislative procedures and the like. It also contains
a prescriptive element, indicating general principles of polity,
personal and social rights, and so on, but the detailed application
of these need not, and perhaps should not, be included. In fact,
Bunreacht na hÉireann could be seen as already somewhat over-
loaded in this regard. Above all, I believe it undesirable to
include provisions of restrictive effect. Thus, while I am personally deeply opposed to capital punishment I would not support
a constitutional amendment excluding it. My basic reason for

saying this is that I believe constitutions should be built to last, and should not inhibit society from acting as it may see necessary in some future situation as yet unforeseen. In the example I have chosen, judicial killing might in some future emergency, be a necessary evil, however deplorable.

Statute law, on the other hand, may well be admirably suited to a specific and perhaps passing concern and in periodic need of amendment, perhaps ultimately of repeal. In proposing the adequacy and indeed appropriateness of parliamentary legislation for dealing with the 'substantive' question of abortion – and this is the second of my 'considerations' in regard to a further Referendum – I am far from regarding the problem in itself as of 'passing' importance. But the way in which it now presents itself may well be.

Basically what has brought the whole matter to the attention of concerned people, has been the relative ease with which a legal abortion can in recent years be obtained in Britain, and the increasing number of Irish women who appear to be taking advantage of this. Clearly Irish society cannot ignore this, and it was inevitable that, sooner or later, some legal action would be proposed. The 1983 amendment was a well-intentioned but, I believe, misguided attempt to meet the situation on the part of those who saw the extension of abortion facilities to this Republic as a very present threat, and believed that the amendment would prevent this happening. In the event, the Supreme Court ruling has shown that (as some of us foresaw in 1983) it does nothing of the sort. But this is not my present point: rather would I wish to suggest that the context of concern may change within the near future, as, for instance, with the possible general availability of a foolproof abortifacient pill.

And I would submit that the problem of abortion, in either the present or a future context, can be most appropriately and efficiently dealt with by legislation, carefully drafted and discussed by our legislators. I have already suggested in these pages that those of us who are concerned with the maintenance of Christian and human values in our society, and specifically with the right to life, in the womb and outside, as with the welfare of mothers and everyone else concerned, should seriously address the question as to how best these values may be ensured.

...

This is the question I should wish to see submitted to general debate, and more especially debate in the Dáil and Senate. Were it to come about it would, I believe, mark a promising new era in the governance of the Republic. But, on past and present form, I do not see the body of our legislators greeting the idea with any great enthusiasm. It has become too easy to off-load the hard questions on to either the Courts or the people ...

But it is the business of legislators to legislate and of governments to govern: neither Deputies nor Senators, a Taoiseach nor his ministers should be allowed continually to neglect some of the most important tasks for which they have been elected. Obviously, some or most of them will be reluctant to show their hand (or their mind, or, if the word isn't too embarrassing, their conscience) in regard to what is notoriously a hot potato. Fine body of men though they are, the *pomme chaude* is not something that most of them go out of their way to grab. The best hope is that some of the admirable women in both Houses may persuade their reluctant brethren to bestir themselves. And as far as party lines are concerned, surely this is an issue on which they might well be crossed without sacrifice of principle – or interest.

...

The third consideration to which we might give our attention is the unpalatable likelihood that the campaign leading to a referendum will be bitter and deeply divisive. Even on the travel-information question(s), it would be too much to expect that a formula can be devised which would gain general approval. The informational aspect of any proposed amendment is sure to be controversial, to say the least of it, in as much as the thorny matter of referral is almost certain to be raised. Here again I am struck by the fact that the problem is probably a passing one, if it doesn't already belong to the past. I mean that short of banning the circulation of British Telecom directories, the basic information can hardly be held at bay. And on a more sophisticated level, information technology has already reached a stage of development making censorship well nigh impossible. In principle, at least: in practice, I am aware that only a small minority has direct access to computerised outlets (or, is it inlets?). However, where there's a will there's a way ... In any case, the arguments against incorporating any kind of restrictive clauses into a constitutional declaration are powerful: if only on the grounds of future feasibility. And in the not very distant future at that.

So I am led to ask my legal advisers (if they're listening)

whether there isn't an alternative to a referendum even as a way of dealing with travel and information? Is it naïve of me to suggest that the right to leave the jurisdiction and the right to be informed, are anterior to the constitution? I should have thought that the first could be curtailed only in the case of those in legal custody, and the second only where it clearly offended or endangered the common good. Surely the common and regular infringement of these rights on the part of the Soviet and allied regimes was regarded by the rest of us as gravely wrong!

I suspect that I am being naïve, and that our betters will insist on submitting us to ordeal by referendum, at least once before the year is out. May I then make an appeal to all concerned to do everything possible to moderate the bitterness and the divisiveness which such occasions seem to generate? And to stop demonising those who disagree with us.

Those who argue honestly for a woman's right to chose, and all who would regard legislation for limited (very limited) abortion, should make the effort to recognise that the 'pro-life' lobby are also honest people, who are deeply concerned at the mounting abortion statistics in so many parts of the world, and who honestly believe that constitutional 'copper-fastening' is the way to avoid it here. I think they are mistaken, I dislike much of their propaganda, and I resent their appropriation of the 'pro-life' title: I resent it in the same way that, as an Irish Republican, I resent the Provos (and their allies) calling themselves the 'Republican Movement'. But I respect the honesty of their concern.

So I would ask S.P.U.C. and their allies to recognise that we too, who may disagree with them in several ways, are also Pro-Life. In fact, I don't know anybody who isn't – although I've found it hard at times to believe it of certain nuclear warriors! And I would also ask everybody involved – including those in the media – to drop the label 'pro-abortion'. Again I know nobody who would accept it, without serious qualification ...

As issues come to be stated, or are heard to be stated in uncompromising terms of black and white, honest people come to believe that they are either all black or all white. The middle ground comes to be despised on both sides, and anyone who takes a stand there is liable to be shot at from left and right, as well as being regarded as a weak, disloyal compromiser.

One other important consideration is the ecumenical dimension of the debate. From the start the Archbishops of the Church of Ireland, and Protestant leaders of differing traditions have made their positions clear ... Our legislators are bound to have due regard to these positions, along with that of the majority Church, when they come to legislate – either directly, or in drafting a constitutional amendment. Any new measure which failed to take the rights of these or other minorities into account would be a grave offence against justice.

(July-August 1992, vol. 42, no. 6, pp. 386-392)

St Bartholomew's Day

A remarkable ecumenical event occurred in Dublin near the end of August. This was the celebration in St Bartholomew's Church in Ballsbridge of its patronal feast in the 125th anniversary of its foundation. St Bartholomew's has always been seen as in the vanguard of the Catholic movement in the Church of Ireland, and hence long regarded with some suspicion by hard-core Irish Protestantism. I remember attending the centenary celebrations in 1967, honoured by the presence and preaching of the great Michael Ramsey then Archbishop of Canterbury and a pioneer of Anglican-Roman rapprochement. But ecumenical developments here were still in their infancy and there was no representative present from the majority Church.

It is then a happy sign of how far we have come on the ecumenical road – in some lanes at least – that this year's commemoration began with First Evensong on the eve of the feast, with no less a preacher than Cardinal Cahal Daly. I am also happy to note that his address did offer that Christian leadership, in our present social and economic situation, which I have called for here. At the Solemn Eucharist the following evening the preacher was Dean John Paterson of Christ Church, who referred to the Cardinal's words, especially on unemployment, as 'both Christian and deeply caring. Rightly they have made the headlines this morning.'

The Dean himself made some headlines the following morning when he was reported as claiming that 'Roman Catholic teaching on birth control' could be seen as partly responsible for a population increase which had been 'a major part of the cause of our unemployment crisis'. And I must confess that this report (which I heard first on morning radio) dismayed me considerably: not to put too fine a point on it, my first reaction was 'What has got into John Paterson?'

My thought was not inspired by any deep devotion to *Humanae Vitae*, or the like, but because whatever the Dean had in mind, or whatever he had said, would be bound to be greeted in certain quarters as an example of the die-hard anti-Catholicism of Irish Protestants, and, perhaps especially, as suggesting that the Catholic working classes, under the influence of their priests, breed beyond their means – and 'ours'.

Of course any such sentiment would be light-years removed from the thinking of Dean Paterson (or indeed of the Church of Ireland in general). But there are those who would like to believe otherwise, and would happily devour any evidence that seemed to support them ... And so I was dismayed, and perhaps rather cross with the Dean for, however innocently, giving comfort to the enemy.

Thank God I didn't tell him so. So all I can do is apologise for what I didn't say to him. And now that I've read the whole text of his very fine sermon, I am ashamed that I didn't keep my own rule of postponing judgement till you've seen the original!

In fact the *gravamen* of his argument was at one with that of Cardinal Daly ... It is certainly clear that Dean Paterson was not engaging in any divisive confrontational approach. *Au contraire*, his remarks serve well to remind us that doctrinal and liturgical convergence may, contrary to past expectations, be much closer then a similar consensus on all questions of Christian living.

The reporting of both Cardinal and Dean indicated an awareness of the importance of what they had to say. Unfortunately the Dean was reported 'out of context', since the greater part of what he had to say was perhaps seen as of interest only to his fellow-churchmen. This was an error of judgement, and an unhappy one.

And, sadly, the ecumenical significance of the celebrations as a whole went unreported. I cannot recall any reference to the St Bartholomew anniversary beyond the minimum indication of where and when the two preachers spoke. In particular, the unique historic importance of the Cardinal's participation was completely overlooked. And so, what might have been highlighted as a memorable moment on the way to Christian unity seemed only to emphasise our divisions.

(October 1992, vol. 42, no. 8, pp. 516-518)

Obstacle or challenge?

The historic decision taken by the Church of England to admit women to the priesthood will have been warmly welcomed in their sister Church here in Ireland where women have been 'priested' over the past few years. The Australians seem to be following suit, and indeed the practice is now common in most provinces of the Anglican Communion. And also in all the provinces, in varying proportions, there are those who find the development quite unacceptable. However, if the Irish experience is anything to go by, talk of schism would appear to lack much substance. But can one take the Irish or other precedents as valid for the 'mother' Church? There have already been strong indications that the disaffected may find it difficult, even impossible, to remain in communion with those who ordain women, with women who undergo ordination, and with those who accept their ministry. And among the options canvassed by and for those concerned is a movement, not just of individuals, but of whole parishes – even dioceses – into the Roman Catholic communion.

There have been proposals – not altogether without precedent – for a 'Uniate' solution. This would enable those who 'come over' to retain much of their traditional order, not least in liturgy, while submitting to the Roman obedience. The response to this idea so far has been, to say the least of it, cautious. As one bishop put it rather bluntly: 'There's more to being a Roman Catholic than a refusal to ordain women.'

On the other hand, there are voices in the Church of England raised in favour of maintaining the Church's integrity, while making every effort to respect the feelings, and more seriously the consciences, of what is after all a not inconsiderable minority. It is quite impossible for an outsider to judge whether this objective can be achieved, but none of us would rejoice in a further fragmentation of the Christian community. Such a fragmentation would almost certainly be something of a disaster for Anglicanism as a whole, since the English Church is seen not only as parent but as centre and focus.

It will be interesting, by the way, to see whether the other two non-Roman 'episcopal' bodies in Britain itself follow the English lead. Neither the Episcopal Church of Scotland nor the Church in Wales – *Yr Eglwys yng Nghymru* – is established: their situation is analogous to the Church of Ireland, and indeed they are both minority communions within their respective nations. The (established) Church of Scotland is of course Presbyterian, but there is no established body in Wales (shades of Lloyd George and Irish Home Rule!). There is a strong Catholic dimension to both Welsh and Scottish Anglicanism (especially the latter), and it is possible that innovators in both may point to the Irish precedent as especially relevant and reassuring. It is I believe true to say that supporters of women's ordination here have included some (though by no means all) of the most Catholic-minded members of the Church of Ireland. In fact, one may be inclined to dismiss the idea that the question is really a 'Catholic' versus 'Evangelical' issue at all.

Nevertheless, the argument that such a major departure from tradition as has now come about in one sector of Christianity should not have been pressed home without the agreement of the Roman and Orthodox sectors, is one which might be expected to recommend itself to those who look to the ultimate unity of all who profess belief 'in one, holy, catholic and apostolic Church.' And this view is certainly held, if only in the most negative terms, by the Roman establishment, as witness the immediate response by the Vatican to the English synodal decision as placing a further regrettable obstacle in the path of unity.

I don't suppose this surprised anyone. It would have been quite a *volte face* for Rome even to have said that such a development needed 'further study'. The ordination of women, like that of married men, appears to be high on the list of Closed Questions.

Still, how much more encouraging to us all it would be, had the word 'challenge' been used instead of 'obstacle'. And, in the long run, how much more sensible and, if I may say so, more humble as an expression of discipleship. In the face of the great cultural changes which are transforming the world we live in, it is surely quite foolishly presumptuous to pretend to any clear view of how the Church's pilgrimage must proceed.

Nothing that is not patently contrary to God's law and the teaching of the Gospel should be excluded as hostile, or even unsuitable to the life and welfare of God's people. And at a time when the very real challenge of a new evangelisation gives urgency to the Church's mission, it may well appear unwise, not to say irresponsible, to ignore the God-given gifts and talents of women as well as of men, as of no consequence in the immense task which lies before us ... The question is by no means 'closed'.

(December 1992, vol. 42, no. 10, pp. 634-635)

1993

Unity – but not yet?

Church Unity Week is now as much a part of the Catholic parish calendar as is the Novena of Grace but with apparently only a fraction of the Novena's impact or influence. I say 'apparently' because Unity Week is after all a week of Prayer, and we must hope that none of it goes unheard. And as I write, an impressive programme of joint services with, in many cases, an exchange of pulpits, is in train in Dublin and other centres. But the slightly cynical friend who suggested that the whole enterprise should be placed under the patronage of St Rita, 'saint of the impossible' was only expressing what many of us are tempted to feel.

Certainly the excitement, the high hopes, the sense of setting out on a great new adventure which marked the early days of ecumenism – among Catholics – has gone like the incense of our youth. And as most of us get a whiff of that nowadays only after a *Requiem*, so too the one continuing sign of Christian solidarity is the funeral service. We're no longer afraid to hear that 'which' for 'who' in the Lord's Prayer and, as Austin Clarke said, 'risk eternal doom'. (If 'which' is ever used now!).

It may at least be counted for gain that we acknowledge the rites of passage observed by other Christians, that we recognise that other Churches have a life of prayer, and that we treat these institutions and communions with courtesy and respect – as, to be fair, most of us always treated their individuals, lay and clerical. It does represent an advance that we may join them in common prayer, and are at times even encouraged to do so. Joining them in sacramental communion is still normally forbidden, though in exceptional cases individuals may be admitted to our Eucharist: the sacrament of Baptism is a different matter, the appalling act of re-Baptism is now very rarely practised, and then only in cases of serious doubt.

So, with some notorious exceptions we now have reached the stage of behaving to each other as Christian neighbours, if not friends. To have reached the point means we have come a long way, far longer than those who have grown up in the recent benevolent atmosphere may realise. But it's still a far cry from

Christian Unity and from what Jesus himself prayed for at the
Last Supper ...

...

Officially, of course, unity is still the aim. And to confine ourselves merely to the Roman-Anglican sector, an immense amount
of hard work went into the proceedings of what we know as
ARCIC I. The hopes engendered by the remarkable degree of
convergence achieved in this process is now sadly a matter of
history, as the Vatican's response, scandalously long delayed,
finally damned it with frigidity and faint praise.

New 'conversations' known as ARCIC II, are indeed in process, but it would take an incurable optimist to see them, however
successful that may appear, as cracking the hard negative Vatican
wall. One may well be tempted to regard the whole proceeding
– and others like it in various parts of the ecumenical spectrum
– as a cynical exercise in procrastination with little expectation
of, or desire for, a positive result.

A temptation to which it would be wrong, indeed disastrous,
to submit. To give up hope at this stage would be a betrayal both
of our mission and of those who have worked so committedly,
and continue so to work, for the realisation of Christ's prayer.
And it is no mere sentimental cliché to remember that the
straight lines of God's writing may seem crooked to us. Thus, I
have heard genuine ecumenists deplore the ordination of women
in the Anglican Communion, not from prejudice or theological
scruple, but as an 'insurmountable' obstacle to the reunion of
that Communion with Rome and with the Orthodox. What the
Church of Ireland and sister Churches have done may, on the
contrary, be a sign of God's will for all of us – not least at a time
when we bewail a 'crisis in vocations'.

Perhaps a far more negative development, and one with
potential consequences of some gravity in this country as elsewhere, is the apparently widening gap on moral issues between
Churches approaching doctrinal convergence. I need only refer
to our pre-Referendum debates on the problems of abortion.
But I would stress that the gap is only apparently widening: I am
convinced that all our Churches are in agreement on the fundamental issue – that abortion is always an evil.

It is on the complex question as to when it may be a necessary
evil, or the lesser of two, that differences of opinion may exist.
And I am also convinced that serious, unprejudiced, detailed

discussions among moral and pastoral theologians, on an inter-
Church basis, could make a very valuable contribution to the
further debate which will be necessitated when the unresolved
aftermath of the Referendum comes to be dealt with by legislation. The mistake would be to look for a neat and easy formula.
But a prudent, considered statement on the moral dimensions of
a real and urgent dilemma could be of immense value, as well as
a sign of the compassion and reverence for life of all Christians.

(February 1993, vol. 43, no. 2, pp. 110)

Moral imperative

The Irish national airline Aer Lingus, which had over several
years become one of our most successful public enterprises has,
as I write, fallen on hard times. Any recovery plan would appear
to demand a substantial State investment, and this is at present
under discussion. But it is also taken for granted that several
hundred staff 'redundancies' will also be inevitable.

Taken for granted by all, except those most closely involved:
the Aer Lingus work force and their trades unions. From that
quarter have come not just the usual protests which are to be
expected in such circumstances, but a more radical demand,
based not unreasonably on the fact that redundancies cost quite
a lot of money. At a time of mountain-high unemployment, it is
asked, why should the community be asked to invest heavily in
redundancy – in other words, adding to the roll of the workless
– instead of in the maintenance of existing jobs, and the creation
of new ones? Similar questions are no doubt being asked in many
other corners of our troubled economy, but the size and scale of
the Aer Lingus case make them sound louder and more urgent.

I suppose the immediate reaction in high places is to dismiss
the mentality behind the questions as impossibly naïve, however
one might sympathise with those concerned. For 'redundancy'
has become one of the o.k. words in our socio-economic thinking: it seeks to palliate the harsh reality of undeserved dismissal,
of losing one's job, of bringing a hopeful career to a sudden end.

It's a word which we first began to hear, in its present usage,
in the 1960s, and its early applications seemed to be fairly
benevolent: 'packages' were devised and offered to quite senior
white-collar workers, some years ahead of their normal retirement age, and in very many cases were accepted more than
willingly. Even then, some of us were uneasy at the thinking

behind all this, and especially its social potential which could develop into something far from benevolent. And more and more, the word 'voluntary', when attached to the R-word, seemed less and less meaningful. But gradually, the received economic wisdom began to hail each new set of redundancies as a step forward while, in another part of the forest, the ever-rising number of the unemployed was piously deplored ...

Now that unemployment is seen, at long last, to be an economic as well as a social problem, one might have reasonably expected that the received wisdom would have been quietly buried. But, apart from a few heretic voices, there seems to be little recognition on the part of the economic establishment – in either the public or the private sector – that it just won't do. And redundancy is no longer (if it ever was) an answer.

That, in a rapidly changing technological context, certain trades and skills must, sooner rather than later, become obsolete is a fact of life. Alternative employment, probably involving retraining, is not always a practical proposition. Early retirement, however unpalatable, will sometimes be inevitable, but it should be a last resort. The same must apply to the sudden, often widespread, job-losses, resulting from a cost-cutting move by a long established multinational employer. National enterprises too are often faced by the necessity of cutting down their operations, owing to a sudden and brutal collapse. Job losses are inevitable.

None of these unpleasant realities can be denied, and our society is not alone in having to face them. But facing them need and should not mean the continued acceptance of and reliance on sterile policies and reach-me-down solutions to our difficulties.

One of the saddest spin-offs of our currency problems in relation to European exchange and to the fortunes and misfortunes of Sterling is this: that, instead of inspiring fresh socioeconomic thinking which might set us on a more hopeful way forward, we have indulged in an orgy of blaming everyone else for our woes. Granted that neither the extraordinary antics of British economic policy nor the criminal activities of speculators, domestic or foreign, can be laid at our door, our reactions have been disappointingly passive and fatalistic.

...

It has surely been evident to all but the most intellectually

hidebound that the science of economics without a social direction can be of no practical value outside the lecture room or
examination hall. It is certainly a *sine qua non* of social planning
and policy making, but of itself it is of no greater use than the
equally necessary science of mathematics is to the practical
business of building a bridge. But with rare exceptions – a
Maynard Keynes, or, in the Ireland of the 1960s, a Ken Whitaker
– most economic gurus seems to regard social purpose as an
irrelevant if not dangerous interference with the laws of the
market.

But social purpose is something which the Christian in politics
must see as a moral imperative, not just an optional extra. I don't
mean social dogma – whether of the left or of the right: I do mean
such simple and obvious aims as providing work for the optimum
number of members of our society in their own country. Does
that sound impossibly romantic and old-fashioned? It was certainly understood to be the objective of those who strove for
'Irish freedom' for the better part of a hundred years. The socio-
economic dimension of 'freedom' was not always articulated,
except during the Land War, but it was surely taken for granted.
Emigration was seen as a direct result of foreign misrule, and
would melt away once we achieved control of our own destinies.

Again, the word 'naïve' seems sadly called for. But however
unrealistic and sentimental the approach, the Irish were by no
means unique in seeing political freedom as ending poverty,
exploitation and dispersal. Patriotic Catholic expectations may
have looked to a cosy, mainly rural, future of simple prosperity
and happy families: such an over-simplified vision was out of date
before it could be realised. But the core values were sound.

Our own age too has produced over-simplified ideas and
ideologies, many of them lethal in their social consequences.
The economic theory encapsulated in the phrase 'a rising tide
raises all boats' is one such. Our blind if well-intentioned pursuit
of economic goals has resulted too often in the kind of successful
operation whereby the patient dies. We can't afford any more of
these.

The Irish Catholic Bishops' joint pastoral letter on 'Unemployment in Ireland' was admirable in its tone and in the urgency
of its message. But not unexpectedly it failed to crack the policy
barrier, and quite properly would see any attempt to do so as
beyond the authority and competence of its authors. The docu-

ment on social and economic exclusion issued by the Conference of Major Religious Superiors was not so inhibited, and
pointed quite sharply at certain necessary departures from established thought and action.

Surely the time is ripe for a concerted Christian lead on
practical social policy, by those who are free to do so, and are
qualified academically or by experience or both. This is a moral
issue, and must be addressed by those who pretend to serious
moral conviction. There are 300,000 reasons why they should do
so.

(March 1993, vol. 43, no. 3, pp. 179-181)

Clandestine ministry

I have often commented on what I have come to regard as a
preoccupation with secrecy on the part of the institutional
Church. A preoccupation at times amounting to an obsession.
One of the best-know and most irritating examples of this marks
the procedures followed in relation to the appointment of
bishops. Secrecy is canonically enjoined on those drawing up lists
of suitable candidates and on those involved in consultations,
both among clerics and among 'lay persons of outstanding
wisdom' (Code, canon 377). And this secrecy extended to a point
of furtiveness seems to colour the whole process up to the
moment when the plain people of God are informed as to whom
their elders and betters have chosen to be their pastor. Even then
they must remain in the dark as to how this choice was arrived at,
what other candidates were considered and how and why these
were passed over.

And, immediately, I can hear defenders of the system point
out the virtues, indeed the necessity of discretion in relation to
this last matter. Nothing should be said which could embarrass
the 'unsuccessful', or possibly belittle them in the eyes of parish-
ioners or others.

The point is of course well taken. The protection of the
individual and the assurance of his privacy are considerations of
no small importance, and should not be – although they all too
often are – easily brushed aside when the 'public interest' is
deemed paramount. And it is altogether proper that Church
authority should give especial attention to such considerations.

Unfortunately, wherever justice is seen to be done, conceal-
ment may well be to the disadvantage of the individual and, in

fact, cast doubts on his position. When access to the facts is
unduly restricted rumour has a field day. But it may be difficult
to decide on when precisely the word 'unduly' applies. Or when
discretion becomes secrecy.

. . .

This reminds me of another very different example of institutional mishandling of a situation, one in fact of great positive
potential for the Church in Europe, and perhaps elsewhere, but
which has been allowed to drift into the half-light of rumour. I
refer to the clandestine practice of ordaining married men
which obtained in what was then Czechoslovakia during the years
of Communist repression.

It was commonly accepted that a succession of regimes in
Prague and in Bratislava had, since the late 1940s, been among
the most rigid in that part of Europe which was within Moscow's
sphere of influence until the collapse of the Soviet Union. Some
slight relaxations occurred from time to time but were of short
duration: only during the Dubcek interlude (1967-8) did 'socialism with a human face' come to life like a sudden springtime.
And socio-political rigidity included an anti-religious dimension
hardly equalled for its brutal efficiency in any of the other
'people's democracies'.

The Polish *Pax* organisation of priests, willing to collaborate
fully with the regime had its equivalent, *Pacem in Terris*, both in
Catholic Slovakia and among the Catholic minorities in Bohe-
mia and Moravia. Non-collaborationist clergy were subjected to
continued, severe restrictions, and at times outright persecution,
leading inevitably to an 'underground Church' which maintained a sacramental and pastoral life in conditions of great
difficulty. To ensure an active ministry for the faithful, priests and
bishops were clandestinely ordained in considerable numbers –
very many of them being married men.

With the normalisation of Church life in very recent years this
clandestine ministry has to a great extent survived, but it has not,
it would appear, been fully integrated into the diocesan structures. There may indeed be questions about these men's 'formation', theological and otherwise, in the absence of an adequate
seminary system for many years, and the extraordinary circumstances in which most them performed their ministry will have
given rise to certain problems.

But there can be little doubt that the main problem, now, in the case of the vast majority, is that they are married. And I am given to understand that while individual accommodations have been made here and there, the overall situation still remains a headache to the Vatican as well as to the Czech and Slovak Churches.

I know that to speak of 'mishandling' what must be a complex situation may appear an over-simplification, indeed an impertinence, at such a distance. But the very fact that the situation has been allowed to remain in such an obscure state is in itself a sad reflection on Vatican attitudes.

Surely the ministry of so many committed married men, whatever their lacks or failings may have been, must form a chapter of some splendour in the history of the Church in Europe, and, more importantly, a sign for the future of Christian mission. Unfortunately, there has been little recognition of this, rather have the survivors been condemned to a kind of ecclesiastical Limbo. We don't apparently have any exact figures as to their numbers. One has heard of perhaps a couple of hundred priests and over twenty bishops ... Rumours, rumours!

(July-August 1993, vol. 43, no. 6, pp. 365-367)

Vatican sources

A Vatican secret, not (as far as I know) yet shared with the world advertising industry, is the extraordinary knack of making two words at the beginning of a 'release' universally memorable. Just think of them: *Rerum Novarum, Mirari Vos, Quadragesimo Anno, Veterum Sapientiae,* and of course *Humanae Vitae.* It doesn't seem to work so well when there are three words to remember: *Mit brennender Sorge* never really caught on – or maybe the Nazis had a secret antidote. Oddly enough – or maybe because the Curia refused to part with what was their secret – none of the documents of Vatican II achieved the same bi-verbal fame. *Lumen gentium,* yes: but only among insiders.

And now, the biggest coup of all. The name and fame of *Veritatis Splendor* have been long well-established from Alaska to South Africa before publication of the document itself. What flair! Or, as Myles na gCapaillín might say: 'How is it done?' What would the boys and girls on Madison Avenue give to know the answer? These days, probably a billion or two ...

...

Pope John Paul's intelligence and human concern are no less
sensitive to the diversity of current realities than were those of the
architect of *Humanae Vitae* in his own time. He is also sharply
aware that times have changed since then, and that *HV* itself has
been unintentionally, but inevitably, a serious force for charge –
in perhaps an unwelcome direction.

Neither is Pope John Paul, as some of his less informed critics
imagine him to be, the prisoner of a debased and outworn
scholasticism, with a mechanistic view of human motivation and
behaviour. On the contrary, some would wish that his thinking
were closer to that of St Thomas, and to those who in our own
time have rescued the Thomistic Tradition from the jejune
pronouncements of the manuals. Some indeed would go further, and wish the Pope were more of a theologian and less of a
phenomenologist.

We are frequently reminded that he is very much a Pole, a
product of Poland's special brand of Catholic culture, and that
by instinct and sympathy he inclines heavily to the East. All this
is true, and it should also be remembered that his personal
curriculum vitae reads like something from a heroic age. Throughout his ministry he has been the very type and figure of the
Faithful Servant. To question any part of this would be both silly
and impertinent.

But one may, with all respect and admiration, still be in some
doubt whether to *'semper fidelis'* we should add *'semper prudens'*.
The fearless are not necessarily always wise, and it would be
dishonest to pretend that everything done by this brave man, or
done in his name, since he succeeded to the papacy, has been to
the obvious benefit of God's People. Much of what he has had to
say over the past fifteen years has been of very real value, but
much has also been, to say the least of it, problematic.

It is only right and proper that, at this point in a pontificate
which has witnessed so many changes for good and ill in the
Church, in Europe, in the World, our chief pastor should address
some of the problems which these changes have brought about
or intensified, and offer guidance to his flock worldwide. And
again one thinks of Paul VI, with whom the present Pope clearly
shares a profound sense of responsibility to the integral tradition
of the Church in matters of faith and morals, and to the role of
the papal office in the preservation and unfailing promotion of
this tradition. It would be hard to conceive of a more striking

contrast in temperament, style and personal impact – especially in public – than these two men. But in their view of papal rights and duties they are almost identical.

Almost, but not quite. Paul was after all the Pope of the Council in action, and had to preside over the ecclesial upheaval which John XXIII had set in motion. He accepted, indeed encouraged the evaluation of the collegial ideas, as was evident in his approach to an institutional development of this idea in the first episcopal Synods. But he also had reservations about how far collegiality should go, how fast, and in what direction. But, where Paul had reservations, his present successor seems to have made his mind up very firmly early on: collegiality in any real sense, in theory or in practice, was not and is not on. ...

...

By far the worst response to the voice of authority, when it seeks to teach or explain, commend criticise or condemn, is not that if should be actively defied or challenged, but that it should be ignored. Ignored as unimportant or irrelevant or incompetent. And I very much fear that this is the most frequent response to both papal and episcopal teaching on the part of very many Catholics today, including some who are deeply committed to the faith and the community of word and sacrament.

And this is nothing less than tragic, on at least two levels. First because of the many excellent things said by pope and bishops on a variety of contemporary issues of great concern. In this country, for instance, social questions have been dealt with in recent years with a strength and lucidity of vision which one might look for in vain among our political thinkers and activists. And Pope John Paul's reflections on the present social situation in the post-Communist world have been both typically courageous and sharply critical of conventional wisdom.

But I would suggest that the crisis in authority goes far deeper than any lack of awareness of Christian social leadership. It pertains to the nature and necessity of authority itself, which is hardly acknowledged in contemporary society, at least on the level of popular social thought. And the fault must be laid fairly and squarely at the door of those who have abused the authority entrusted to them, have too often identified it with power, and have allowed what should be a service to society to become degraded, self-justifying and corrupt.

That this should be the case in secular society may evoke

nothing but the cynical comment of those who have few illusions. But surely it is of the very nature of the Church's mission, that her authority, rooted as it is in God's promise, should continue to be a light to the nations. And so, those who exercise this authority must at all times submit to a discipline of service, a 'self-denying ordinance' which will seek to maintain their ministry free from the corruption of power, of venality, and from that insidious form of self-deception which allows these corruptions to wear masks of justice and holiness.

It is, thank God, some time since the grosser forms of corruption disgraced the structures of Church authority, to any serious extent: such financial scandals as have been revealed have hardly touched the heart of the matter. But Acton was right: all power does tend to corrupt. And those who partake in forms of power which touch the fringes of the absolute are always seriously at risk.

The anti-Modernist witch-hunt which disfigured, one may say disgraced, the pontificate of Pius X should be a solemn warning to all who care for truth. It may serve also to remind us that even the saintliest of men may not be proof against evil counsel, plausibly offered, or against confusing what someone seems to say with what he is really saying. Dreadful errors, dreadful injustices, were committed in the name of orthodoxy: names and reputations were blackened and good servants of the Church punished, and silenced. The loss was ours. The insights of many, if not all, of those condemned remained hidden far too long, and later generations continued to suffer from the siege mentality which had been inculcated. Not until the Vatican Council did the process of rehabilitation begin, when some latter-day 'rebels' and 'dissidents' were restored to favour.

We have lived to see the old bad ways make a partial comeback. Honest people have been declared 'suspect', and some have suffered 'disciplinary measures' in a process of enquiry more appropriate to a totalitarian state then to Christ's Church.

There have been other indignities. A 'Catholic University' proposed to award honorary degrees to an American archbishop (who is also a Benedictine monk), and to a South African Dominican friar, once elected Master-General of his Order but who opted to stay with the people he served. Word came from the Vatican forbidding the awards. No reason was offered: the sane mind can hardly guess at what tortured pervert-in-office was

responsible ... We do know that at least some cases of bureaucratic injustice were executed without the Pope's permission, or
even his knowledge. But surely somebody consults him when
obviously suitable candidates for bishoprics are passed over in
favour of, at best, nonentities ...

All is far from well in the corridors of Vatican power, but who's
going to do anything about it?

(September 1993, vol. 43, no. 7, pp. 431-436)

1994

Half-way there?

A cynic might be tempted to observe that the month of January is singularly appropriate for the annual celebration of Church Unity Week, expressing as it were a collective New Year Resolution, reassuringly repeated each year, with little long-term effect. Or, some might say, intention. Others still might even more cynically suggest that such would be of considerable embarrassment to those most nearly concerned.

One may of course argue that while to some the cup of Unity is, after so many decades of prayer and action, still half-empty, to the more sanguine among us it is already half-full. Is it then merely a matter of temperament? Thus, the fact that at the funeral of yet another victim of 'Northern violence', there was a joint inter-church prayer service. 'It couldn't have happened thirty years ago,' was a comment I heard more than once. But I also heard a number of remarks, all suggesting – mildly or with a certain fury – that it apparently takes a couple of decades of murder to make Christians pray together.

As ever, the truth is divided. The cup is both half-full and half-empty: we have a long way to go, but we have also come a long way. Self-deception, refusal to re-examine our entrenched attitudes, reluctance to abandon cherished but untenable positions, all these – and sheer hypocrisy among both leaders and led – add up to a dismal record among all quarters of our professedly Christian society. And yet this is only half the story. The appalling inhumanity which has disgraced all elements of our divided community would have been worse, much worse, were it not for the long, hard, thankless work of brave untiring Christians – within and outside of the ordained ministry – who have tried to preserve or rebuild some fragment of *pax Dei* in their own corner. They have at times succeeded, often at real cost to themselves and their families. If and when a longer, wider peace is established, it is unlikely that these men and women of mercy will be remembered in 'marble or conventional phrase'. But what they have done will remain 'a blessing and a holy inheritance' to those who come after them.

In the meantime the ecumenical vision, however remote it
may too often appear, demands our service and our loyalty. The
academic labours of the Irish School of Ecumenics (I.S.E.) are,
one might think, a world apart from the realities of Christian
disunity, as lived and suffered in the Northern ghettoes. But
peace studies and ecumenical theology are the essential, intellectually disciplined, co-relative to pastoral and social action which,
however admirably intentioned, may, without these, be more
dangerous than useful on the ground. Theory, far from being
irrelevant to practice, must be its complement and indeed
usually its prelude.

So I am delighted to learn that the valuable work of the I.S.E.
proceeds apace and, it may be said, has recently entered a new
phase of development. Not alone has the School's headquarters
in Dublin – named Bea House, in memory of the great Jesuit
cardinal to whom Pope John XXIII initially entrusted his own
ecumenical project, in advance of Vatican II – now been re-sited
on the Milltown Park campus, but new institutional status has
been given to the School by the four main Christian Churches in
Ireland.

(January 1994, vol. 44, no. 1, pp. 29-31)

The waiting game

Hope deferred continues to produce its own sparse, dry fruit. As
I write, there is little expectation of peace in the North, or of a
new beginning which could bring new vitality to a tired people,
all over the island. The very fact that the I.R.A. have continued
their bloody campaign, while their own process of internal
consultation is in progress, might indeed give the impression
that all that has happened over the last number of months,
beginning with the Hume-Adams conversations, has been nothing more than an elaborate propaganda exercise, a black farce
into which two prime ministers and their cabinets have been
drawn, under the skilful direction of the Sinn Féin leadership.

I am convinced that this reading (and various versions of it) is
quite wrong. I believe that Adams and several of his colleagues
are sincere in their desire to end the conflict, provided they can
strike a bargain attractive enough to sell to the 'army' leadership,
and to a substantial majority of those on 'active service' (including those serving prison sentences). But I am very much afraid
that a hard core of 'hard men' who believe that time is on their

side make such a conclusion highly unlikely this time around. Things are likely to get worse before they get better.

One cannot fail to be aware of the widespread desire for peace among ordinary men and women of the Republican tradition all over the North, and indeed all over Ireland. The strength and depth of this desire have been eloquently and movingly expressed by Cardinal Daly and others, and we may be assured that everything possible is being done, quietly and discreetly, by clergy and other community leaders, to persuade the men of violence to turn to a better way. I am certain also that this work for peace is under way on all sides, and among militants of both traditions. Unfortunately so far, Provo irredentism continues to provoke further sectarian violence on the part of 'Loyalists'.

So where do we go from here? Clearly the two governments cannot be seen to wait indefinitely for a response to the 'joint declaration'. Already it has been announced in both London and Dublin that the 'three-strand' talks process, involving constitutional political parties, is to be resumed, with or without Sinn Féin. But the prospects on that front seem little brighter: Mr Paisley and his Democratic Unionists have, if anything, regressed into the lumpen philosophy of 'not an inch'.

Once again, there are few grounds for optimism. But one must continue to hope ...

(March 1994, vol. 44, no. 3, pp. 179-180)

A lack of vision

The substitution of circuses for bread is a long-established ploy of those in office at times of public exigency. The past couple of months have witnessed serious industrial disorders in the public sector in Dublin and Cork, not to mention continuing violence in the North at a time of especial national concern for peace. Against such a background, the Taoiseach's [Albert Reynolds'] intervention to insist on a large scale celebratory homecoming for the World Cup team, however well-intentioned, laid him open to accusations of cynical populism. It certainly did little to ease the lot of those families faced with the repayment of loans incurred for the American expedition.

One thinks of the employees of Team Aer Lingus and Irish Steel, two enterprises whose recent affairs have made sorry reading. Some of those occupying positions of leadership in the trades unions concerned do seem to have proceeded in a short-sighted manner, and can hardly claim to have engaged public support. But even a cursory study of the recent history of both bodies leaves one in serious doubt as to the quality of management in a period of serious, not to say traumatic, change in the international scene. All in all, the conduct of industrial relations, as it has appeared to the outsider, has seemed less than appropriate for dealing with the urgent demands of what is clearly a long-festering situation.

One is forced to ask whether in fact our cadres of leadership on both sides of industry have what it takes. There appears to be a certain tired reiteration of attitudes whose relevance to contemporary needs is at best doubtful, and a poor substitute for original thinking. In such circumstances it is, I suppose, understandable that some of those concerned should reach for such panaceas as privatisation or 'partnerships' with sources of foreign capital. But one takes leave to doubt the long-term value of these policies.

If one may so describe them. It does appear that any fundamental rethinking of our industrial situation is blocked on the one hand by the received wisdom of market economics, and on the other by the painful need to keep the unemployment figures from mounting any further. Any suggestion of a radical change of course may appear to be, to say the least of it, untimely: but, in the long run, it will be less painful sooner than later.

Most commentators would agree that the desire for change which seemed to power the remarkable successes of the Labour Party (and to a lesser extent the Democratic Left) at the time of the last general election has cooled considerably – or rather that it has been overtaken by that sense of popular disillusion to which I have earlier referred. Actually, the record of the Labour ministers in government has been more than creditable, but it is unlikely that this will be generally recognised. It would be good to think that the present inter-party differences might lead to a clearer tendency on Labour's part to define its political vision, and thus to rekindle the enthusiasm of a couple of years ago. At present, however, I regret to say that I cannot see any evidence of this development.

Indeed an understandable reaction against overblown political rhetoric promising new heavens and new earths has led to the substitution of *pragma* for *dogma* among progressive and even radical politicians at home and abroad. The British Labour movement is an apposite example of this: ironically, doctrinaire socio-economic policies had, during the Thatcher era, become associated with the right wing – I say ironically, since socialism was the noun with which the adjective 'doctrinaire' had formerly long been associated.

Over here, lofty political ideas and ideals were long associated with the Fianna Fáil party, focused particularly on the 'national aims' as classically defined by the late Eamon de Valera. Fine Gael tended to eschew political rhetoric, relying rather on simple, if not simplistic, objectives and statements of intent. It's a long time since a former Agriculture Minister preached the prescription 'one more cow, one more sow, one more acre under the plough' – which was, I suppose, in its own way a rhetorical proposal.

It was not until the late sixties that the Irish Labour Party began to use the words 'socialism' and 'socialist' with any freedom. They had long been tabu words, due to the disapproval – one might say the anathemata – of the Catholic Church.

One should remember that, little more than a decade earlier, Catholic social teaching, as pronounced in the encyclicals of Leo XIII and Pius XI, and locally interpreted by episcopal pundits, had declared sharp opposition to 'welfare state' policies not to speak of socialism. What has been described as the 'Noel Browne affair' has more recently been open to some historical revisionism, but it may at least be agreed that it marked a decisive watershed in the story of Catholic Church authority in contemporary Ireland. Rightly or wrongly, a traditionally docile people began to entertain the feeling that the bishops had overreached themselves, and the psychological foundations were already being laid for the cultural revolution which began in the nineteen-sixties, and in which the proceedings of Vatican II was one of the most powerful agents of change.

Be that as it may, we were told by an over-optimistic Labour Party that 'the seventies would be socialistic'. Things didn't turn out quite that way, and for one reason or another even the increasingly vague vocabulary of socialism seems to have been quietly abandoned. Undoubtedly events following the collapse of Soviet power in eastern Europe have once more given all forms of Marxism a bad name, and 'market economics' is the new shibboleth.

But socialism should not be equated with Marxism, still less with Soviet Communism. One need not ignore the very considerable contribution of Marx's thought to our understanding of socio-economics, nor indeed deny the positive achievements of the Soviet experiment, while recognising the appalling enormities of the latter – not just in the Stalinist period but in the corrupt regime which followed the dictator's downfall. As to Marx, someone has pointed out that while it was he who made us aware that the rich will always exploit the poor, he cannot show that to do so is morally wrong. Certainly in Britain at least, socialism owes at least as much to the moral conscience of Methodism as it does to Marx or even the Fabians. And it is interesting that the new British Labour leader, Tony Blair, is a member of the Christian Socialist group as was his sadly short-lived predecessor John Smith.

A socialist vision is not necessarily the only ideal to offer a younger Ireland, eager for justice and change. But it is better than none at all: the old dictum that without a vision the people perish is still one we ignore at our peril. Certainly the vacuum which obtains at present must sooner or later be filled, and the anti-ideology that greed is good for you seems ready and waiting to fill it.

(September 1994, vol. 44, no. 7, pp. 428-430)

Heart of darkness

It needs of course to be said that our national misadventures, as well as our hopes for the future, seem of very little consequence against the background of what has been happening in Rwanda and – but for the grace of God – may, as I write, be spreading to Burundi. And while the Irish people have been generous in their response to appeals from the bishops, and from the various relief agencies – I think of a sum of £11,000 plus subscribed in one Dublin parish on one Sunday – one is frighteningly aware that the best we can do must be only the proverbial drop in the ocean.

The larger political issues from which we as a free Republic cannot prescind, as members either of the European Union or of the United Nations, are of a terrifying dimension and, as we move closer to see them in some detail, of an even more terrifying intensity of violence. Ever since the Holocaust, we have come to see largeness of scale as implying a significant difference of kind in matters of evil as of good. (Marx was aware of this.) And this largeness, this difference of kind, only seems to have paralysed the international will and our communal ability to bring our huge resources – and they are huge – to bear on the present situation.

Here again I'm afraid popular disillusionment takes over. The tremendous efficiency with which the West – meaning the United States and their clients – rallied to punish the aggressor in the case of the Gulf War can be seen in retrospect as only confirming what at the time was suggested by the more cynical among us: that it was all really a matter of oil.

Certainly, the record of the international community since then, both in the matter of Bosnia and now in Rwanda, offers little hope to those of us who had believed that, even if it took a little time, aggression would not go unpunished and – more immediately urgent – famine and death would become an inescapable challenge. Alas! the response has been muddled, reluctant and inadequate. We are clearly still far from a time when the claims of a common humanity, rather than those of individual national self-interest, will be paramount in situations of international crisis.

It becomes more and more apparent that neither the executive of the United Nations, in the person of the Secretary General, nor even a clear consensus in the Assembly can force the centre of power to act in pursuit of justice in clear emergencies, however serious. Even the Security Council as such is impotent, if and when one of its members with the power of veto chooses to exercise it. It is high time that this arrangement, however necessary or desirable in the immediate post-war situation, is seen to be a dangerous and frustrating anachronism. It is further desirable that the powers of the Secretary-General should be, as a matter of urgency, increased and sharpened to a degree which would make him capable of meeting real emergencies.

Can a small nation like ours do anything about this? I believe we can, in alliance with others like us. In Europe alone, it should be possible for us to help in the construction of a coalition of like-minded peoples with the aim, first of all, of making the European Union itself more effective, and secondly of presenting a united European front in the larger forum. I do not believe that this is an impossible dream: I am sure that we could call on potential allies from Norway to Greece.

(September 1994, vol. 44, no. 7, pp. 430-431)

That justice be done ...

Sunday November 20th, 1994, was a much-needed day of rest at the end of an extraordinary week, in which the Irish body politic was convulsed to the point of implosion. Coincidentally, or perhaps, providentially, it was also the feast of Christ the King. Preachers will not have been short of material, and the word 'apocalyptic' must have trembled on the edge of many a homiletic lip. But I imagine most if not all will have resisted the temptation to prophesy. For the buzz-word at the weekend, among all who had taken part in or were closely touched by the week's events, was one rarely heard in a political context: reflection.

The leading players were opting for it, and recommending it to each other. Only the media pundits speculated (loudly and at length) or offered suggestions on what should happen next. But even they seemed happier reviewing (again at considerable length) what had already happened, each with his own 'insight' to contribute, or his version of what 'really' happened. Actually, once the Taoiseach [Albert Reynolds] had resigned, most if not all passion was spent, and the election of Bertie Ahern as the new leader of Fianna Fáil, came almost as a welcome anticlimax ...

A friend for whose shrewd and humane judgement I have considerable respect, had suggested to me that Mr Ahern's personal marital situation would exclude him from the party leadership. For once he has been proved wrong; nor do I see this matter as an impediment to a future election as Taoiseach. With all our faults, we seem to order these things differently if not better than they do in the United States. Both Mr Ahern and the alternative candidate – Máire Geoghegan-Quinn – have impressive records in ministerial office, but while his rival has many qualities that would make her a formidable Taoiseach, I suspect that Mr Ahern's proven talent and experience in socio-economic conciliation would be especially valuable at this moment in our history.

I refer of course to the 'peace process'. It may be gathered that my personal preference would be for renewal of the Fianna Fáil-Labour partnership as the best available in the Dáil as at present constituted. And I believe that the opinion polls have got it right in suggesting that, on the whole, such would be the popular preference throughout the country.

The programme of joint political action which formed the

basis of the partnership when it was formed merely two years ago
had by no means been completed, but real progress has been
made in many areas. Some of the Labour ministers have done a
particularly good job, as have the new leader (once he got over
some early problems) as Minister for Finance, and one or two of
his party colleagues as well. Certainly, if appointments to a new
coalition were in my gift, I would make some changes, and I'm
sure that changes will be made (if not all to my liking!). But,
looking at the realities of the situation, I feel we could fare further
and do very much worse. And in the matter of the peace process,
it would be a pity to renew discussions fielding a team which did
not include the Tánaiste, and also Mrs Geoghegan-Quinn, who
played an important role as Minister for Justice.

...

Having said all that, we cannot, and must not attempt to ignore
the issues which brought about the crisis, which was not merely
a crisis in government but, as I have said, in the whole body
politic. Matters of trust, of accountability, of transparency in
conducting affairs of state are, heaven knows, of enormous
importance: they touch the very core of our democratic society.
But of at least equal importance are the independence of the
judiciary, and the necessary, delicate, subtle relationships which
link it to the legislative arm: that relationship also calls at all times
for the utmost transparency.

If a politician, however highly placed, is perceived to have
betrayed his trust, or to have lost the confidence of the people
whom he was elected to serve, there are at least clear and effective
remedies to hand in the democratic process. But if a member of
the judiciary becomes subject to a measure of popular misgiving,
especially in relation to that delicate relationship with the legis-
lature to which I have referred, society may be damaged in a
manner not easily patient of effective restoration. And, in both
judicial and legislative arms, society suffers at its essential and
most vulnerable point: the exercise of authority.

Reference to this may bring many of us to another area of
reflection, occasioned by what was perceived to be a key element
in the recent crisis. I mean the fact that the subject of the demand
for extradition, whose handling by the former Attorney General
was at the centre of debate, was a Catholic priest now serving a
prison sentence in another jurisdiction for paedophile offences.

But my immediate concern is not the substance of that

unhappy affair, rather the effect that a number of incidents involving sexual behaviour have had on yet another vulnerable authority, that of the Catholic Church, local and universal. I suppose the fact that a generation ago 'vulnerable' would be the last word likely to be used in this connection is itself a sign of the times. Certainly, Church authority was often subject to attack, but always from without: now, it might appear that any damage or decline is due to 'the enemy within'.

Some would have little hesitation in identifying that enemy: quite obviously, those who have brought the institution into disrepute, most recently those public offenders from Bishop Casey to an unfortunate elderly Dublin curate who died suddenly in a gay social club. But also, and more to be condemned were those theologians and other critics who have questioned and even opposed authoritative statements and decisions, not excluding those of the Holy See itself.

There is however an alternative reading which I dare to find preferable. Briefly, this reading would suggest that the 'enemy within' who have damaged Church authority and brought about its declining power and influence are in fact those, whether in Ireland or in Rome, who, charged with the exercise of authority, have abused it to the point of bringing it into disrepute. This is not the time or place to list some of the more glaring examples of what I have in mind. I will confine myself to suggesting that the former common practice of certain Irish bishops, current in my youth, to 'invent' mortal sins and threaten damnation for what were at worst trivial offences, had the inevitable effect of debasing the whole currency of pastoral rule and judgement, of sacramental practice, and of grace itself. Inevitable also was the gradual erosion of credibility, not alone with regard to episcopal pronouncements, but, far more seriously, the gospel message to which their pronouncements purported to relate.

As to recent 'scandals', evidence of human frailty does less damage than might be imagined. Only when perceived to be linked to public dishonesty, hypocrisy or pharisaism do ordinary people (as distinct from professional carpers) condemn. And only then is authority further damaged.

...

It was good to hear the potential leaders of the next government promising greater 'transparency' in state affairs, and specifying measures which would provide for radical reforms of official

secrets legislation, as well as establishing full and free information to be made available to all citizens. This was one of the main
burdens of a fairly detailed interim declaration by the Labour
Party leader, Dick Spring, and would I think raise few objections
across the political spectrum.

It would be equally good if we could, *mutatis mutandis*, antici-
pate a similar move towards transparency in Church affairs. I
have often deplored the wall of secrecy which surrounds the
appointment of bishops, but this is only one example of an
obsessive concern with a kind of 'confidentiality' which, however
it was accepted in the past, must nowadays be seen as eroding the
confidence of the ordinary people of God in those who exercise
authority. This can give comfort only to the Church's enemies: it
must surely dismay all those – including many millions of the
wretched of the earth – who see her as a strong light in darkness
and, in a sense that Marx could hardly have foreseen, 'the heart
of a heartless world'.

One does not have to go to Mexico or Guatemala to appreciate
this. I have just received a copy of the most recent publication –
or should I say pronouncement – by the Conference of Religious
of Ireland (formerly C.M.R.S.), whose justice commission has in
recent years been a strong prophetic voice, bringing the Gospel
into the Ireland of poverty, unemployment and exclusion. And,
unlike other less effective though sincere and sympathetic voices,
what we have from C.O.R.I. is a fully-costed programme for
action, a detailed socio-economic review which is also a draft
budget for 1995. This is only the latest of several admirable
statements from different levels of the institutional Catholic
Church in Ireland in recent years. Sadly, their source tends to
mean they are ignored if not regarded with suspicion by government, the media and society in general.

Why so?

(December 1994, vol. 44, no. 10, pp. 625-630)

1995

De mortuis ...

To speak only well of the dead is a maxim so commonly, indeed
universally, observed that any breach of the rule is greeted with
enormous disapproval. This is very much the case in Ireland,
although a cynic might suggest that it's by way of ritual recom-
pense for our notorious inability to speak well of the living – or,
at least, if forced to do so, without adding a qualifying coda such
as 'and isn't he well paid for it!'

However, there is one aspect of the *de mortuis* tradition which
I think calls for comment. I refer to the practice of including a
eulogy of the deceased in the homily at his funeral Mass –
sometimes indeed to the near exclusion of any more general
reflection. And I believe I'm justified for once in confining
myself to 'his', rather than 'his or her', because in my own
experience women are rarely the subjects of at least the more
fulsome eulogy.

When I say I disapprove of the practice, I understand that I am,
for once, in agreement with Church authority. While I can't
quote from the relevant instruction, nor indeed indicate how
grave or how rigorous the ruling may be, its intent is quite clear...

...

It is perhaps worth noting that homilies of any kind were
formerly quite rare at the liturgy for the dead. That they are now
common – as at baptisms, marriages and so on – is surely a
development to be welcomed. It is also right that the Church
should give expression to the humanity of the event which is
being commemorated, whether it be an occasion of mourning or
of joy. What we have come to call the rites of passage are cardinal
occurrences in the life of a family or community, as well as for the
person or persons directly involved. It is only proper that this
should be recognised by the officiating minister, in his capacity
of *persona ecclesiae* and what he chooses to say forms an important
dimension of the Liturgy of the Word ...

...

The immediately bereaved are of course the closest object of this

ministry and those most susceptible to whatever of sensitivity, of
tact, of warmth, of personal concern may mark the minister's
words. They are also the most vulnerable to insensitivity, to the
empty platitude, to hollow sentimentality, to pious generalities,
to the threadbare sympathy of one who clearly neither knows nor
cares about the circumstances of the one who has died, or of the
family.

But, for both good and ill, the minister will often have a wider
audience, which can and does sometimes include men and
women who have become distanced from, indeed alienated from
the Church – as well, of course, as some who have never been part
of it. To these also he has an obligation, and a mission so to
celebrate the liturgy that it will be a true sign of the mystery it
enshrines and commemorates. And the homily is an integral part
of this.

So, the homily should be particular rather than general or,
better, a correlation of the two: a reflection on death, based on
Scripture and the liturgy, but with a personal application to the
one whose body lies before the altar. An act of thanksgiving for
his life, as of all life: to include perhaps some record of his deeds
or even his talents. But never a eulogy.

Why not? Well, there are many good reasons, but, most
basically perhaps, the injunction not to judge anyone, and that
this applies as much to positive as to negative judgements. Those
qualified to do so may and sometimes must judge an individual
act, or a sequence of behaviour, but no human being (I would
argue) has the right or the competence to pass judgement on the
totality of a life, even in its more public manifestations. And it
should be noted that homiletic eulogies tend mainly to be
offered at the funerals of 'public men' and of others who had at
least some public dimension to their lives. Mainly, though not
always: I have heard husbands and fathers preached about as
models and exemplars in their conduct of family life.

The problem is that you never can tell. I confess that I say this
remembering certain occasions when, even at the time, I would
have entered a *caveat*, and others when subsequent revelations
have, to say the least of it, cast a very doubtful light at what was said
at the Requiem.

But, even where the eulogy may never be open to amendment
or contradiction, I would insist that it is still out of place in the
Church's liturgy. The good a man or a woman does is certainly

a matter for thanksgiving and praise and rejoicing. But nobody is all good.

There are of course occasions when someone whose work has been of such national or social significance that it demands public recognition in the form of an address or tribute, delivered at or after the funeral rites. Obviously the gathered assembly offers an appropriate and convenient occasion for this. I have been the speaker myself more than once, and while appreciating the honour, I have been less than totally at ease in performing my task. But I would agree that there can be no substantial reason for excluding the possibility of such a tribute, provided it is clearly not part of the liturgy. Ideally, perhaps, it should be delivered after the actual interment.

It may be suggested that what I propose smacks of a certain ritual dishonesty. I would reject this. I am of course aware that the public tribute may be more than a little panegyrical in tone, but I am certain that it is important that the Church, assembled to share in God's word and sacrament, should not appear to judge any man or women. I have recently heard a well-know professional man eulogised by the presiding celebrant of his Requiem in terms that would have been more appropriate to a canonisation. There may indeed have been something of the saint in the man we mourned, but then there's something of both saint and sinner in most of us ...

To balance the premature 'canonisation' to which I referred above, I should mention an occasion when friends and former colleagues joined the family of a distinguished musician whose unexpected death had shocked us all. It was a moment, one might have said, when eulogy could be counted forgivable, but the homilist, while speaking warmly of his deceased parishioner, and sympathising with his widow and children, went on the praise the art of music, to rejoice in the God-given talent whose exercise had so often given delight to so many people, and in return had so graced the liturgy itself. It was in this context he spoke of the man we mourned, and it raised our hearts far higher than any eulogy.

(April 1995, vol. 45, no. 4, pp. 316-319)

Collapse of an institution

It appears that Irish Press Newspapers has collapsed, taking with it two daily titles – *Irish Press* and *Evening Press* – and one weekly,

the *Sunday Press*. The passing of an institution which has played
a considerable role in Irish life over the past sixty-four years is to
be regretted, and will be deplored on all sides. Equally if not
more deplorable will be the loss of some six hundred jobs, about
a quarter of them among journalists.

And while those involved in administration, advertising, and
general office work may find alternative employment, and the
same may to be true of those in the printing trade – note I say
'may' not 'will' – reporters, sub-editors, sports writers, specialised
columnists and the like cannot hope to be easily absorbed. It is
then to be devoutly hoped that, following the liquidation of the
present company, another group or individual entrepreneur
may come forward to purchase one or two or even all three of the
titles.

And however desirable such a move would be from the point
of view of employment, it would be seen as of even greater
importance across a wide social and political spectrum. The loss
of any newspaper, maintaining even a minimum standard of
professional decency, is to be lamented. And while it has to be
said that the *Irish Press* in particular had declined in quality as to
both content and style over recent years – especially since it 'went
tabloid' – nevertheless it did manage to hold on, if precariously,
to the niche in Irish journalism which it had achieved and held
for so long.

With certain outstanding exceptions, I suppose that standards
of journalism are not significantly higher (or lower) here then
elsewhere. Some individuals will inevitably be more gifted than
others, but where accuracy, balance, honesty and general profes-
sionalism are concerned, journalists are not easily categorised as
goodies and baddies. But if some newspapers are obviously
'better' or 'worse' than their rivals, the credit or otherwise must
in great part go to the leadership of senior management.

Happy indeed the journal where leadership and management
are personified in an editor-in-chief, with or without the benevolent support and overall direction of one who, in American
practice, is known as the publisher: one who, while not necessarily a practising journalist, knows what journalism is or should be
about. One who recognises that long-term aims can best be
achieved by men and women whose vision is matched by their
craftsmanship. And that long-term aims should involve something more than the narrowly economic. A good newspaper

should not have to run at a loss; but neither should profit-making be the main motivation....

The masthead of the *Irish Press* when it first appeared in 1931 was nothing if not idealistic. The titles in English and in Irish (*Scéala Éireann*) were supported by phrases in the two languages, '*Dochum Glóire Dé agus Onóra na hÉireann*' and 'Truth in the News', which were open to cynical comment. And, no doubt, there was an amount of this, not least among the journalist fraternity itself.

But it has to be said that among the broad constituency of readers and potential readers to whom the masthead and the paper itself were directed, the response was more than positive. It should be remembered that this constituency consisted mainly, if not wholly, of those whose loyalty to the regime which governed the Irish Free State, since its foundation at the end of 1922, was at best reluctant, and at worst non-existent. And I do not speak of the 'ex-Unionist' minority, as it was called, *Irish Times* readers to a man (and a woman). The disaffected element, who, for the first time, found a daily voice in the new newspaper were of course the unreconciled anti-Treatyites, and especially those who supported the entry of Eamon de Valera and Fianna Fáil into Dáil Éireann in 1927.

And the fact that the general election of 1932 enabled Fianna Fáil to form a government (in time for the Eucharistic Congress!) was, it was generally agreed, due in no small measure to the vigorous political journalism of the *Irish Press*. After that it went from strength to strength and was widely accepted as a lively newspaper, modern in lay-out and tone, and socially radical with a fresh approach to events at home and abroad. It served Fianna Fáil well during the Blueshirt years as well as carefully maintaining the party line against movements of dissent – violent and otherwise – within the Republican majority.

The Spanish Civil War was a testing time for the new paper. De Valera who, as head of government, had played an active and significant part in the councils of the League of Nations, was a strong advocate and supporter of non-intervention in that conflict. One effect of this was that the Saorstát continued to be represented in Spain by a Minister Plenipotentiary accredited to the Republican government: this policy came frequently and violently under attack from a coalition of the main political opposition (Fine Gael), many Irish bishops, and a lay Catholic organisation called the Irish Christian Front. To all of these,

Franco was Spain's saviour from 'atheistic communism' and as such should have the unconditional support of the Irish government and people.

This is not the place to rehearse some of the more tragic and comic episodes of the period, ranging from the fate of several of the Republican volunteers to the story of 'O'Duffy's Brigade' who set out to fight for Franco. But it must be recorded that the *Irish Press* played what was perhaps a crucial role in maintaining popular support for De Valera's consistent refusal to switch diplomatic recognition: this in fact did not take place until the conflict was over, and the Franco regime had gained *de jure* recognition from most western states.

The *Press* was of course supportive of Irish neutrality in World War II, though the practical effect of this support was minimal, since censorship suppressed any opposition to government policy. I do not propose to trace the paper's post-war history except to note two points: at a number of periods in the '50s, '60s and '70s, nobody who cared for good journalism, or who wanted to be fully briefed on current affairs, the arts or sport could afford not to read it. And secondly, it slowly but surely, for good or ill, became less and less recognisably a party organ. General support for Fianna Fáil became at times mildly critical, and later, occasionally, quite strongly so. One occasion when this happened is worth remembering here.

It was some time in the late 1960s when there was a certain amount of social unrest in Dublin, centred mainly on a lack of adequate housing available to those trying to live on very small incomes. Two Catholic priests supported public protests on the matter, one of these being Michael Sweetman, S.J., the other the then editor of *Doctrine and Life*, Austin Flannery, O.P. Two members of the Fianna Fáil government in power made foolishly slighting remarks about Fr Flannery, one of them describing him as 'so called cleric'. To the credit of the editor of the *Irish Press* he criticised the Minister concerned quite bluntly.

But while very many readers were glad to see the paper's party ties being loosened, it was also observed that its radical national ethos was gradually diluted: so that it became difficult to discern it as having any positive identity. The move to make it more 'popular' in competition with imported tabloids failed, I believe, to attract the new readership that was hoped for, while the paper's traditional constituency became sadly disillusioned, tending to defect to other organs or – as sometimes happened in rural areas – to depend solely on radio, television, and local journals...

(July-August 1995, vol. 45, no. 6, pp. 436-439)

Liturgy and integrity

As a fine an example as I can remember of Roman fiddling while all around the flames rise higher, was the decision of the Congregation for the Doctrine of the Faith, recently announced, that two categories of manhood must not be admitted to ordination *viz* alcoholics and (wait for it) coeliacs. And while the first of these exclusions may represent nothing worse than a muddled misunderstanding of a human condition, the second can be seen only as rubricism gone raving mad. The 'thinking' on which it appears to be based resists all sane argumentation: one can only hope and pray that higher and wiser counsels may act to obliterate the ordinance by *fiat*.

All this, mark you, at a time when the Church's life of worship, in word and sacrament, should 'shine before men' so that the beauty of holiness is not clouded over or disfigured by institutional folly. Like the Church itself, liturgy is always in need of purification and clarification, *semper reformanda*. The great Mystery is no more enhanced by mystification than it is by pettifogging trivialities: the aim, as proclaimed by Vatican II, is, or should be, a 'noble simplicity'.

And for a very pertinent reason. Liturgy can be defined and described in several ways: adoration, thanksgiving, intercession, anamnesis, celebration. But one word of special relevance to our time and situation is: communication. This might appear to some as reductionist. Far from it, the communication is of course both vertical and horizontal: the common act of communion is with all creation, but also with creation's Lord.

This at least is what good liturgy tries to be, tries to do. For, like all human activities, liturgy moves between failure and success, but always striving, fuelled by a faith and hope rooted in the promise that where we gather, He will also be. But an incarnational faith must recognise the human limitations to the efficacy of the *opus operatum*.

I am fond of quoting the Irish saying: *D'ordaigh Dia cúnamh*. Indeed God does command, demand our assistance, not least when we meet specifically in his name. And that assistance must involve all our talents, all our insights, all our skills, personal and social – remembering that these are his gifts, given for our use and grateful return.

The Eucharistic Liturgy, in particular, needs to be celebrated in such a way that it is, clearly, a celebration. And celebrating, on every level, is something that should not be left to, on the one hand, formulaic performance – the kind that earns the description 'empty ritual' – or, at the other extreme, a reliance on the mood of the moment: just as structures are necessary but not of themselves sufficient, neither should we depend on spontaneity however desirable. Slipshod informality is just as deplorable as formalism.

Indeed form itself is as necessary to matter as the body is to the soul. The two are in fact inseparable, not least in liturgical celebration where sign is of the essence, and where the sacramental sign makes present what it signifies. Thus, it does matter that the eucharistic bread is a credible piece of food, in a way the average 'host' is not, and this is immeasurably more important than the kind of flour that goes into its baking. It does matter that the central account of Christ's breaking of bread should be matched by a meaningful action – rather than by a recourse to the tabernacle, which signifies nothing so much as getting something from the larder or the fridge for guests who were not expected or catered for.

Again it does matter that the invitation to all 'to take and drink' should not be ignored, as it nearly always is. I have heard it suggested as a 'reason' for denying the Cup to the people that to grant it 'would weaken their faith in God's presence, body and blood, in each kind'. This of course is not the point. Jesus, apparently, thought it right to offer us the double sign: it would be near blasphemous not to accept it.

Of course, whether admitted or not, the real reason for confining Communion to the Bread is one of inconvenience. This hardly needs to be spelt out. I would only suggest that, where numbers are a real 'problem' (we should be so lucky!), the availability of lay ministers provides an obvious solution in the vast majority of cases.

...

Modes of eucharistic participation, while at the heart of the matter, are far from being the only area of liturgical concern, by impoverishment or distortion of the sacramental sign. We too easily forget that the ministry of the Word has a sacramental dimension also, and that this is often seriously diminished in practice.

There are a number of aspects to this of which the most notorious, is, rightly or wrongly, the composition and delivery of the Homily. On which, readers will be happy to hear, I do not propose to pronounce – at this point in time, as they say! But before describing the dimensions of the splinter in the preacher's eye, any of us who, regularly or occasionally, may read the first or second lesson, might well consider the sizeable block in our own. And we might profitably recognise that reading, no less than preaching, should not be attempted off the cuff. Both Old and New Testament texts demand a minimum of study beforehand, if for no other reason than that both canons boast a remarkable variety of material, in style as well as in content. History, prophecy, poetry, pastoral instruction, meditation, each needs to be placed in context – at least in the reader's mind – and presented with due regard to its distinct function and impact.

The American usage, now becoming common over here, by which contributors to public discourse are invited to 'share' their opinions or insights, is one of which I am personally not enamoured. But I must admit it has a certain appropriateness in relation to liturgical reading – with echoes perhaps of the Reformed phrase 'dividing the Word' – for it does emphasise communication. I often wonder what the visitor from Mars would make of what goes on in so many of our churches: somebody 'up there' reading, apparently for his own personal information or edification, since nobody in the assembly appears to be listening – they're all engaged in a personal reading from their 'missalettes'. Once again, *opus operatum* at its most pointless.

I strongly suspect that the problem is rooted in a lack of any real conviction that proclaiming God's word is of the same order of importance as the 'administration' of any sacrament. Hence the ministry concerned is undervalued and, subconsciously perhaps, relegated to the role of 'optional extra'. Indeed the very word 'proclamation' is hardly ever used, perhaps because it seems to have a ring of rhetoric.

A session of regular scripture study, with particular emphasis on the appointed liturgical passages, would surely be of immense value to both pastor and readers. To place this on, say, a weekly basis might seem to overload an already busy parochial schedule. But I am convinced that it is of sufficient importance to be given priority over other activities, in which the pastor's personal involvement may not be of the essence.

...

A funeral Mass, at which I was very recently present, was notable for the fact that most of the singing was of plainchant, rendered by members of the Palestrina Choir from Dublin's Pro-Cathedral of Saint Mary. This was arranged by the family of the man whose life and death we gathered to celebrate. During the Mass, I was made happily aware that a proportion, at least, of the very large congregation were glad to join in the singing, and I am certain that this was no mere exercise in nostalgia. Rather, in my own case and I believe many others, it was a recognition of the unique quality of Gregorian chant, an almost perfect expression of the 'beauty of holiness'.

There is no doubt in my mind that we will be cursed by future generation for our impious philistinism, if we continue to neglect these riches which it has been our good fortune to inherit. 'Neglect' is indeed far too weak a word for this collective sin of omission.

And let us not blame Vatican II and the long-overdue introduction of the vernacular. As long as I can remember, few of us had much opportunity of singing or even hearing the chant in the liturgical context for which it was designed. A few monasteries and friaries, a very few cathedrals, a number of scattered parishes and other churches where an enthusiast was in a position to do something about it – apart from these, a plainsong Mass was hardly more common then than now.

Undoubtedly, vernacularisation has had an adverse effect on the situation, but almost by accident. For the 'either/or' mentality, which seems endemic among Catholic, in this country anyway, saw to it that the arrival of English and Irish meant the disappearance of Latin. This was not the Council's intention – most certainly not as far as music was concerned. And it is sadly ironic that conciliar encouragement of congregational liturgical singing, more effective perhaps than ever before, should have coincided with the new linguistic totalitarianism. It is to me a bitter reminder of the popular abandonment of the Irish language in the last century, mistakenly seen as a necessary concomitant to learning English.

Music in the old Latin tradition, both plainsong and polyphony is truly 'part of what we are' and have been. It must be allowed to live and flourish, alongside new vernacular settings of comparable quality: so far, only a very few contemporary works merit consideration. And there is no shortage of second- and third-rate material, including a plethora of new hymns in English which for sheer awfulness rival the worst of Victoriana. Irish (language) congregations are much more fortunate ...

...

In seeking to respond to the problems and challenges which beset the Catholic Church in Ireland, I am convinced that we must resist the temptation to take refuge in a shallow and adventitious 'relevance', and take a hard look at fundamentals. When the Soviet Union faced its moment of truth some few years ago, a major project for reform and renewal was proposed, offering two major strategies, *glasnost* and *perestroika*, openness and restructuring. It came too late.

Perhaps the Church could do worse than explore the potential of these two ideas. Nationally, but especially internationally, difficulties – some long brewing, others of recent development – in the whole area of authority, signal an urgent need for new structures. These involve a very wide range of ecclesiology, from hierarchy, subsidiarity and collegiality to the whole clerical fabric, which has become so generally regarded as inseparable from the concept and exercise of ministry that its replacement may appear unthinkable.

But *glasnost* may well be of greater and more urgent importance. Translated as 'transparency' it has recently become one of the buzz-words of Irish politics, and, though often reduced to a mere slogan, it does reflect a genuine *desideratum* of Irish society. And of course the Church's troubles over the past couple of years have, perhaps inevitably, triggered off a demand for something similar, particularly as between hierarchy and people. A number of inept cases of 'news management' or mismanagement, have added fuel to this demand. There are indications that some lessons have been learned, some new skills acquired, and, most important of all, some recognition that concealment begets gossip begets scandal begets 'revelations', whose impact would have been much milder had the initial concealment never taken place.

I do not however suggest *glasnost* as a politic ecclesiastical strategy, but as an essential dimension of the Church's communication with the world, for which another name is 'Mission'.

And at the core of Mission, evangelical outreach must be rooted in an evangelical sacramental witness, borne by and in the Church's own life. The Church is the Sacrament of Christ, a sign whose meaning must be always open to the world.

This is why liturgical integrity is of the essence. Christianity is not a mystery cult, and the Christian assembly meets to share the bread of life with and for the world. It is here that the sacred and the secular join and communicate, where flesh and spirit may hope to be reconciled, as they were and are in the man who is Christ. We must take care not to cloud that hope.

(November 1995, vol. 45, no. 9, pp. 624-629)

1996

Ecce sacerdos

A friend reminded me recently of a remark I had made some years ago about the late, great Cosslett Quin [died 6 December 1995], to the effect that he was 'a wonderful combination of sinew and warmth'. I had completely forgotten saying this, but I'm proud that I did.

Born in Antrim in 1907, a graduate of Dublin University, he was ordained to the priesthood in the Church of Ireland and served for many years in parishes, rural and urban, in four provinces: his final pastoral appointment was as rector of Dunganstown, Co. Wicklow, where he was buried early last month, following a service in St Patrick's Cathedral. The address was given by his Methodist friend, Risteard Ó Glaisne, and the final prayers were led by Archbishop Donald Caird.

Ó Glaisne has speculated on what might have been a quite outstanding academic career, if Cosslett (as we all knew him) had not followed his pastoral vocation so devotedly. He was in fact sometime Professor of Biblical Greek in TCD, but it was as a theologian of considerable scholarship and originality that one might envisage him as making a signal contribution to contemporary Christian thought. Indeed such a contribution was there in embryo, in remarkable essays on the Eucharist and on Christian living – as well as in his work as a biblical translator.

In the whole art of translation, both secular and religious, his gifts were quite outstanding, in a range of works from Latin, French, Spanish and German originals. He introduced aspects of the Gaelic literary tradition to a wider audience: he was perhaps at his best when translation was supplemented by highly perceptive critical comment – as in his work on Brian Merriman. And he was, I think, among the first, if not the very first, to bring Seán Ó Ríordáin's work to the notice of English readers – ironically, through the medium of an English Jesuit publication.

His own sympathetic awareness and appreciation of the Gaelic tradition were very much in the manner of his immediate predecessors among Ulster Protestants, who recognised and accepted the significance of Douglas Hyde's invitation to share in what should and could be seen as the common intellectual and aesthetic inheritance of all Irish people. Like Hyde he applied himself to the living language, which in his youth was still spoken in some part of each of the nine counties of Ulster and we are all indebted to his work in this area. But, again like Hyde, for him the written and oral traditions were all part of one seamless garment.

But of course he was also one of those who in every generation have given the lie to the accusation of 'insularity' too often cast at those devoted to the cultivation of the Gaelic language and culture. To him Irish was a window on Europe and the world, and his conversation bore constant witness to the fact that this was a window rarely closed or even curtained.

And it was in his conversation that both 'sinew' and 'warmth' were so apparent. He was never vague or woolly in his opinions or his judgements. Anything less like the 'muscular Christian' of legend it would be hard to imagine, but there was a splendid intellectual toughness in everything he said and wrote.

But there was also the warmth of the true humanist, a warmth which embraced all those many men and women, of all sorts and conditions, who had inspired him and whom he admired – living and dead. And among the living, how many of us did he inspire: how many of us sought to repay him with our admiration and our love! Doreen, with his daughter and his sons, must know this, and know too that in some way we share their loss, and the joy he brought them and us.

Solas Chríosta ar a chroí is a aigne feasta.

(January 1996, vol. 46, no. 1, pp. 42-43)

Damian Byrne, O.P.[1]

It would be difficult to imagine a greater contrast in the style and performance of their ministry than the two Irishmen who came to lead the Dominican family worldwide in the past half-century. Michael Browne was the very type and figure of a senior religious superior at the end of the Tridentine era. His very considerable theological and philosophical scholarship were firmly in the scholastic mode: his understanding of religious discipline was equally firmly fixed in a traditional reading of rule and constitutions, and in a profound sense of loyalty to the Holy See.

1. Master of the Order of Preachers, 1983-1992. Born in Galway in 1929, Fr Damian had served in Argentina, in Trinidad and Tobago and in Mexico before being elected Provincial of Ireland in 1977. Died 18 February 1996.

Damian Byrne whom we now mourn would not count himself a scholar. But his great pastoral experience in Latin America and the West Indies, as well as in Ireland, provided a unique base for his achievement in securing the unity in diversity of the Order, at a time of radical change and challenge. His work on his return to Ireland was equally crucial in offering guidance and leadership, over a wide range of missionary experience, to the men and woman whom he served as secretary general to C.O.R.I. He too was a man of his time, and a huge loss to the Irish Church. *Requiescat.*

(March 1996, vol. 46, no. 3, p. 184)

Coping with divorce

Now that the result of the divorce Referendum has been confirmed, following Des Hanafins's quixotic appeal to the Supreme Court to have it overturned, the time has come for urgent detailed thinking on the issue. The government's Divorce Bill, drafted to implement the constitutional amendments, has been published; but this should not be regarded as heralding a final, formal ending of what has been a lengthy procedure. It is in fact essential that an informed, non-partisan debate on several crucial issues should now take place.

And this debate, while it will of course be conducted in the Dáil and the Seanad, must not be left to the political parties. Public opinion must make itself felt now as perhaps never before since the amendment was first mooted: I don't mean the kind of populist expression which masquerades under, on the one hand, 'traditional', 'Christian' banners, or alternatively, 'liberal' and 'progressive' labels. I rather urge a process of consultation, not just with 'interested' bodies, but with groups and individuals whose experience of hard cases might, against the received wisdom, help us to improve bad, or even fair-to-middling law.

In saying this I do not want to imply that those charged with drafting the Bill – or such amendments as the Opposition may have prepared – will have done their work *in vacuo*. Consultations will undoubtedly have taken place, and I am sure that such a conscientiously fair-minded and concerned minister as Mervyn Taylor will have seen to it that these consultations should be as far-reaching as appeared appropriate.

But 'appropriateness' may have its limitations, and I should like to see a genuinely popular movement of opinion – stimulated by the Churches, the women's movement, the I.S.P.C.C., Combat Poverty, marriage guidance and mediation groups, and other concerned bodies – on a range of very pertinent questions...

...

We have already had a salutary example of the fallibility of parliament in the matter of governmental funding of the 'Yes' campaign during the Referendum itself. I remember at the time arguing that this was a rather dicey proceeding: the fact that it had the support of Dáil parties (on both sides of the House) was not sufficient to legitimise it. The referendum was a matter closely touching the Constitution, which belongs to the people, not to the Oireachtas. Other democracies may be built on a doctrine of parliamentary sovereignty; ours is not.

My reservations were subsequently justified by Patricia McKenna's successful Court action. I hope that the implications of the judicial decision on that occasion, which extend far beyond the matter then in question, will serve to remind our parliamentarians that they are guardians, not proprietors of our constitutional rights. Which does not mean that the Dáil and Seanad are the only forum where the detailed consequences of these rights should be discussed before being enshrined in law. But it is highly desirable, indeed vital, that such discussion should be based on the realities of the human situation, here and now, as well as on considerations of social polity and moral principle.

It would be dangerous to neglect these considerations. Marriage and its ending are matters of more than personal or family concern. And, for Christians especially, the larger social aspect cannot be neglected with impunity, if only for the sake of the individual relationship. 'My' happiness, 'my' fulfilment, can never be self-sufficient or self-justifying goals. This is not a dogmatic imposition: experience shows that to deny or ignore it just doesn't work.

Having said this, we must of course immediately agree that marriage is or should be about fulfilment, and the pursuit of mutual happiness – if not its attainment. To deny or belittle this is to revert to the worst kinds of pseudo-scholastic moralising, with its emphasis on procreation as the 'primary' end – or worse, on a purely legalistic contractual view of the marriage relationship in which the act of love is reduced to the payment of the 'marriage debt'!

And so, when fulfilment eludes the partners – or one of them – and that elusive thing, happiness, is palpably absent; when in short, what we call irretrievable breakdown has taken place or appears inevitable; when living together, in almost any sense of that word, has become practically intolerable; then the larger social context appears to be a less than compelling reason for maintaining the relationship.

Christians, including Roman Catholics, have long come to accept this, however reluctantly. 'Separation' in its various forms has become an accepted if unwelcome fact of life. But of course the Catholic position remains that separation, even if it's called divorce *a mensa et thoro*, does not allow for a second chance: the marriage is still a legal and moral fact – unless of course annulment procedures are seen to find that it never existed in the first place ...

...

An increasing number of young men and women all over Ireland, but especially perhaps in Dublin and other large centres, are tending to postpone marriage indefinitely, and this is not confined to those who have no wish to bear or rear children. The word 'partner' is becoming more and more common as the ordinary generic name for the man or woman with whom one 'settles down'. I am not suggesting that marriage has yet reached the stage of being a minority option, but it is certainly no longer taken for granted as the norm. And, in urban society at any rate, this situation seems to transcend most class and cultural differences. Neither does there yet appear to be any significant reverse in the trend.

So, it would appear that even without the impending problems arising from the legalisation of divorce, the institution of marriage is not quite the bulwark of Irish society that it so long seemed. In fact the availability of second marriages may possibly concentrate the minds of all concerned in a way which has not taken place over the past quarter-century of social and cultural upheaval. If Christian leadership faces the facts of the present unstable situation, we may see a new, more honest and healthier appraisal of what sex, human love and marriage mean and could mean to Irish society, as we approach the second millennium.

A certain honesty and frankness of approach have already been forced on us by way of the unveiling of an underworld of abuse and perversion which have subsisted just below the surface of 'conventional life'. It is of course sad to think that this has been brought about only at the cost of human suffering on a scale that we are only slowly coming to measure. It is also sad, and indeed shameful, to have to admit that the stripping away of layers of self-deception, hypocrisy and institutional deceit has owed little to specifically Christian or Catholic initiative,

We have heard much in recent times of the desirability, indeed the urgent need, of involving the ordinary faithful in the active life of the Church. This should not be seen as any mere process of organisational reform, of 'democratisation', even ecclesiastical *glasnost*, desirable though these be. What is basically at stake is the fundamental matter of mission, of translating the gospel into personal and social reality in our society at this time. And this means that we join – all of us, ordained and unordained – in taking a hard look at law and practice, at principles and policies in the light of Christ's testament of love.

One would need to be blind, deaf, or invincibly stupid not to recognise that Christianity is in crisis in the Ireland of today: not just in the erosion of our Christian culture, not just in the declining power and influence of Church authority, but in the faith of the people. And those whose faith remains are finding it increasingly difficult to communicate their convictions and commitment to those who have 'lost' it. Even the common language of inherited assumptions seems to have slipped out of use.

It is to a great extent, though by no means completely, a matter of generation. And the lack of a common inter-generational discourse is perhaps currently most evident in relation to the whole area of sexuality. There is, you may say, little new in this: parents and children have always been notoriously ill at ease in discussing such matters, and the problem has often been aggravated by a variety of cultural tabus. But I would argue that the present communication block is different in kind, not just in degree, from past difficulties: indeed the generational aspect seems almost accidental to what is basically a clash of cultures with little in the way of common ground.

I have personally little doubt that one of the crucial factors – perhaps the essential one – in bringing about this state of affairs is the contraceptive revolution. I am also convinced that in 1968 the Catholic Church, as so often before, missed a golden opportunity to provide an ethic, and promote a discipline, in the use of the new facilities, based on a vision of sexual activity which, while open to the creation of new life, and eschewing self-centred gratification, would seek to find a reconciliation of individual love and social commitment.

But that was nearly thirty years ago and today we have to respond to today's challenges. It is, I think, important that we do not identify Christian faith with a 'narrow' morality – in the sense of a code of behaviour such as befits members of the Christian club. Rather is it vital that the new evangelisation which our society so sorely needs should point to the Christian way as leading to a full life as Jesus himself taught. It is only within such a life, nourished by prayer and sacramental encounter, that our human nature, and not least our sexual nature, can find fulfilment.

I don't believe that it's impossible to convince the new generations of our people that this message is at the core of a fully human future. Clearly many seem to be quite happy, at least in the short term, without any reference to spiritual ideas, But those who do accept such ideas are often willing also to accept that they may have a positive bearing on how they should live. Unfortunately, the ideas are often second-hand, ill-digested versions of non-Christian philosophies. Their 'exotic' origin does not of course discount their value: there are many roads to truth. But why have we failed to gain acceptance for the riches of the Christian gospel and the Christian heritage?

It is not a matter of offering a soft diluted version of Christ's message. Even the youngest among us cannot live long in ignorance or doubt about the fact of evil in our world: sin, pain and death are ever-present realities. But we believe that He has conquered these by his life and rising: we believe he is with us in his Spirit till the world ends. He offers us life, and we must share it.

(July-August 1996, vol. 46, no. 6, pp. 362-368)

Pioneers

The remarkable contribution of Edmund Ignatius Rice to the Christian apostolate of education is being duly, if somewhat belatedly, recognised in Rome this month. But it would be nothing short of tragic if his equally significant role at a crucial moment in the making of modern Ireland were to be ignored or undervalued.

It might appear that there's little danger of this happening and undoubtedly there will be no shortage of rhetorical panegyrics of what Rice and the 'good Brothers' have done over a period of nearly two centuries. We may take it, however, that the rhetoric will be less fulsome and the panegyrics less wholehearted than they would have been if the beatification had taken place thirty or forty years ago. And none the worse for that, you may say: the 'praise of famous men' gains rather than loses from being based on a sober assessment of their lives and works.

Unfortunately, in the climate of the present time, the prevailing view of the place of the Church in education is less favourable than one might wish to such assessment. I sincerely hope that I'm over-pessimistic, and that a month from now we will have gained a new and generous, but balanced and unblinkered, appreciation of what Edmund Rice and his followers have done for us. But I doubt it.

Criticism of the Christian Brothers and their schools is indeed nothing new. Some of it arose from the pathetic snobbery of twopence looking down on three-ha'pence. There have been allegations of a narrow nationalism, even to the point of inculcating a positive hatred of the English. There may have been grounds for this abuse of the class-room: if so it must have, in the nature of things, been confined to certain periods and places – which of course would not make it less reprehensible. I can only say that I never came across it myself, except in the case of one teacher – and he was a layman.

Much more serious are accusations of other kinds of abuse, mainly relating to class-room cruelty, some of it deserving the epithet 'sadism'. Again, where this occurred it must be unreservedly condemned, but it was by no means confined to the C.B.S. – some diocesan schools ('minor seminaries') and other educational establishments, religious and secular, have been equally to blame.

And let us frankly admit that out-and-out disapproval of corporal punishment of the young, and of other institutional cruelties suffered by children is something quite new in Ireland, as elsewhere. The culture of the birch, stick or 'leather' prevailed until very recently.

More serious still, of course, is the matter of direct sexual abuse. This has inevitably been mainly alleged in relation to residential institutions, ranging from élitist public schools in the

English tradition via their Catholic imitators, to orphanages and 'industrial schools'. Once again, it would be unjust to single out the Brothers: one can only hope that the new *glasnost* in these matters would deter those inclined to such crimes. But where harm has been done it cannot or must not be lightly passed over: the effects can be incalculable.

In so far as the victims of fanaticism, uncontrolled temper, frustration or outright perversion may condemn the Christian Brothers, or any other teaching community, they must be heard and heeded. But frankly, I must say that a great deal of contemporary disparagement of such communities is a mere rehearsal of fashionable prejudice, and sadly lacking in any recognition of the positive side of the story.

Indeed my own remarks so far may seem to be less than positive. So let me say without equivocation that were it not for the work of Edmund Rice, Nano Nagle and Catherine McAuley, the fate of the Irish poor in the years of the great population explosion, 1770-1845, would have been unthinkably appalling, with equally ghastly consequences for the post-famine generations. It is no exaggeration to state that, while their best efforts were limited by considerations of human and financial resources, as well as by time and place, theirs was the crucial intervention, in the fields of both teaching and the care of the sick, that made the difference between the bottom rung of the human ladder and utter bestial degradation.

Edmund Rice died on the eve of the great famine, but his work was already placed on a solid basis, so that it could continue in the 1850s and throughout the following decades. It is indeed darkly ironic that the Brothers' mission was made somewhat easier by the awful purge of those at the bottom of the social pyramid, brought about by mass starvation, disease, and of course emigration. Although the latter factor opened new missionary challenges to which the Brothers were not slow to respond.

I have long regarded the epic work of both Sisters and Brothers as a shining exemplar of the Church's ongoing mission to and in society. This may be summed up, rather crudely I admit, as: see a need that is not being served; go in and serve it without stint; and, when society as a whole can and will take over the work, get out and move on to the next need. The last part is of course the most difficult, especially when a vested interest has been built. And by 'vested interest', I don't mean something selfish or

sinister: the investment of years, perhaps many decades of labour, must produce such an interest. Abandoning it may not
merely be painful but may appear unjust and even irresponsible.
But the problem has to be faced.

In the case of Irish schools and hospitals, 'moving on' might
appear especially wrong and unfair since the Irish state was for so
long all too willing to 'leave it to the Brothers and Sisters', making
use of them in a manner which bordered on exploitation, while
loudly proclaiming the 'debt of gratitude' due to them. And now
that a range of new attitudes and policies have taken over, the
debt is unlikely to be paid ... Perhaps a further irony may be seen
in the fact that moving on has become easier, and perhaps
inevitable, by the decline in 'vocations', across the board.

Which is not to suggest that there need be or should be a total
abandonment of either education or sick-care. However effi-
cient or enlightened the intervention of the state, or of subsidiary
social institutions in these fields, religious communities have still
much to contribute, not least in training and orientation. Indeed
the maintenance and future inculcation of a holistic approach in
both fields of activity is vital, and is very much in the spirit and
tradition of the founders of these works.

Let me also say this in relation to Edmund Rice. It is easy to
forget that the work he pioneered was initially a lay enterprise
fuelled by lay resources, mainly those accumulated by his own
very 'secular' activities. To stress this is not to undervalue the
specifically religious aims and ethos of the organisation he
founded, but rather that it was an independent growth within the
Church. (And its relations with the Irish bishops were not always
easy.)

I would add that the Brothers' role in Irish education continued in importance long after their pioneering days. When they
moved into secondary teaching, they set in motion a process
which liberated hundreds of the intelligent children of the less
well-off from the prison of social immobility, and continued to do
so for nearly a hundred years.

Sé do bheatha, a Éamoinn bheannaithe!

(October 1996, vol. 46, no. 8, pp. 483-486)

Alternatives to jungle justice

'Catholic social teaching is the Vatican's best-kept secret ... ' I
forget who said it first, but the phrase has been often quoted by

way of reassurance that the Church has strong views on matters other than sex. In fact, it makes little sense to those of us who grew up in the pre-war or even pre-Vatican II Ireland. *Quadragesimo Anno* (1931) which was Pius XI's contribution to the subject, was more than a confirmation of Leo XIII's pioneering *Rerum Novarum* (1891): the onset of the Great Depression, of Soviet Communism and Italian Fascism provided a context which gave a timely significance to what seemed to be a 'middle way' forward. Its relevance, of course, hardly extended beyond what we later came to call the First World: concerns for justice further afield, not to speak of 'liberation' – political or social – belonged to the future.

In this country, the corpus of papal teaching in both encyclicals, especially that of Pius, was translated into school text-books, into lectures and sermons given by the more 'socially conscious' clergy, and into the proceedings of a small but influential range of 'social' weeks and weekends, where the implications of the teaching were expounded and discussed. On the organisational level, the most popular articulation of the spirit – if not of the letter (mainly urban-directed) – of the encyclicals was the movement for rural renewal *Muintir na Tíre*.

During the war years, what little there was of forward thinking and planning continued to follow Catholic social guidelines. The trade union movement was sadly divided and, indeed, with a later corresponding division in political Labour, the split became represented in some quarters as one between those loyal to Catholic teaching and Marxist sympathisers. This interpretation was not discouraged in certain quarters that should have known better, and became the received wisdom of the *Standard*, then a lively Catholic weekly paper which, in fairness, had some positive attitudes also.

What was at the time seen as a serious attempt to bring Catholic principles to bear in a radical way on the structures of Irish society in the 1940s was the setting up of a government commission to consider the possibilities and problems of socio-economic reorganisation on 'vocational' lines. The choice of the Bishop of Galway, Michael Browne, as chairman of the commission was itself indicative of the thinking behind this development, although some of its members were more than a little doubtful of the direction to which that thinking pointed. The words 'corporatism', and even 'corporate state' were, it was suggested, the logical objectives to which vocationalism might be directed, and, even in neutral Ireland, neither Mussolini's Italy nor Franco's Spain, both corporatist in ideology, recommended themselves as models of society, Christian or otherwise.

In the event, the report of the commission duly presented to the government (1943) remained a dead letter. As did (though for quite different reasons) a more modest and less controversial proposal for national social insurance, presented by another bishop, Dr Dignan of Clonfert, then chairman of the National Health Insurance Society (1944). Perhaps the only positive response by government to all the ideas and ideals which Catholic teaching had produced were the eventual introduction of 'children's allowances' as a small practical recognition of the family as 'the basic unit of society'.

Looking back on those years. I think I would be right in saying that while the many positive features of both *Rerum Novarum* and *Quadragesimo Anno* did awaken many Catholics to the importance of social justice and emphasised its centrality to the apostolate, their practical influence on Irish political thinking remained marginal. And indeed it was probably the most negative aspects of their teaching which impinged on the public consciousness – condemnation of socialism and the like. It was also unfortunate that the valuable idea of subsidiarity, erected into an immutable principle, became a barrier against state intervention, however desirable.

In fact the very word 'state', at least in a socio-economic context, was regarded askance. Hilaire Belloc's *Slave State* became a primary source for many of this way of thinking, and was a convenient weapon with which to snipe at 'godless' socialism, particularly at a time when even the most democratic of socialists were doctrinaire nationalists.

But as things turned out, the demonising of state intervention and state control was the rock on which aggressive Catholic social doctrine perished. This was the doctrine on the basis of which Noel Browne and his health schemes were attacked and condemned, with the full solemnity of an Irish Catholic bishop's *pronunciamento.* As we all know now, the actual story is full of political and bureaucratic ambiguities. But the near-universal popular perception of what happened was that of an unholy alliance of Church, medical profession and conservative politicians: Noel Browne was cast as the scapegoat – hero – and there was no shortage of villains. But when it was all over, and the dust of conflict had settled, we were left with a distinct and widespread feeling that the bishops had finally gone too far, as had the secular authority in accepting their judgement.

I am personally convinced that this was the beginning of the end of Irish Catholic triumphalism, although the last Hurrah! wasn't sounded until the end of the Patrician year, on the very eve of Vatican II. Catholic social teaching suffered a near-complete, if temporary, eclipse: its reappearance, changed apparently beyond recognition, had to await the new era of 'The Church in the Modern World' and the great encyclical of Paul VI, *Populorum Progressio* (1967)

I say this in full awareness of the truly epoch-making *Mater et Magistra* (1961) and *Pacem in Terris* (1963) which were the legacy of John XXIII. The first of these, as has often been remarked, internationalised the social teaching of the Church, and this extension of Christian concern invoked the human solidarity of 'all people of good will' in Pope John's great charter of human rights (as articulated by the United Nations), issued in the year of his death. But it took the Council to open the Church's eyes and ears and mind to a new vision of *shalom.*

'The new name for peace is development.' This perhaps has been the most enduring idea deriving from *Populorum Progressio.* Even though the word 'development' itself has become somewhat problematic, the basic imperative of the encyclical still holds: that the disparity between rich and poor nations must be addressed by placing the superfluous wealth of the former at the service of the latter – the alternative being violent revolution. And in Pope Paul's 'call to action' in *Octogesima Adveniens* – issued in 1971 for the eightieth anniversary of *Rerum Novarum* – he urges Christian people everywhere to analyse injustices in their own countries 'in the light of the Gospel' and proceed to act as the situation demands, rather than expect a papal blueprint to suit all circumstances.

All this was new and refreshing, and seemed to reflect the conciliar vision. If that vision appears to many of us to have faded, this is certainly not for lack of prophetic action, especially in the Southern half of the world where the 'option for the poor' has been vigorously pursued.

This biblical concept, by the way, seems to have been first institutionalised at the Medellin conference of 1968. It was confirmed as a principle by the present pope in his own first social encyclical *Laborem Exercens* in 1981 – followed by *Sollicitudo Rei Socialis* in 1987, and, in yet another commemoration of *Rerum Novarum* – this time the centenary – *Centesimus Annus*, 1991.

Pope John Paul's social thinking has, it would appear, been undergoing a certain process of evolution responding to the changing international scene. His early understandable preoccupation with Marxism has given way to a no less critical reaction to unbridled capitalism and the evil of market-worship, and he has followed Paul VI's condemnation of the exploitation of the South by the North. It is also noteworthy that he has given his blessing to the idea of 'structures of sin' (in *Sollicitudo*) – a phrase whose social implications were seen by some as an abnegation of personal responsibility: very properly he sees these structures as rooted in personal sin, and equally demanding of conversion.

All in all, it is clear that today's 'social teaching' has come a long way since 1891, and not all of it would immediately recommend itself to Leo XIII or Pius XI. And there are features of the two early encyclicals which would raise eyebrows – not to say hackles – today. The notion of 'frugal comfort' (which, incidentally, was taken up with some approval by certain Irish statesmen!) is not one which would be chosen as a rallying-cry by the socially active nowadays, though we must remember that it once represented a considerable improvement on the lot of the poor in most countries, if not all. (And still would, alas.) And 'Socialism' is no longer a word deemed offensive to pious ears ...

Still, it would be foolishly unhistorical, as well as ungracious, to belittle those early expressions of the Christian imperative of social justice, or to fail to recognise their seminal influence. As we look at the international horizon in these final years of the second millennium, there is little enough for our comfort, even in 'Christian lands', and there would be far less were it not for the continuing efforts made by those Christian leaders who have set about the awakening of the social conscience, in the Churches as well as outside.

In this country the renewal of social thinking was marked in 1977 by a joint pastoral, *The Work of Justice*, issued by the bishops to commemorate the tenth anniversary of *Populorum Progressio*. Three years later, there appeared a second document whose title speaks for itself: *Christian Faith in a Time of Economic Depression*. And this in turn led to a further initiative involving a procedure of consultation, unprecedented, I believe, in the Irish Church.

This entailed a series of 'listening days' held at various centres throughout the country – during which representatives of the bishops met representatives of a wide range of socio-economic interests: trades unions, employers' groups, the unemployed, farmers and so on. The value of such a process towards preparing an adequate response to the social situation is Ireland can hardly be exaggerated, and its symbolic importance does not need to be stressed. A discussion document based on the consultations was issued in 1990, and two years later saw the publication of the pastoral letter itself, *Work Is the Key*.

Another process of consultation and discussion has been inaugurated by the Taoiseach, Mr Bruton, as a preliminary to drawing up a successor to the *Programme for Competitiveness and Work*, including, for the first time, a fourth participating party 'representing the unemployed, women, the underprivileged and youth'. A submission on behalf of the 'fourth party' was made by one group involved, our old friends from the Justice Desk of the Conference of Religious of Ireland. CORI have been the most consistently vocal, informed, and active of all Church groups campaigning for social justice, and the most innovative in exploring and proposing new approaches on behalf of the poor and excluded of our society ...

The constant incantation of the words 'job creation' to which employers and employed are both addicted as to a mystic mantra, conceals the unpleasant fact that the equation 'work = jobs' is no longer universally valid.

The 'job for life' is rapidly becoming a memory of other days – except, that is, among a tiny privileged section of the work force, especially in the higher bureaucracy. The unstable character, not alone of the economic context in which we live, but also of our socio-cultural environment, cannot be ignored. Its effects are all too plain in a whole spectrum of situations, from family relationships to sexual 'partnerships' to religious vocations. And an employment policy which relies heavily on foreign industrial (or 'services') enterprises and investment is, as sad experience continues to show, a very frail foundation on which to develop an economy.

In such circumstances the CORI plan centred on a guaranteed minimum income for all, with appropriate tax adjustments for those who are owners or earners, seems to be one of the few current economic proposals to make sense. Sooner or later

something of this kind is the only alternative to jungle 'justice'.
Why not sooner than later?

(November 1996, vol. 46, no. 9, pp. 548-554)

Michael Sweetman, S.J.

Sad news: the death [23 October 1996] of the great and good
Michael Sweetman, S.J. In the early 1960s, when our economic
miracle produced a rising tide which left many boats grounded,
he gave of his remarkable talents and energies in the service of
Dublin's homeless poor. Along with our own Austin Flannery he
helped to disturb the false 'peace' which hung like an evil cloud
of unknowing over the city's housing scandal. Both priests were
criticised in high places for what they did, but their work was
honoured by their collaborators – Christian, communist, or
both – and by all those who may never have known them, but
whose lives they touched and in some way redeemed.

More recently, Michael Sweetman continued his work for the
homeless with a special focus on our street children. He was one
of the founders of the Los Angeles Society: in this and other ways
he has been one of the first exemplars of the 'new' Jesuit
apostolate. Nor did age wither his commitment. *Euge, pastor bone!*

(November 1996, vol. 46, no. 9, pp. 554)

Something borrowed

'The Church must learn from democracy,' said the Bishop of
Kerry in a recent address, 'just as in the past it borrowed from
societies with imperial, royal or feudal systems.'

He might have added that many of these former borrowings
became so much part of the Church's life that the fact that they
were borrowings was soon forgotten, and some were – and are –
treated with the reverence due (as the Catechism used to tell us)
to all holy things. And I don't just mean the ritual acts and
gestures which became part of liturgical practice – most of
which, though not all, were gently removed or allowed to lapse
after Vatican II – nor even the secular titles and ceremonies,
most of which have fallen into disuse, though some linger on.
Forms of address such as 'Your Grace' and 'Your Lordship' are
rarely heard nowadays, nor is the kissing of rings the normal way
of saluting our fathers in God, but the remarkable thing is how
long they persisted even in democratic societies. Some of us will
remember how, in the summer of the Patrician Year 1961, a Lord

Mayor of Dublin who was a member of the Church of Ireland so greeted the Cardinal Legate, to the scandal of some but to widespread approval. And of course his own Church, as in the Anglican Communion generally, also retained feudal titles.

More serious than any of that, however, is the way in which 'imperial, royal or feudal systems' were adopted, whether consciously or by infection, to become the very structural framework of the institutional Church. It would be very difficult to find warrant in either Scripture or early tradition for the hierarchical, legislative, disciplinary or even ministerial arrangements which have become part of the very fabric of the Church, east or west. It was of course inevitable that the Christian faith should have taken on the integument of the cultures in which it flourished: indeed we may see it as providential that the Roman empire, and the political entities which succeeded it, became the vehicles through which the gospel came to be preached 'throughout the whole world'.

But while faith and culture may be inseparable, it is essential that they be rigorously distinguished. To say that this has not always happened is an understatement, and the ensuing confusion of secular with sacred has been responsible for many of the accretions and distortions which have disfigured Church organisation and practice – not excluding liturgical practice – over the centuries. One serious consequence of this has been the misunderstanding and condemnation of ideas and activities regarded as heretical or even blasphemous, simply because they were culturally different from what was seen as the norm.

Even more serious has been the clericalising and professionalising of the ordained ministry. The roots of this are clear to be seen in the structures of imperialism, and in post-imperial regimes in which the clerics played an important role. The ambiguity of the word 'clerical' in common discourse today bears witness to these origins. And, as I have suggested before, the question of women's place in the ordained ministry can be satisfactorily resolved only when that ministry is declericalised and ceases to be seen as a profession, albeit a 'sacred' one ...

...

That we celebrate Christ's birth at the time of the winter solstice has a greater significance than just the 'Christening' of an ancient festival. It also marks the beginning of the event which changed our whole relationship with time and with the seasons, whose cycle of growth and decay, of light and darkness had long dominated human life. Long generations of men and women had, with the turn of each year, hoped and prayed and offered sacrifice to the gods of time that light would once again conquer darkness, that new growth would spring up where all was decay. But, since the Lord of Light came to conquer darkness and death and time itself, all has changed: we live with the cycle of the seasons, but we are no more subject to it.

Time is no longer an absolute; like all created entities its existence and significance are relative. The only absolute is God. Taking our stand on this, we can look with confidence at the findings of the scientists, as they explore this universe of miraculous detail – a miracle of chance, some would say, but we would claim to know better! But what is of importance is not that we should engage in fruitless controversy, but that our sense of wonder should be deepened and enlightened as we look and learn, always remembering that a mystery is not that of which we can know nothing, but that of which we can never know everything. Which does not relieve us of the tasks of knowing as much as we can – another example of *fides quaerens intellectum.* And, far from undervaluing what God's word has revealed to us, we may become the more 'aware that we live within the drama of the Bible'.

I am indebted for the phrase I have just quoted to the late George Otto Simms, whose last written work, *Exploring the Bible,* has been released under the joint imprint of the Columba Press and the Association for the Promotion of Christian Knowledge.

George Simms was Archbishop of Dublin in the Church of Ireland from 1956 till his translation to Armagh in 1969. In both primacies he was known and loved as a caring and quietly authoritative pastor.

(December 1996, vol. 46, no. 10, pp. 619-623)

INDEX